The Play of Sun and Shadow

A memoir by Brian Esr

Table of Contents

Preface

Hi. This is a memoir based on journals I have kept for over forty years from my early twenties through my early sixties. If you're looking for a whodunit, look elsewhere. This story is more of a whoami, if you will, an account of my maturation process and spiritual journey.

I have attempted to include enough of my life story to create dimension by including everyday pleasures and pains, thrills and spills, along with significant detours, dead ends, roundabouts, and rest-stops. Various themes are developed and how they evolved and/or devolved. Thus, this story is best read from beginning to end.

I have no fame, fortune or particular talent. I am nothing special. In fact, I am an egotistical mess; an ex-problem drinker who is occasionally crude, clumsy, and cocky. If that isn't enough to dissuade you, I am a pessimistic optimist, liberal Democrat, astrology aficionado, fickle sports fan, and a spiritual-but-not-religious guy. This is a story of joy and woe, a play of Sun and shadow.

> Life can only be understood backwards; but it must be lived forwards. (Søren Kierkegaard)

Chapter 1: Initiation

1971 was a mixed bag. Disney World in Florida opened. Intel produced the world's first microprocessor. A ban on cigarette ads was instituted on TV in the US. The NPR radio program was broadcast for the first time. The People's Republic of China joined the UN. The Soviet Union launched the first space station. War between India and Pakistan erupted over a border dispute. *A Clockwork Orange* was a popular movie. *All My Children* and *Mary Tyler Moore* were TV hits.

And, there was a lot of political unrest in the United States stemming from the anti-war and civil rights movements. The Vietnam War which started in '64 was slowly winding down but still with close to 200,000 US personnel involved from a high of over 500,000. Over 50,000 US military personnel and hundreds of thousands of Vietnamese had been killed, both military and civilian. Most Americans considered the war to be a mistake; opposition was growing exponentially. As the historian Howard Zinn said, "...the greatest antiwar movement the nation had ever experienced, a movement that played a critical role in bringing the war to an end".

Adding to the tempest was the upcoming presidential campaign between the incumbent Richard Nixon, the Republican, and the unknown nominee for the Democrats; a contentious selection process was dividing the party. And, the 26th Amendment to the United States Constitution was passed giving "citizens of the United States, who are eighteen years of age or older" the right to vote. In large part, the amendment's adoption was fueled by the military draft and the elimination of the college deferment. Up to that point, young men between the ages of 18 and 21 had no say, no vote, on issues such as the war in Vietnam. I would be voting for the first time in the upcoming presidential election.

The summer of '71, after high school graduation, I drove cross-country with my girlfriend, my first love, and her family from Ft. Lauderdale, FL, to Palo Alto, CA. We lived in a sorority house on the Stanford campus near their old neighborhood where they used to live. They rented the house much like folks do with vacation rentals near an ocean or lake. Another sorority house down the street was rented by the Esalen Institute which was an innovator in the Human Potential Movement. One day I happened to walk by the house and heard my first rendition of the chant Om. I became quite fond of the Bay Area and surroundings from San Francisco to Santa Cruz. One afternoon while I waited for my draft lottery number to be announced over a local radio station, I busied myself with a paint-by-the-numbers landscape. My heart dropped when my low number was announced; there was no doubt I would be drafted into the Army the following year. I never finished the paint-by-the-numbers landscape.

Later that summer upon my arrival in Gainesville, FL, to attend my freshman year at the University of Florida, I consulted with a draft-dodging agency off campus. They informed me that I didn't qualify for conscientious objector status since I didn't' have a religious background such as Quaker. However, they told me about a psychiatrist involved with the anti-war movement that dispensed diagnoses guaranteed to get one disqualified: drug and alcohol addiction. After a brief consultation where I described my frequent marijuana usage and infrequent beer consumption, he gave his diagnosis as promised: drug and alcohol addiction.

However, I opted not to use the diagnosis for fear it would upset my parents and negatively impact my future job prospects. Also, a few months earlier draftees had been exempted from serving in Vietnam, so I didn't have to worry about that prospect. Having lettered in three sports in high school, I figured the Army would be akin to playing for a sports team.

The University of Florida wasn't my first-choice college. I was accepted at Tulane, but my father decided against such because of its anti-war movement and, especially, the burning of an effigy of Nixon the previous year. Dorm life quickly proved not to my liking. Within the first two weeks, I was placed on social probation because I was caught by a resident assistant with a woman in my dorm room while smoking pot; both were rule violations. Yep, both. Marijuana was against the law, but women? Some fundamentalist Christian state legislator had gone on a rant about dorms at state universities being dens of sexual misconduct which resulted in *all* visitation between men and women being banned. The social freedom that college life promised proved to be an illusion. However, I did enjoy one of my classes, English 131. The professor, a grad student, required all of us to write papers which we would deposit at the English department offices, Quonset huts from WWII, so classmates could read them and comment. I wrote an 800-word paper provocatively titled "I Don't Need Him" which elicited quite a few comments, mostly negative. Basically, it was an explanation of why I didn't believe in religion. I ended the paper with a passage from the popular poem, *Desiderata*, that expressed some of my sentiments.

> You are a child of the universe, no less than the trees & the stars; you have a right to be here. And whether or not it is clear to you, no doubt the universe is unfolding as it should. Therefore, be at peace with God, whatever you conceive Him to be and whatever your labors & aspirations, in the noisy confusion of life keep peace with your soul. With all its sham, drudgery & broken dreams, it is still a beautiful world. Be careful. Strive to be happy. (Max Ehrmann; *Desiderata*)

It was easy for me not to believe in religion; neither one of my parents subscribed to a religion or, for that matter, a belief in God. Mom and Dad didn't discuss religion even though they were quite capable of doing so since both had been reared in church-going families. Mom's upbringing was Mormon and Dad's Catholic. I felt no attraction towards such nor did I feel inferior or disadvantaged by my lack of religion or belief. Actually, that is somewhat of a misstatement. Occasionally, I wouldn't understand a word or a concept that was from the Bible. Because of that, to this day I think it helps to have at least a cursory understanding of religion and the Bible. Beware of the side effects.

By spring of '72, the presidential campaign was in high gear between incumbent Richard Nixon, the Republican, and George McGovern, the Democrat. Nixon had a substantial lead in the polls; the Democrats weren't optimistic about the result come November. Meanwhile, the war in Vietnam wasn't going well; a humiliating defeat was a real possibility. The peace negotiations in Paris had broken down. To get the North Vietnamese to compromise, the Nixon administration conducted a massive bombardment of North Vietnam, Laos, and Cambodia. Anti-war demonstrations, sometimes violent, were held throughout the country.

On May 9th word of an anti-war demonstration spread through the dormitory. The protest was planned by an assortment of organizations and individuals from Vietnam Veterans Against the War to various faculty and clergy members. At first, it was kind of fun; sort of spring frolics with a political twist. We were smoking weed and drinking beer openly. The demonstration was held in front of the administration building on 13th street, which in effect shut down the thoroughfare. This didn't go over well with the authorities, so they brought in police along with water cannons and batons to clear the street. Then we, the protesters, moved caddy-corner and occupied University Blvd. The police regrouped and cleared University Blvd. We went back and forth in such a fashion a few times.

Since county and city police weren't allowed on campus, we were protected. It was a cat and mouse affair…we thought. As the protest progressed, the police started targeting individual protesters and arresting them. They used excessive force which angered many of us. With nightfall, the dynamics changed; anger morphed into a riot. Barricades were erected with benches, and some of us threw stones and bottles. The police responded with a massive charge. Seeing the oncoming onslaught, I ran towards the library and the supposed safety of a crowd of onlookers when I sprained my ankle on a curb. Hobbled, I continued to make my way until a plainclothes cop stepped out from the spectators and hit me across the back of my head with a baton. I blacked out. When I came to from my concussion, I realized I had pissed in my pants, and that I was surrounded by a handful of policemen ready to beat the shit out me if I resisted. I didn't. They handcuffed me and dragged me by my long hair to a bus filled with other protesters.

Close to four hundred of us were arrested and fined $50 each for our overnight stay at the city jail. I gained some admiration among friends and faculty but felt disaffected. The Vietnam War would drag on for another three years resulting in a debilitating brew of bitterness. It would be one of many rude political disappointments in my life.

On September 1st, I reported to the draft board in Coral Gables, Florida. It looked and smelled like a government building with uniformed men barking names and ordering young men to go this way and that. This was accomplished by following colored lines on the floor, converging and diverging down various halls. I was told to sit until my name was called for a physical. While waiting, a guy my age approached the desk I had just left. He had a shaved head except for an equilateral triangle of hair above his forehead with one angle pointing towards the back of his head and the other two pointing toward his ears. I was still wearing my hair long. We made eye contact along with an unspoken acknowledgment that we might have something in common. He sat next to me. I asked him about his hairstyle which he explained had something to do with the Egyptian Book of the Dead which was Greek to me. Matt and I became fast friends. I was told to follow the yellow line.

After the classic "drop your shorts and spread your cheeks" routine, I went through a series of tests which I did my best to flunk. No luck. After more waiting around, forty or so fellow recruits and I boarded a bus for Miami International Airport. We landed in Lexington, Kentucky, around

11:00 PM. We got to Fort Knox around 2:00 AM. We were immediately put through a series of orientations with men in uniform barking various admonitions. We were assigned barracks based alphabetically on the last name. Matt and I ended up in barracks across the road from each other.

The next day was the beginning of physical training and orientations on how to become a GI; that is, government-issued not gastrointestinal. The physical training part was a breeze; that wasn't the case with most of my fellow GI's who were in horrible shape. Unfortunately, the barber shop was backed up, so I was still sporting long hair which attracted the attention of various drill sergeants. The result was many pushups in cadence with "One drill sergeant, two, drill sergeant…" And, so on.

Before lights out that night, I visited Matt in his barracks. I found him in a yoga posture chanting something unintelligible. In a subdued voice, he told me that he was trying to figure out how to get out of the Army, even if it meant going AWOL which left me feeling out of sorts. Sleep didn't offer much comfort. I was awakened by a disturbing dream in which I was climbing a chain link fence to escape boot camp. My emotional hangover worsened when I found out later that morning that Matt was no longer going through orientation. A fellow GI heard it was due to medical reasons and that he would join us later. I wondered if he'd gone AWOL. I felt very alone.

That evening the dynamics shifted considerably. The commanding officer (CO) held an impromptu meeting. As he pranced around like rooster extolling the virtues of the Army, he said, in a surprisingly routine manner, something to the effect that if anyone "felt they couldn't handle the Army" they should speak with him. I was stunned. Could it be that simple?! I reflected on my encounter with two guys a couple of months before who'd secured early discharges from the Army for outrageous behavior (i.e., stuffing peanut butter up his ass and eating it). I started considering my options. I had no doubt the Army and I weren't a good fit.

The question was what to say to the CO to get out the Army. I decided to feign some sort of mental/emotional problem; peanut butter wasn't considered. I figured I had to attract the attention of my fellow GIs. My bunk mate was the lucky mark. I rolled up my recently issued towel the required length of a dollar bill and quizzically looked him in the eye and said, "Doesn't this look like a cockroach?" I purposely distorted my description to create a buzz. A short while later I heard him whispering to some guy that he thought I was weird. Then I initiated a hunger strike by refusing to go to the mess hall.

My mission to create chatter about my mental/emotional state had taken shape. However, to speak with the CO, I first had to talk with my squad leader due to the chain of command procedures. Finally, I got his attention and told him I needed to talk to the CO. He informed me I'd have to wait until Monday because the CO was off for the weekend. I knew there would be ramifications because of my request; I was essentially broadcasting that I didn't want to be part of the team. My primary concern was avoiding a "blanket party" (a form of retribution for not being a team member which had resulted in a recruit's death a couple weeks before). Though not officially stated as punishment, that weekend I was given two days of sixteen-hour KP duty shifts.

Monday morning, after our early morning run in which I purposely underperformed, one of the drill sergeants called me out of formation after I let him butcher my last name a few times. He was a big linebacker-sized guy with a gruff attitude. He had been informed about my request to see the CO which meant I wanted out of the Army. He asked me why. I told him I couldn't "take the Army." With contempt in his voice, he countered by saying he couldn't take the Army either with a few "fuck the Army" declarations for effect. I felt like things were going downhill fast and I'd probably end up in the brig. However, I kept repeating my contention that I couldn't take the Army. Then he looked at me and asked if I was "doing drugs." Damn, I had tried to avoid that categorization before getting drafted when I refused to use the psychiatrist's note. Not this time; I told him yes.

The drill sergeant sent me to the CO's office. To meet with the CO, first I had to speak with the master drill sergeant. I gave him the same line of reasoning, and he blasted me. With tearful conviction, I told him that if I weren't discharged, I'd go AWOL or commit suicide. For emphasis, I was considering jumping through a nearby large double hung window that I had checked out the night before on fire watch. However, that proved unnecessary. Unknown to me, the CO was listening behind an office partition. He stepped out from behind partition and sent me to the chaplain's office at the interfaith chapel. I felt a surge of relief which I tried to mask.

I knew where the chapel was located. The previous day, Sunday, I was given a choice of picking up cigarette butts or going to Sunday services. I opted to attend services. During the sermon, the minister asked the attendees to raise their hand if they felt they had been replacing God with other things. Much to my surprise, I found myself raising my hand. Back to the chaplain; he wasn't there when I arrived. Emotionally exhausted, I sat in a pew and cried and prayed; it was transactional, the only form of prayer I was familiar with. Something to the effect that I'd believe in God if I got out the Army.

I thought the interview with the chaplain would be a breeze compared to what I had been through. I was mistaken. He had been on a couple of tours in Vietnam and had seen guys in much, much worse shape than me. Every time I said I couldn't take the Army, he'd counter by saying that's how most GI's felt. Finally, he asked what kind of drugs I had been taking. I listed marijuana, speed, *and* LSD. His whole attitude changed when I mentioned LSD. He drove me to the "psychiatric unit."

The "psychiatric unit" had an ominous tone. I was afraid I'd get drugged or hooked up to some electronic equipment to make me Army material. My appointment was with a young Army Corporal who had graduated from the University of Kentucky with a degree in psychology. Much to my relief, he was a genuine guy who advised me to learn from the experience I was having. With his approval, I was sent to the Army hospital on base where I was to perform orderly duties until the paperwork for my discharge was completed which I was told took two weeks.

While registering at the Ward 5A reception desk in Ireland Army Hospital, I heard some footsteps approaching me. By the sound, I could tell they weren't standard Army issue. I turned towards the sound and saw Matt walking towards me wearing slides! As we made eye contact, he put his forefinger to his lips indicating proceed with caution. Later, Matt warned me that certain individuals might not have our best welfare in mind; namely, the Specialist 5 in charge of supervising us. He was a mean-spirited son of a bitch.

My twenty or so ward mates were a mixed bunch or, better yet, mixed nuts; some had obvious psychological disorders. Others had physical issues such as heart problems which begged the question why they were drafted. Except for a couple of guys, most ward mates were less than friendly especially when I was in the company of Matt. I had no idea why and didn't give it much thought. Matt was a breath of fresh air. When we were not on orderly duty, we'd go to the USO suite and listen to music or talk about spiritual things. Matt would do most of the talking. He introduced me to meditation, chanting, and some guy named Ram Dass.

One afternoon as Matt and I got on the elevator a couple of ward mates made a point of getting off because of our presence. I asked Matt what he made of that. He proceeded to tell me that his discharge was due to homosexuality. Matt was married! However, he knew admission of homosexuality would get him out of the Army. I didn't question his motives one iota. The problem was that one of our psychologically unbalanced ward mates found out about the nature of Matt's discharge and went out of his way to be an asshole. He caused a stink when he accused us of stealing some of his music cassettes even though none were found missing. You would think that would have dissuaded him from further irritating behavior. It didn't.

So, there I was in Ward 5A; a heterosexual whose best friend was a heterosexual pretending to be homosexual to get out the Army. This made me homosexual in the opinion of my fellow ward mates. However, much to the chagrin of my heterosexual ego, I couldn't go around explaining the truth. I had to maintain the ruse for Matt's sake. We were told if we screwed up in any way our discharge would be rescinded, and we'd end up in the brig. Later, I found out that probably wasn't the case. That lie was the work of that mean-spirited SOB Spec 5 I mentioned earlier.

On the lighter side, a gay Army nurse found out about Matt's supposed orientation and asked him whenever possible to help with tending to the patients. Matt couldn't tell him the truth either. Apparently, to curry Matt's favor, he gave him some pot. Matt and I proceeded to light up in a bathroom on the fifth floor of Ireland Army Hospital. What were we thinking?! A couple hours later Matt and I were lounging around Ward 5A stoned when we heard our names announced over the intercom along with orders to report to Ward 5B. We thought we had been set up and busted. That walk from Ward 5A to Ward 5B was one of the longest walks of my life. I thought I'd end up in the brig. It turned out Matt's gay nurse friend wanted some help with bedpans!

Two weeks later I received an honorable discharge from the Army. Matt had been discharged a couple of days before me. We promised we'd hang out as soon as possible. Five years would pass before we'd do so at a mutual friend's wedding. I was living in Miami again with my wife as did Matt with wife and child. We hung out occasionally for a couple months then went our separate ways due to lack of sympatico in our spiritual paths.

After my discharge, I returned to Miami and my parent's home. They were concerned about my mental welfare and suggested I seek psychological help. I declined knowing there was nothing wrong with me. Dad had hoped the military would be a beneficial experience. He was an officer in the Navy in the Pacific Theater during WWII; my brother was a Navy pilot. The military was held in high regard in my family. Little did they know what a clusterfuck the Army had become due to the prevailing practice of giving criminals the choice of enlisting instead of going to jail. Eventually, I would view my getting an early discharge as my first significant adult decision; albeit, enhanced by some government-issued ego reduction!

A week or so later I headed back to Gainesville and worked as a maintenance man at an apartment complex until the next academic quarter started In January. During those next couple of months, I found out how shallow the post-hippie culture had become. Because I no longer had long hair, old acquaintances didn't consider me cool. I found myself shying away from social situations. Thankfully, I was living with my best friend, Stan; his friendship was much appreciated. Oh, Nixon defeated Democrat George McGovern in the presidential election of '72. It was one of the largest landslides in U.S. political history.

Over the Christmas holidays, I stayed at my parent's home in Miami. On Christmas Eve morning Stan and I ingested some LSD. By the time we got to the beach, everything was sparkling, and we were feeling carefree. Around dusk, having come down from our trip, we went looking for a place to get a bite to eat. Most restaurants were closed for the holiday except for a greasy hamburger place on US 1. We walked in and promptly turned around. The greasiness was overwhelming. We returned to our car in the parking lot where we ran across three guys from Canada. They were on their way to the Keys. We invited them to smoke a joint with us. Stan climbed into their car, and one of them got in mine. We drove down to Biscayne Bay next to a power generating station, an old favorite fishing spot.

While we passed the joint back and forth between the two cars, I tried to carry on a conversation with my passenger. He didn't have much to say; he worked at a Ford plant. I told him about my majoring in religion even though I was nonreligious. Casually, I expressed my doubts about my course of study with the offhanded remark, "maybe it's a lot of shit." Then I corrected myself out loud saying it wasn't. Suddenly, I felt this tremendous rush of energy well up in my heart. I looked at the fellow from Canada seated next to me and told him that "something very special was happening." I think that freaked him out, but I couldn't help it; I had to close my eyes. In my inner eye, a beautiful yellow hibiscus flower arose and bloomed, engulfing me in a resplendent love beyond anything I had ever felt before. In a state of ecstasy, I crawled out the car window (because the cars were too closely parked to open the door) and danced down the street. Stan caught up with me and expressed concern; I assured him I was okay but didn't have the words to describe my euphoric experience.

My initial major was history which was in part due to Dad's influence; he had all but dissertation in early English history. Beginning in late elementary school, I began reading history books for fun including my brother and sister's high school history texts; biographies along with WWII and Civil War accounts were my favorites. The second quarter of my freshman year I took a 300-level history course to get a feel for what a college level history course was like. It was a disappointment. However, I found my Asian religion course captivating. I encountered numerous scriptural passages as well as statements by various sages that corresponded with my LSD experiences; descriptions of a scintillating reality that was my very being beyond belief and conventional sense of self.

> It is the underlying truth of all that exists, the reality on which all name and form depend. (The Upanishads, circa 800-200 BCE)

A month or so before Spring break, I helped move a piano at a community center. A couple days later while drying myself off after a shower, I noticed a lump just above my penis in the pubic hair area. My first thought was cancer which I feared would adversely affect my sex life. The doctor at the student clinic laughed when I shared my concern. He informed me that it was a hernia and that I should have it corrected as soon as convenient.

During Spring break, I returned to Miami to visit Mom and Dad and to have a hernia operation. The operation was scheduled for late afternoon. I was assigned a room with one other patient. Part of the pre-operation preparation was the shaving my pubic hair which I hoped would be performed by a sexy candy striper. That fantasy was dashed when a very effeminate male nurse entered my room quoting the famous stripper, Rosemarie, about having to "take it all off." The guy next to me reacted homophobically and suggested I call and complain. I wasn't in the mood to hassle. My attitude was "what the hell, it might make a good story." My bravado vacillated when he started to apply the shaving cream and apologized for his cold hands. I told him to get on with it as quickly as possible.

A little while later another nurse gave me an injection of Demerol to calm my nerves before surgery. I was familiar with its effects having used it recreationally a few times in pill form. As they wheeled me down the hall to the OR, I was feeling quite gregarious, making friends with whomever. Once in the OR, the anesthesiologist asked if I had ever experienced anesthesia. I confirmed in a smart aleck fashion. Then, she asked me to count backward from ten. I did so with a smirk. Next, she said, "Okay smartass, count forwards from one." I remember getting to two. When I woke up from the anesthesia in the recovery room, the pain was pronounced and would be throughout the night.

The next morning a nurse awakened me with an inquiry, "Have you had a bowel movement?" Surprised by her question, I replied in the negative. The idea of a bowel movement or, for that matter, using any muscles in the general abdominal area wasn't an attractive notion. Then she inquired whether I had ever experienced an enema. Once again, I replied in the negative. She proceeded to give me an enema; its efficacy, the sense of urgency, surprised me. I got up from bed wincing in pain and stumbled towards the bathroom at the far end of the room. Much to my disbelief and distress, the nurse told me I had to use the bathroom down the hall. I thought I was going to shit all over myself before I made it to the bathroom. Later, I shared that tale of pain with my sister who was a nurse. She found the nurse's behavior questionable; a shitty thing to do.

The following phase of my life was emotionally and intellectually trying to say the least. Via LSD the Ineffable had opened my heart, but my intellect and ego were grasping straws. Questions about various belief systems overflowed. I found myself favoring the mystical approach; that is, the divine as the ground of all being. The anachronistic, mythic, dogmatic theism I had culturally inherited, but didn't believe in, wasn't an option. My reading list included anything written by Stephen Gaskin, Alan Watts, Aldous Huxley, and Ram Dass; *Be Here Now* was one of my favorites. Family and friends didn't understand my spiritual quest; some were openly disdainful. My romantic endeavors fared no better; a few unsatisfactory one-night stands laced with sexual insecurity. It was a period of confusion, self-doubt, and loneliness...a dark night of the soul; one of several dark nights that would follow.

I was out of shape and had gained weight, so I implemented a jogging routine. I experimented with a hatha yoga, vegetarianism, fasting, and became enthralled with synchronicity and the *I Ching*. I tried various forms of meditation from counting my breaths to staring at a candle flame which didn't click, so I signed up for a Transcendental Meditation class. The instructor began the class with a foreign sounding chant. I wondered what I had gotten myself into. Then, he gave me a mantra which I was told not to share it with anybody which was a turn-off, but I went along with it. Next, he showed me how to repeat the mantra silently with my breath. Much to my surprise, I experienced a peaceful state in the allotted fifteen minutes. I became a regular meditator.

Somehow, maybe it was via meditation, I came to the realization that I needed to talk to someone about the changes I was going through. I made an appointment with a counselor, Kat, at the campus mental health clinic. Kat's psychological orientation was Gestalt a la Fritz Pearl's *Gestalt Therapy Verbatim*. She warned me that counseling wouldn't be easy; honesty was required. She asked me to journal about what I was feeling in the moment, not what might be, could be or should be. Little did I know that those initial journal entries would become a lifelong habit and the basis of this memoir.

> I do my thing and you do your thing. I am not in this world to live up to your expectations, and you are not in this world to live up to mine. You are you, and I am I, and if by chance we find each other, it's beautiful. If not, it can't be helped. (Fritz Perls; *Gestalt Therapy Verbatim*, 1969)

The primary emphasis in our sessions was getting in touch with my feelings and learning to express them clearly. Kat used dream analysis which my subconscious seemed to respond to by conjuring up some fantastic dreams. In one dream I killed a guy who was trying to kill me. I felt conflicted. Kat showed me how I was caught up in being a people-pleaser; that is, seeking the approval of others and that I can't please everyone (a longer-term project than I imagined!). We met on a weekly basis for months topped off by group workshops where I was the only undergrad in the group.

Chapter 2: Transmission

The heart is the hub of all sacred places. Go there, and roam. (Bhagawan Nityananda)

On an irregular basis, I babysat aquariums for a couple who lived in a mobile home outside of town. They paid me with plenty of pot to smoke. One hot, muggy August evening Stan accepted my invitation to help me tend to the aquariums. We had tripped on some microdot LSD earlier that morning, and I figured we'd enjoy the quiet of the countryside and smoking some weed. After dealing with the aquariums, Stan and I took a walk in the surrounding woods with the usual high concentration of mosquitoes. The sky was clear except for the occasional passing cloud. At one point I paused and looked up at the stars and mumbled something about yearning for a spiritual teacher. Stan moved on, probably tired of my babbling. Suddenly a triangle with an eye like on the back of a dollar bill appeared at roughly 3 meters up and 3 meters away from where I stood. To my surprise, the eye was human; it wasn't some static symbol. I blinked my eyes, shook my head, thinking I had done too many psychedelics. Regardless, the triangle remained in my field of vision andt started to grow to include a man with South Asian characteristics from chest up. He looked at me with a powerful, unconditional love. Then he disappeared.

When I came to, so to speak, I realized I was covered with mosquito bites so I retreated to the mobile home. While I sat on the living room couch and considered the spiritual significance what had just happened, I vigorously scratched the mosquito bites. Then, as clear as day, an inner voice told me to stop scratching which I did without hesitation much to my surprise. Then, the inner voice told me to sit up straight because I was going to have a "spiritual experience." I felt like I had already hit the mother lode but gladly sat on the edge of the couch with as straight a back as I could muster. Then, I noticed I couldn't feel my feet. I thought I must be sitting wrong and that my feet were falling asleep. I readjusted my posture to no avail.

The awareness of no sensation moved up to my knees. At that point, I realized I was, indeed, in store for something extraordinary. The lack of sensation rose to my abdomen and then to the heart area. I freaked. I thought my heart might stop beating and I would die. Matter-of-factly, the inner voice asked if I was responsible for my heartbeat. I had just finished a course in cellular biology and knew that the heartbeat was involuntary and had to do with the SA node, known as the heart's natural pacemaker. So, I let go of my fear. The lack of sensation rose to my neck; I freaked again. I thought my breathing would stop and I would die. Again, the inner voice asked if I was responsible for my breathing. I thought about sleep where I was not in control of my breathing. I let go of my fear.

I entered the Sahasrara chakra at the top of my head and experienced 360-degree inner vision and the "radiance of a thousand suns." If I concentrated on a ray of light emanating from the splendor, I could discern an amorphous energy body of another person. I thought I was finished with my earthly existence which thrilled me and surprised me (that I was willing to leave my life behind). Suddenly, in the distance, I heard Stan close the door having returned from his walk. I re-engaged with my physical body down through the Sahasrara chakra. I felt disappointed, but the inner voice assured me it was appropriate because I had "lessons to learn."

Fall of '73 I took part in a student exchange program with the University of Utrecht in the Netherlands. A dozen or so fellow UF students lived in Dutch student housing and attended various courses taught in English. It was my first time in a European country. Even though there was considerable anti-American sentiment because of the Vietnam War, I felt comfortable in a way I never did as a child in Venezuela where my father worked for an oil company. Being an American kid, a gringo, with blondish brown hair and blue eyes meant I stood out and on an infrequent basis was cussed at, spat at, or chased. However, in Holland, I was often mistaken for being Dutch by locals. I fell in love with the Netherlands from Maastricht to Friesland. The Hague, Rotterdam, and Amsterdam were only a short train ride away. Naturally, Amsterdam with its hash bars, museums, and canals was my favorite.

On my own I was studying Christian mysticism a la Meister Eckhart, St. Teresa, St. John of the Cross, etc. I found much of what they said corresponded with mystics from other traditions. One night I was awakened by a dream. In the dream, I was walking along a shoreline. Out upon the water was a point of light; I figured it to be a fishing boat. As I continued walking, the light approached me and grew bigger and brighter. Soon the light became a man. Then the man became Jesus with a golden cross on his chest beaming glorious light. I fell to my knees on the sandy beach in reverence as I awoke.

The next morning, I attended a sunrise service at a local Anglican church with a fellow UF student I was dating. Upon entering the sanctuary, behind the altar was a stained-glass window of Jesus as I had just seen in my dream with the morning sun shining through the golden cross on his chest creating surreal lighting in the sanctuary. I sat in the nearest pew and bowed my head in appreciation of the affirmation of my spiritual path.

I ended up leaving the program after the first quarter. The choice in coursework for my religion major was lacking. This was a difficult decision; one that I knew didn't please my parents who were concerned about my direction in life. They figured it best if I didn't return to Gainesville and its questionable influences. Nonetheless, I moved back to Gainesville and resumed my studies at UF. I rented a flea-infested mobile home south of town with Ron who I had met the previous year through a mutual friend. We became friends which we are to this day.

Part of my desire to return to Gainesville was Crystal. In sixth grade, she became my first official girlfriend and the first girl I kissed romantically. After seventh grade, both of our families moved from Miami, and we lost touch. We reconnected my freshman year at UF but saw each other infrequently because she lived in Jacksonville. While in Holland, we exchanged love letters and plans on getting together upon my return. That didn't happen. Over the Christmas holidays, Crystal started dating another guy. This would be our modus operandi for the next couple of years; when one of us was available the other wasn't. I ended up dating Patty who lived in the adjacent mobile home; she was an undemanding lover. We never became a couple in the traditional sense; we dated on and mostly off for the next couple of years.

The following academic quarter Ron, a fellow religion major, and I took a course on Zen Buddhism; the professor had written the preface to a book by the English mystic and philosopher, Douglas Harding. The book was titled *Having No Head--Zen and the Rediscovery of the Obvious*. Douglas gave a lecture which included a demonstration of a straightforward method of self-inquiry called an experiment. Douglas invited us to point our index finger at where we thought we had a face or head. Indeed, I saw space instead of a face or head but discounted the significance of what I saw; it wasn't extraordinary or cosmic enough.

My dark night of the soul continued. I was not content with most aspects of my life including romantic relationships, academic efforts, exercise, diet, etc. One of my religion courses required visiting different church services. I attended Catholic, Methodist, Evangelical, and Unitarian churches. I found it frustrating when believers couldn't see or at least appreciate the truth of other paths beside their own. This was especially the case with fundamentalist Christians and Hari Krishnas (I had visited their temple off campus per invitation of a high school acquaintance who had become a devotee). Basically, they were egotistically preaching "my god is better than your god" as if there was more than one Spirit. I believed that Spirit was the essence of the various religions. Just as there were different strokes for different folks, there were different religions for different folks.

> Because people want something elaborate and mysterious, so many religions have come into existence. Only those who are mature can understand the matter in its naked simplicity. (Ramana Maharshi)

I knew my path had something to do with the LSD vision of the eye within the triangle that transformed into the South Asian man. I figured he was a guru and tried to find out who he was. Every bookstore I came across I would scan the shelves looking for a book about him or by him. In the process, I ended up finding inspiring reading material by Ramana Maharshi, Yogananda, and Vivekananda. Based on my reading, I started to get the impression that gurus were a varied bunch; some could be iconoclastic in their behavior.

During the summer of '74, I worked for the landscape department of UF in lawn maintenance. I mowed yards and trimmed hedges. One week it rained heavily for four days which meant I was stuck inside; however, it provided me the opportunity to read *The Handbook to Higher Consciousness* by Ken Keyes. *The Handbook* provided some analytical tools to better comprehend my psychological turmoil. The most significant insight was understanding the consequences of "emotionally backed demands" or emotionally charged expectations (subconscious shoulds or shouldn'ts about myself, others and/or circumstances). Ron and I became enthusiastic practitioners of Ken Keyes' Living Love system. We took part in workshops and learned to be monitors, which meant helping others spot their subconscious expectations and upgrade them to preferences; that is, seeing life as a "parade of preferences."

Later that summer, I rented an upstairs efficiency in Kat's home on the northeast side of Gainesville near the "Duck Pond." Kat was working on her dissertation and conducting Gestalt workshops in her living room. I would occasionally listen in; unrealistic expectations were popular distractions. Kat expressed concern about my involvement in the Living Love group. She thought the leader was on a power trip. She was right. Frustrated with the power dynamics and feeling indifferent about my classes, I decided to drop out of college, much to my parent's chagrin. I sold my car and flew to San Francisco to live in the Living Love center in Berkeley. Taking part in the workshops and interacting with Ken Keyes was the highlight.

However, after a week at the center, I realized there were several individuals on similar power trips to what I'd encountered in Gainesville; an unfortunate dynamic I would come across repeatedly in other spiritual organizations as well. Also, I realized I hadn't thought through the financial aspect of living in the center. It required getting a job. Attending college while being supported by my parents looked a whole lot better. After a week I returned to Gainesville and re-enrolled in school. Shortly after my return, based on a glowing article in one of the popular yoga magazines, Ron and I signed up for a weekend retreat with Swami Muktananda.

In January '75 Ron and I met Swami Muktananda at the Hillel House just off campus. By the time we got there, the hall was packed with a long line of people waiting to greet him. I got in line and figured out the procedure. Upon becoming first in line, one would kneel, bow, and get swatted on the head with a wand of peacock feathers by Muktananda. Then it was the next person's turn. My turn came; I knelt and bowed. However, there wasn't a swat as I expected. His assistant tapped me on the shoulder and told me to move on. I looked at Muktananda, and he grinned playfully. An open microphone question period followed. A questioner asked whether he believed in car insurance. Muktananda said, "Yes, especially if you have a wreck." I found his answer humorous and practical.

Ron and I attended one-on-one question and answer session the following Thursday. We were told to prepare our questions beforehand. I spent Wednesday evening composing and recomposing questions. Just before going to bed I wrote down a poem inspired by a chant I had heard earlier in the day. When it was my turn to ask my questions, they seemed superfluous. I read the poem instead and became choked up. Muktananda swatted me with his peacock feather wand, and I became peaceful golden light. As I was coming out of my quiet reverie, I noticed a framed picture of a man next to Muktananda's seat. It was the man I saw in the triangle! His name was Bhagawan Nityananda, Muktananda's guru, who died back in '61. Go figure.

Within short order, Muktananda and Siddha Yoga became my focus *and* authority. My meditation experiences differed substantially from TM including spontaneous physical and emotional spasms (kundalini kriyas). In the weeks that followed, I stopped drinking and smoking cigarettes and weed. Feeling silly one day at a retreat near Tulsa, I asked Muktananda why yawns were contagious. He looked at me intently and said, "Because you have great love." That statement was the catalyst in discovering a reservoir of love as my Self. At another retreat some folks were asking Muktananda for Sanskrit names; I figured what the heck. I received the name Mahadev which I shared enthusiastically with friends and family; most were unimpressed or turned off. I didn't care, I thought problem-free Self-realization was just around the corner. I had no idea of the road conditions ahead.

Mom and Dad became concerned about what they perceived to be cult-like behavior. To assure them, I sent them an article from *Time* magazine about how a fellow Siddha Yoga enthusiast's business had profited from his practice. Dad sent me the following note. "If you don't mind, your mother and I would prefer to continue to call you by the name we gave you. I honestly do not think that being called Brian will distract from your holiness. I was given a confirmation name, Joseph, which I never used and I can't think that I'm less saintly, or more than I deserve to be...We are glad that Indian friend has returned to wherever he came from because we think you have your priorities reversed. It simply is not well worth falling behind in school work, so you can go on some kind of emotional jag. Your number one priority is, except you don't know it, completing school, getting an education. I'd like to think you'll be prepared to take care of yourself when you graduate, but I'm very much afraid you've spent so much effort trying to find yourself that you've done little about getting educated. You'll soon have to take care of yourself, you know." I took to heart some of what he said and disregarded the rest; fortunately, they continued to pay for my college education.

I graduated with honors from UF in June of '75 with a BA in religion. As you probably have ascertained, thoughts of a career were few and far between; I got a job as a busboy at the local Hilton and then moved up to exterior/interior painter for the housing department at UF (a skill that has come in handy many times since). I figured I'd work for half a year then secure a student loan and attend the graduate program in elementary education. While at the student union one day, I ran across Ann who was working at the information desk and reading a book on St. Francis. We had met at a yoga retreat a few weeks before. I found her attractive, so I asked her out.

The relationship with Ann sputtered from the beginning. One day we'd talk about coordinating our plans, and the next day we'd debate the merits of going our separate ways. Our disagreements reminded me of my spats with my sister when I was younger; she could piss me off in a nanosecond with her knack for misconstruing situations. I started flirting with other women. Amid this muddle, our lackadaisical birth control caught up with us. Ann, who was finishing her senior year in accounting, got pregnant. She decided to get an abortion which somehow contributed to our feeling more committed to each other. We even started talking about living together; marriage wasn't part of the discussion.

Douglas Harding came through town and conducted another workshop which I attended. This time I saw the simplicity of having no head or no-face. In the Pointing Here experiment or exercise, Douglas instructed us to point at various things like the chair and carpet. Then he had us point at our foot, then our knee, then our chest, and, finally, "point at where others see your face." Next, he asked, "What do you see? Do you see your face? Do you see anything at all there? Do you see any color or shape or movement?" I saw space coupled with subtle calmness. I "got it," the simplicity of the valley experience, of Who I really am already. However, my hankering for euphoric experiences would continue to distract me.

> This meditation is certainly not in itself a mystical or religious experience, not euphoric, not a sudden expansion into universal love or cosmic consciousness, not any kind of feeling or thought or intuition whatever. Quite the contrary, it is absolutely featureless, colourless, neutral. It is gazing into the pure, still, cool, transparent Fountainhead, and simultaneously out from It at the streaming, turbulent world – without being carried away into that world. You can ensure your full share of mystical or spiritual experiences, not by going downstream after them, but only by noticing that you are forever upstream of them all, and they can only be enjoyed there from their Source in you. (Douglas Harding)

On the spur of the moment, Ann and I got married the day after Valentine's by a local spiritual teacher. A recently married couple who were fellow Siddha Yoga devotees served as witnesses. We were broke; our rings were the cheapest we could buy, and there was no honeymoon. Marriage provided the comfort of commitment, but we complicated matters by trying to be sexually moderate, abstinent if possible, as recommended by Muktananda. Ann graduated with an accounting degree and as a certified CPA.

In the meantime, Mom and Dad moved back to Baton Rouge where they met and got married while attending LSU before WWII. We decided to move to Baton Rouge as well in part because of better job prospects for both of us. Ann promptly secured a position with one of the big national accounting firms. And, once I finished my elementary education classes at LSU, I had a significant advantage in securing a teaching position due to one of my relatives being a bigwig in the local public school system.

In April of '76, we flew up to New York to attend a meditation intensive at the ashram in the Catskills. We had Muktananda "bless our marriage." Upon our return, I taught a weekly meditation course at the student union and conducted weekly meditation meetings in our married student housing apartment; neither was attended by more than a handful of people. Ann was dissatisfied with her auditing work as was I with my courses at LSU. When Ann was offered a position at a small accounting firm in Tallahassee, we jumped at it. I resumed my classes for elementary education at FSU. We attended meditation meetings or satsangs at another devotee's home where I met Johnny. Neither one of us had any idea that we'd become friends.

Ann got fired in July which was a professional setback. We decided to move to Jacksonville where she got a staff accountant job at the local junior college. I continued my coursework at UNF, the local state university, and worked part-time at the campus bookstore. Neither one of us was content with our circumstances; moving back to Gainesville was actively considered. And, marriage was proving to be more difficult than either one of us anticipated. We quarreled frequently and threatened divorce often. I started studying astrology hoping to gain insight into our fractious relationship dynamics.

Based on limited knowledge of Johnny's experience of working on oil rigs in the Gulf of Mexico, I decided to give it a whirl. I figured some time, anytime, away from Ann might do us some good, and maybe I could save enough money to visit the yoga ashram in India. However, some of the men on the rig were less than salutary. After a week on the rig, I decided my education studies looked a whole lot better. I needed two semesters to finish the necessary courses to get an elementary teaching certificate. I secured a government student loan for the term starting in January. However, I ended up using some of the student loan to visit the ashram in India. Ann didn't make a big fuss; I would have gone regardless. On my way to India, I stopped in NYC for a three-day stay at the West Side ashram where I ran across two women who were going to India without their husbands. My marriage wasn't the only one on the rocks. Upon my arrival in India, I had crushes on both (in one case it was reciprocal).

The ashram was located in Ganeshpuri, a two-hour drive north of Bombay (Mumbai). It reminded me of where I lived as a child in Caracas, Venezuela, with the tropical flora, heat, and poverty. The ashram experience was profound in unexpected ways. For the most part, I stopped meditating due to the mosquitoes and noise made by other meditators. Chanting seemed nonstop; there was chanting before breakfast, after breakfast, before lunch, before dinner, and after dinner. I thought my legs and ass would become deformed from sitting so much; however, after a week or so I became accustomed. In between the chanting, there was work or seva. I worked on the painting crew which had some truly troubled souls; my problems became less significant in comparison. I also took part in meditation center leader training which included sharing sessions. I found it comforting to hear others' stories that were similar to mine including confusion about career, complications with marriage, and concerns about spiritual growth.

During a question and answer session with Muktananda, I asked about whether Ann and I should live in an ashram in Gainesville. He said, "Do what you think is best." That statement would prove pivotal in reclaiming my authority. I decided to return home sooner than planned prompted by Ann's threat to seek extramarital pleasures. I was ready to finish my elementary teaching certificate and embark on my teaching career. My yoga fundamentalism, the anxious preoccupation with spiritual practices such as chanting and meditating, began to relax. The last day of my ashram stay was Johnny's first day. We had a pleasant chat; little did we know the twist and turns we'd encounter on our journey as friends.

In October '78 Ann moved to South Miami for a tax accountant position with a local firm. She lived with fellow Siddha Yoga members Donald and April. I stayed in Jacksonville until the end of the year to complete my student teaching practicum. The main reason for relocating was Muktananda's six-month stay scheduled the following year at a South Beach hotel that was being converted into an ashram. Those two months without Ann's company provided me plenty of solitude which I enjoyed. Raja, my dog, and I took many walks to the local park where he would chase squirrels much to my amusement. I also got to know Mark better who had attended the meditation meetings a few times. After a while, I began to suspect Mark was gay because he never talked about women. I couldn't have cared less which he intuited. One night at dinner, after some humorous hemming and hawing, he officially came out of the closet.

Chapter 3: Inception

A true seeker never looks upon loss or gain; he only looks towards the inner Self and tries to become centered there. (Muktananda)

I loved being a teacher. However, finding a teaching job in Miami meant substituting which was bonafide student teaching because I encountered numerous teaching environments. I favored 5th or 6th grade due to the kid's sophistication at that level. To help ends meet, I worked part-time at a department store at Dadeland Mall where I sold men's sportswear. Ann and I lived just around the corner from the mall in a one-bedroom apartment with our dog, Raja. He was an attentive companion and possibly the best tennis ball receiver east of the Mississippi or at least in Florida. I was Montana and he was Rice. We won many Super Bowls.

Ann and I continued to quarrel on a seemingly regular basis. It looked like we were going to get divorced when I was offered a teaching job at a local private school for the following school year. Rather than appreciating the valley experience, I continued to yearn for the mountaintops; in other words, I was still hankering for spiritual fireworks. Without consulting with Ann, which pissed her off for good reason, I decided to visit Muktananda at the upstate New York ashram. I stayed at the ashram for a month before returning to Miami. Mark, my gay friend from Jacksonville, was my roommates until he came down with hepatitis and had to be hospitalized. Later, he told me it had to do with his gay lifestyle.

I returned to Miami and taught summer school and did odd jobs here and there. A week before classes started at the private school, I was offered a position in the public school system at the elementary school I attended in 5th and 6th grade. This enabled me to negotiate a raise from the private school which I had determined to be a better teaching environment.

With a loan from Mom and Dad, we bought our first home. I didn't realize how invigorating home improvement projects would become, especially the yard. South Florida was a garden paradise. I would go about the neighborhood looking for free ornamental plants growing in vacant lots. Living in south Florida also provided us with a chance to hang out with other young married couples involved in Siddha Yoga; namely, Donald and April who lived nearby and Chuck and Margie in Boca Raton who had recently become parents to a daughter which prompted us to consider such.

Muktananda's six-month stay at the converted hotel in South Beach was a bonanza, a buffet, of experiences. I was able to visit the ashram a couple of times a week. At one of his talks, Muktananda said, "Life is a play of Sun and shadow." I knew right then that I would use that as a title for "my book" based on my journals. Johnny and Mark stayed with us for a few weeks at a time. Johnny with his Virgo Sun, Scorpio Moon, and Capricorn ascendant was a skilled carpenter by trade and a breath of fresh air. He was particular about things in a grounded, emotional way along with being a baseball fan. Mark with his Leo Sun, Taurus Moon, and Libra ascendant was grounded as well and, when Ann wasn't around, unabashed about sharing accounts of his gay lifestyle.

In May, we found out Ann was pregnant. Along with being excited about becoming parents, a mutual sense of purpose dawned; the option of divorce faded. Finances would be tight but manageable. However, it caused a reevaluation of living in Miami due to the cost of living. Moving back to Gainesville was our first choice. I planned a trip to check out the teaching opportunities.

Maggie, who attended the local meditation center, was considering moving to Gainesville as well to attend graduate school at UF. So, Maggie and I drove together to Gainesville. On the way, we chatted amicably about all sorts of things including sex. I got so horny that I stopped at a market and went into the bathroom and masturbated. I knew I was attracted to Maggie before, but that really brought it to a climax, so to speak. Over the years, Ann and I had fessed up about our occasional lusts. I shared the basic story with Ann. To her credit, she didn't get judgmental.

Our daughter, Layla, was born on January 2nd with a Capricorn Sun, Sagittarius Moon, and Virgo ascendant. Ann's labor was long but without complications. She underwent the entire procedure without drugs opting for the Lamaze breathing technique. Watching Layla exit Ann's body was one of the highlights of my life (cutting the umbilical cord was a lot tougher than I anticipated!). While giving her a LeBoyer bath she opened her eyes and looked at me. It was love at first sight. I've been captivated by her ever since.

The drama that led up to Layla's birth was notable. The night before, Ann experienced a couple of hours of contractions, so we went to the hospital a couple of blocks away. We paid extra for our doctor because he didn't believe in intrusive measures, but he was on vacation. The substitute doctor was old school and immediately started suggesting all sorts of invasive procedures including Pitocin. Ann's contractions hadn't increased in intensity or frequency, so we left the hospital in protest. The doctor called the next morning and said he would work with us on noninvasive procedures. We returned to the hospital assured that our wishes would be honored.

Ann's water broke around 6:00 PM; she knew the significance of the event but tried to downplay it. Rather than make a big deal about it, I made up an excuse to slip out of the birthing room and reported the incident to the nurses. At the insistence of the substitute doctor, an external fetal monitor was attached. Thankfully, our regular doctor showed up around 8:00 PM in his tropical shirt just back from his Caribbean vacation. At 9:00 PM Ann started pushing. Forty-five minutes later Layla was placed on her mother's stomach. The afterbirth of the placenta was the most difficult to witness. "That is one bloody piece of liver!" was my thought.

Back from the hospital, Layla's first diaper change was my privilege, and I was all thumbs. For the most part, she was an easy baby to care for compared to Chuck and Margie's (i.e., baby colic: crying for hours on end often in the middle of the night). Not that there weren't some trying times when she was fussy. After the second month or so, she usually slept through the night except for waking up around 2:00 or 3:00 AM which was my exclusive period to tend to her. Parenthood was proving to be simultaneously rewarding and exhausting. However, our bickering remained the same.

Because of my minuscule pay as a teacher, Ann had to go back to work after a few weeks. We started looking for childcare which proved more difficult than we expected; the caretaker of our precious child had to be right. A few interviews later, we found a mother caring for three other babies that suited our needs. Later that month, Mom and Dad drove into town to visit their new granddaughter and old friends. They were happy for us and, as a bonus, parenthood granted us legitimacy in their thinking. As a parting gift, they gave us a small black and white TV. Neither one of us had watched TV since high school. That was the beginning of my love affair with sitcoms. Reruns of *I Love Lucy, MASH, Barney Miller*, and *Three's Company* became favorites.

Due to cardiovascular disease which had resulted in a heart attack and stroke, Muktananda decided to pass the yoga lineage on to two young Indians; they were a sister and brother who had traveled with him extensively. For me, the transition wasn't a big deal. I had been gradually detaching from Siddha Yoga and its management policies which at times smacked of fundamentalism (i.e., sanctioned reading lists, etc.). However, detaching from my desire for extraordinary spiritual experiences was still problematic.

> I had been blind to the one thing that is always present, and without which I am blind indeed—to this marvelous substitute-for-a-head, this unbounded clarity, this luminous and absolutely pure void, which nevertheless is—rather contains—all things. (Douglas Harding)

Layla was growing like a weed. Her crawling stage quickly morphed into walking. We visited Chuck and Margie on a frequent basis because they had a young child as well. These visits highlighted the differences in our parenting philosophy. They didn't believe in saying "no" to their daughter. One afternoon at their home I had Layla in my arms when she grabbed my glasses. I issued a quick no; they thought I was a barbarian. Ann and I differed on discipline as well, though it wasn't an issue. She was more lenient than me. My experience as a teacher had shown me that kids responded well to firm limits and loving discipline.

In May of '82, I received my teaching contract for the upcoming year. My raise was a whopping .8%; that's point 8 percent. This instigated my investigation into jumping ship and teaching in the public school system. And, the notion of moving from Miami was dusted off again because of the cost of living and the local elementary school Layla would attend; I had substituted there before and considered it inferior. I took another trip to Gainesville to check on teaching opportunities. While in Gainesville I stayed at Maggie's. Once again, we dealt with a strong sexual attraction which probably would have materialized had it not been for Maggie's reluctance due to my being married.

During summer break I helped supervise a day camp for kids 6 to 11 years old. That meant keeping the boys from hurting each other with bats, balls, rackets, and pretty much anything else they could weaponize. The girls were a breeze in comparison playing hopscotch, four square, etc. I became friends with Ricardo, the tennis coach. He was a gregarious guy with a manic/depressive streak. His marriage was rocky as well. We'd hang out, smoke weed, and discuss our similar situations. This didn't go over well with either wife. Ann didn't like Ricardo, ostensibly because of his chauvinism but augmented by her insecurity issues. Despite my increasingly sophisticated astrological analysis and insights provided by various marriage manuals, our marital problems hadn't improved.

My brother's pilot schedule enabled him to stay over one night. I really didn't know him except as an older brother from childhood. As adults, we hadn't spent any significant time together. After Ann went to sleep, we proceeded to get drunk (which I hadn't done in years) while he told me about his dysfunctional marriage. As he described his feelings, I had the sensation of depth charges going off in my subconscious; explosive confirmations of what I had been feeling for years. It was a heartfelt exchange that resulted in our first hug as adults. With that unexpected insight, I decided if things weren't better between Ann and me in six months, I would pursue divorce. I was tired of the bullshit. Another dark night of the soul was dawning.

The new school year started in August. In addition to the pay, I wasn't happy with my teaching load and certain administrative decisions. Instead of Gainesville, Ann and I decided to move back to Jacksonville due to familiarity and friends. We put the house up for sale. Due to rapidly escalating real estate values in Miami, there was a chance we could make a nice profit. However, there were two circumstances not in our favor; the economic recession and the house across the street. The owner of the property, our realtor, rented the small house to a mother with three single teenage daughters and two grandkids. The late-night parties punctuated by fights among the suitors resulted in the police intervening a few times. We hoped he would get a better tenant soon.

Swami Muktananda, age 74, died on October 2, 1982. It came as no surprise; he had struggled with cardiovascular disease for a handful of years. Regardless of his sexual misconduct, I was grateful for the pivotal role he played in my spiritual evolution. His spiritual power was indisputably palpable and profound. His discourses were perceptive, transformative, and his basic message priceless: "Meditate on your own Self, understand your own Self, attain your own Self. The Supreme Truth dwells within you as you." Yes.

Chapter 4: Division

It's not possible to "get away from it all" 'cause everywhere I go...there I am! (Ziggy)

In January of '83, I jumped ship for a teaching position at one of the best public elementary schools in the county as a fourth-grade teacher. I replaced a teacher who had burned out years before but due to moribund union regulations had been maintained unconscionably. (That isn't an anti-union statement; teachers need unions as do many other professions. School boards are necessary too, but problematic because of their function as springboards for political careers, and parents mean well but are frequently the problem and clueless about such.) There were no lesson plans or grades that I could discern. The students were out of control. However, within a couple of weeks, I had the situation under control. The principal thought I walked on water.

The teaching environment left a lot to be desired. I had 35 plus students (it varied by the week). I had at least three grade levels to teach due to the disparity in reading level. I broke reading into three groups; second grade, third grade, and fourth grade. I couldn't accommodate the kids above grade level; they were stuck at the fourth-grade level. The real problem with the multiple reading levels was in other subject areas where I couldn't group by reading level. A social studies textbook written for a fourth-grade reading level would probably pose problems for a student reading at a second-grade level. The amount of cover your ass (CYA) paperwork required by the administration left a lot to be desired as well. Our decision to move to Jacksonville was reinforced when I found out that I wouldn't be able to teach there the following year because of racial quotas for teachers. I would be the low man on the totem pole **seniority wise** and could be assigned anywhere in the Dade County, a big county.

Digestive problems cropped up with abdominal cramping and odorous gas, especially at night. I mean, I had farts that could melt the paint off walls. **My general practitioner** misdiagnosed my condition and prescribed an acid blocker that masked the symptoms. After a couple of months, out of desperation, I went to a chiropractor who correctly diagnosed my condition as digestive enzyme deficiency. He prescribed an over-the-counter diet enzyme; within a week the symptoms disappeared. He also advised me to drink more water and eat more protein (I was still trying to maintain a vegetarian diet) and suggested that the reason for the imbalance was due to stress. What stress? I was going through a marriage crisis, career changes, and relocation logistics.

In April we closed on the sale of our home and made a nice profit. We rented a house down the street and started planning our move to Jacksonville. Our primary concern was Layla's daycare. I drove up to Jacksonville to find an apartment with a decent daycare facility nearby and interview for a teaching position. I stayed at Mark's and with his help found a comfortable apartment complex with daycare right down the road, and I accepted an offer to teach at a local parochial school.

We moved back to Jacksonville in August. In January of '84, we bought a home on the south side of town in a suburb with good schools. Layla's eventual elementary school was within walking distance. Ann and I continued trying to make the marriage work; the six-month deadline I set was on hold. In addition to the astrological analysis and marriage manuals, I researched various ways of enhancing our sex life. One technique, based on a book recommended by my brother involved backing off from the edge of orgasm repeatedly to produce a more powerful orgasm by using breathing to help control the orgasmic reflex. Ann wasn't enthusiastic about the recommendations and accused me of being oversexed and selfish.

> We see that it's all natural. Our selfishness doesn't make us feel separate. We see how naturally we're selfish, but there's no self-condemnation. We see it as just how it is. Perfect. No need to be separate because of it. Full of self-forgiveness, full of letting go, full of understanding. It is there, but it's not us. It's just more stuff. There's room in us for all of it. (Stephen Levine)

We tried marriage counseling; actually, we attended only one session. The counselor started by asking me to share some brief reflections about Mom and Dad. I obliged. Then he asked Ann to share her feelings; specifying that she start with her father. Ann refused. The counselor declined to work with us. It dawned on me that some of the dysfunction in our relationship had to do with Ann's unresolved issues about her father. I was a convenient target.

In addition to the discord between the brother and sister, inheritors of the yoga lineage, rumors surfaced about Muktananda's sexual impropriety with young women before his death. The national organization reacted by circling the wagons, so to speak, which was disconcerting. We hosted a monthly meditation meeting in our home which was attended by most of our friends. All of us, I think it safe to say, felt stunned, stumped, and/or saddened to some degree or another. For me, what had been a gradual distancing from the organization became a dissolution. I figured it was the Universe's way of encouraging me to focus on Self rather than guru or group. It was time to drop the wishy-washy stuff and become 1st person-centered. In other words, embrace my spiritual authority; a longer-term project than I anticipated.

> The majority of men are curtailed 'I's; what was planned by nature as a possibility capable of being sharpened into an 'I' is soon dulled into a third person. (Søren Kierkegaard)

The new year dawned with an offer from the public school system for better money teaching eighth-grade physical science. And, once again, I replaced an incompetent teacher who had burned out. My worst fears were realized. Most of the students were undisciplined, disrespectful, and contemptuous of learning. The physical facility was a clusterfuck of monumental proportions. It had one continuous roof with 3 meter high cabinets for walls that didn't reach the ceiling. The noise was deafening. There were no windows either. And, to top that off, the middle school was one half of the building; the other half housed the high school. Occasionally, high school boys would walk through the middle school and terrorize the middle school students. Yep, a nurturing learning environment...not!

At the end of the school year, my teaching position with the county school system was eliminated due to budget cuts. I was substitute teaching and considering jobs outside of the profession for the first time. Then the public school system in Gainesville requested an interview with me for an elementary teaching position. Even though we had just purchased a home, I thought it might be worthwhile to investigate due to the unstable nature of my marriage. I might need options, so I drove down to Gainesville for the interview. It went well. Afterward, I stopped by Maggie's to say hi. She was upset about how some guy had treated her the previous evening. My attempt to comfort her evolved into us fucking which we thoroughly enjoyed having lusted for each other for a handful of years. Feeling no contrition and without hesitation, I decided not to tell Ann about my infidelity.

One of Ann's girlfriends and her ex-husband came over for a visit. Both were familiar with Siddha Yoga having visited the Oakland ashram. Tom and I quickly became friends; along with playing ping-pong, we would drink beer and smoke weed along with the occasional cigarette. He sympathized with me about my divorce deliberations having gone through his own the previous year. Knowing Tom's astrological chart was quite helpful in dealing with him. He had a Gemini Sun and ascendant, Virgo Moon and four planets in Cancer. Intelligent, curious, and critical along with a manipulative conversational shtick.

Tom considered himself a spiritual teacher; he had spiritual insight but was seemingly unaware of his egotism. He could be a real jerk at times. Regardless, we had some good fun. One evening we did some LSD. As we chanted Om Purnamidam, I went through a vortex of sorts; I found myself sitting at a fire ritual wearing the white lungi of a Brahmin priest. Tom was seated across from me wearing the orange robes of a swami. We continued chanting Om Purnamidam. Then I returned through the same vortex as did Tom followed up by us communicating telepathically for a while.

The interaction between Tom and Ann had strong sexual overtones. I wondered whether it had evolved into outright sex but wasn't getting out of sorts considering my recent tryst with Maggie. Furthermore, I was actively trying to hook up with another lady that had caught my eye. My marriage with Ann was all but over. I had moved into the guest room. Our primary concern was Layla's welfare; we felt that living separately would provide a better environment than growing up with parents who didn't get along. Just before Christmas of '84 we officially divorced.

It was an emotionally trying phase; a dark night of the soul. I was living in a funky garage apartment above Tom's sprawling house which he shared with his parents who owned and managed an RV park. I missed my daughter, my dog, and the comforts of my home. I was broke and unemployed; I had to borrow money from Mom and Dad. Fortunately, in February, I started teaching middle school math and science at an all-girl prep school. Ann and I decided to give our marriage another go. However, within a few weeks, we found ourselves bickering even more than before.

> We cannot hope to work out of this human sense of existence without making mistakes. We may make many, but will profit by them all. We are at liberty to change our belief of things as often as we get new light. We should not let our vanity compel us to adhere to a proposition simply because we have taken a stand therein. We should be willing to relinquish our former views and change our thought as wisdom furnishes us enlightenment. (Adam H. Dickey)

One evening Tom came over for dinner; afterward, we sat around the living room smoking weed. Tom and Ann were massaging each other's feet when I went to bed. I fell asleep but was awakened a short while later by a dream. I ambled back into the living room and noticed that Tom and Ann were sexually compromised. I went back to bed. Ann came to bed shortly after and guilt fucked me. The next morning Tom called worried about the impact on our friendship; I told him not to. Ann and I met for lunch. She was remorseful, so I decided to tell her about my affair with Maggie a few months before. It worked; she stopped feeling guilty. Without a doubt, I knew my marriage was beyond resuscitation. I moved back to the garage apartment at the RV park.

It wasn't long before a few rays of light started to shine through the shadows. One of those rays of light was Caroline. I met her at the hair salon I frequented when I was married. She worked in the chair next to my hair stylist. I made a note to myself that when I got divorced, I'd look her up. It turns out Caroline had the same feelings for me. She was brash and blessed with a bodacious sex drive. She was just what the doctor ordered after the ordeal I had been through. We took advantage of our sexual compatibility as often as possible along with a non-exclusive agreement.

Renting the garage apartment at the RV park had its pros and cons. Tom and his parents were Christian Scientists. Occasionally, we would gather in their living room and discuss *Science and Health* by Mary Baker Eddy. It offered a more metaphysical conception of God than standard Christianity; that is, God as the Divine Mind, not unlike Vedanta with its recognition of Brahman as the ground of Being. The emphasis on denial of disease struck me as over the top and not taking advantage of medical science questionable (apparently optometry and dentistry were okay--the entire family wore glasses and frequented the dentist). I also had the privilege of meeting Will. When Tom returned from his summer trip to California, Will had tagged along having recently gone through a divorce as well.

God is at once the center and circumference of being. (Mary Baker Eddy; *Science and Health*)

The main drawback, the con if you will, with living at the park was dealing with Tom. He didn't have much of a work ethic but had plenty of spending money from the RV business. He didn't appreciate my limited finances and was clueless about my responsibilities as a parent. Tom also had a curious companionship dependency (due to four planets in Cancer?). For instance, he'd ask me to accompany him to the store for a "short errand," and we'd get back four hours later. Or, he'd show up uninvited when I was staying over at Caroline's. Eventually, I learned how to be more assertive about my boundaries. That is, how to say "no."

A few months later Tom, Will, and I went to our favorite restaurant/bar at the beach. After milling around the smoky bar, Will and I stepped out to get some fresh air. Seated on a nearby bench were two fine looking women, so we introduced ourselves. I exchanged pleasantries with Mary; her beauty was breathtaking. I secured her phone number. The following week we went on a date; it wasn't smooth. Her Sun in Virgo conjunct Pluto resulted in strong introversion and reticence about sharing her feelings or thoughts as opposed to my expressive ways. However, she was an unselfish, soothing, sensuous lover. We proceeded to fall in love and after a few months spent most weekends together at my apartment.

In August Mary, Layla, and I drove to Baton Rouge to visit Mom and Dad. We stopped in Tallahassee and visited Johnny, Patty, and their new baby, Edward. They were stressed out with new parenthood and not happy with each other. Mom and Dad were thrilled to see Layla. Mary and I spent a couple of days in New Orleans. One night, after a couple of Hurricane drinks, we wobbled down Bourbon Street, one of the most aptly named streets in the USA. A beautiful lady dressed in a bright yellow chiffon dress caught our attention. We walked towards her to get a better look. She was a he who was a very pretty she.

Frank, Tanya, and their child, Liz, lived at the RV park as well. Frank and Tom had known each other since their early teens. Born eight hours apart, they shared the same Sun in Gemini and Moon in Virgo resulting in personality similarities; however, their rising sign or ascendant sign which changes every two hours differed. Tom's was in Gemini and Frank's in Taurus which meant a substantial difference in tonality. Frank wasn't reticent about sharing his criticism of Tom (and vice-versa); he had already figured out years before the necessity of setting boundaries with Tom. Frank and I would become friends.

One night we had a party at Tom's place with a handful of folks in attendance including Mary, Will & girlfriend, Frank & Tanya, and Jenny, Tom's new girlfriend. Everyone was having a good time altering with weed and/or drinking various types of alcohol. At one end of the living room, I was seated on the carpet listening to the *Yes* album, *90125*, which was my favorite at the time. Suddenly, I felt a sharpened focus. I had seen or experienced the scene before; everybody and everything---a déjà vu. *And*, I remembered when I saw the scene back in ninth grade in Puerto Rico waiting with the rest of the JV team for the bus to take us to the football practice field. I was sitting on the curb with my head on my knees sort of napping when I had what I thought was a curious daydream, a vision of the party scene just described. Call it a wrinkle in time.

My relationship with Ann, my ex-wife, continued to be strained, laced with bitterness and anger. Our conversations were akin to walking through a minefield. Without warning, one of us would hit a mine, and an explosion of emotion would occur. Meanwhile, Mary and I had begun living together full time; she was magnanimous with Layla. Unfortunately, Ann felt otherwise and, to complicate matters, would speak disparagingly about us in Layla's presence which she told us about. Mary and I had doubts about whether we could weather these difficulties.

I enjoyed teaching at the all-girls school with the small class sizes and daily interactions that in many cases were graced with genuine rapport. As you might imagine, being a male teacher in an all-girls school meant some girls developed crushes. I always kept a professional distance. However, one girl stands out. Even though Nora wasn't one of my students, she had a big crush on me. As part of an English assignment, she was required to keep a journal which they shared in class. Her journal had many mentions of me which other students told me about. So, to pop her inflated idea of me, so to speak, I invited her to be part of a lunch cleanup crew which I supervised. I was hoping she'd see me in a more realistic light which didn't work.

My financial situation was strained. Teaching at a private school meant even less pay than the public sector. I started considering other alternatives including, much to my surprise, sales. What brought about the change in my attitude was a conversation I had with Will months before when I was dating Caroline. He stopped by to chat while I was on the phone with her. I was trying to convince her to come over to my apartment rather than vice-versa. I was unsuccessful. When I finished my conversation, Will illustrated how I was trying to *sell* my idea of her coming over to my place. That insight would percolate in my subconscious and eventually evolve into the realization that I had been selling something or other since I could remember.

Chapter 5: Attraction

> Truth is by nature self-evident. As soon as you remove the cobwebs of ignorance that surround it, it shines clear. (Mahatma Gandhi)

In January of '87, Will recommended me to the sales manager of an in-ground swimming pool company that he had sold advertising to. The interview went well, and I was offered the position which would start in April. Once again, it would require me leaving my teaching position before the end of the school year which would be frowned upon by current administration and, more than likely jeopardize my teaching career. However, my justification was simple—financial. In March my contract for the next year was issued. They offered me a bit less than a 1% raise. My decision to change professions and sell pools was made easier.

Selling pools was an education. First, I learned product knowledge. Then I got a grip on the typical buying cycle. Most customers opted for home improvement loans which I helped process through a local bank. The amount of debt the average homeowner carried was an eye-opener. The most difficult challenge was getting along with a couple of fellow salesmen who proved less than trustworthy (they got caught trying to steal leads by the sales manager). My first customer was the wife of Navy sailor stationed at Naval Station Mayport. I presented the various options, and without hesitation, she picked one; my first sale. It couldn't have been easier regardless of my clumsiness. Working on straight commission was a radical shift from the salaried position of teaching. However, I made more money in my first month than I did in three months of teaching.

On the home front, Mary and I were enjoying living together having put aside our lingering doubts. I quit smoking cigarettes and only occasionally drank beer or smoked weed. My morning meditation was regular. However, coordinating with Ann continued to be a challenge given her mercurial sometimes volatile moods. However, around this time, Ann and Will started living together having dated long distance while Will had a temporary job in Miami. I was pleased with the development figuring his influence would be beneficial.

A couple of months later Mary was informed that her job at the title company would be eliminated due to corporate shuffling in August. Her options were another administrative job or going back to school for a nursing degree (she already had a BA in psychology). Meanwhile, back at the pool company showroom, a gorgeous advertising representative with the local newspaper started flirting with me, something that didn't happen much before. I was flattered. Over the next couple of weeks, our flirtation grew into a plan to rendezvous regardless of her engagement. Eventually, she got cold feet. I was disappointed in myself. Mary was a beautiful woman who loved me and deserved better; my wandering eye worried me.

When I hired on as a pool salesman, I didn't realize the pool sales season lasted only six months; come fall I would be without income. I interviewed for a manager/salesman position at an unfinished furniture store. The owner and I hit it off immediately which resulted in my accepting his offer. He had made his fortune in medical supply sales and purchased the franchise operation thinking it would be his retirement ticket. The first month was spent preparing the store for the grand opening in time for the Christmas season. I had never worked such long hours; 14-hour days, every day. Mary and I moved to an apartment nearby in my old burb. She decided to go to nursing school.

Nine months after I had resigned from my teaching position, one night after a long day at the furniture store, Nora's mother called me, much to my surprise. She was worried about her daughter's well-being. She knew about Nora's crush on me and thought I might be able to talk some sense into her. She asked me to meet with Nora; I hesitantly agreed. Nora and I met at a pizza shop for lunch near where I lived. After the initial nervous how-do-you-dos and a bit of conversation, Nora burst into tears. Yep, right in the middle of the restaurant. To alleviate the embarrassing situation, on my suggestion, she accompanied me in my car to a local pier on the river where we were able to talk with less self-consciousness. With as much compassion and firmness as I could muster, I told Nora that she had to adjust her behavior and that I would file a report with the dean of students. On the way back to her parked car I had the awful notion that she could accuse me of whatever and I would be left proving my innocence. I didn't hear from her for decades.

My daughter, Layla, had matured into an inquisitive, enthusiastic, and intelligent seven-year-old who excelled in school. She loved games; we spent hours playing UNO and gin rummy. My concerns about the negative effects of the divorce on Layla's psyche were fading. However, my worries about Ann's anger management problems did not abate. After one particularly repugnant scene, Layla asked me why she behaved like that. I mumbled something; I was ashamed I didn't have a cogent answer and couldn't protect her from such ugliness.

In my day to day encounters with potential customers at the furniture store, I met many attractive women; Ruth was one of them. She was considering the purchase of a dining room table and chairs which happened to be the most elegant ensemble on the floor. A couple weeks later she returned to examine the set again...and me. I invited myself over to her home, ostensibly to check the fabric match. We talked little about fabric and much about ourselves. She was an ex-Catholic practicing Christian Science; I considered such a sign that we were meant to be together because of my familiarity with Christian Science. I decided to pursue my attraction.

Breaking up with Mary was emotionally wrenching. I felt horrible but had a gut feeling that I had to move on, regardless whether the attraction to Ruth panned out. If it weren't Ruth, it would be some other woman; my wandering eye had worsened. I also decided to leave the retail furniture business. The money wasn't as good as promised and retail hours sucked. I ended up securing a sales job with a local computer peripherals company. The learning curve was treacherous. I knew little about computers and nothing about the large mainframe environment, namely IBM System 36s and 38s. For the first time in my professional life, I was working in an office setting; there were two fellow salesmen, two administrative assistants, two technicians, one accountant, one vice president, and the president.

The dating routine with Ruth was different. We spent most of our time on home improvement projects and cooking; sex wasn't an option until she was sure we were marriage material. I was decompressing from breaking up with Mary, so I went along with her conditions. We would kiss and caress but nothing south of the waist. Finally, after six weeks we had sex; it was stilted. Shortly afterward, **she had a herpes flare-up which put a hold on our fledgling fucking for a month or so. Regardless, we engaged in the typical courtship rituals. We visited her parents in upstate NY. Warning: The Finger Lakes are cold even on a hot summer day!**

In August Dad had surgery on his prostate cancer followed by chemotherapy which was debilitating. Dad had always been a formidable, vibrant man. To see him depressed was depressing. Also, Mom's drinking problem, which had not been openly acknowledged for years, became impossible to ignore. Her mental clarity had deteriorated noticeably. My siblings and I spoke to Dad. He realized his drinking was part of the problem and instituted a moderation program. At that time, I had no inkling that alcohol would become an issue for me. There were warning signs; even though I drank infrequently, my propensity when I drank was to drink to excess.

There were warning signs in regards to my relationship with Ruth which I didn't pay attention to as well. Four months after meeting her I moved into her home. Sexual problems surfaced immediately; namely, her lack of desire which resulted in less sex than I preferred (a few months later I found out she masturbated daily but wasn't willing to her save her libido for fucking). Oral sex wasn't an option either; she didn't enjoy receiving or giving. Then, she decided to stop taking the pill and changed her mind about wanting a child. Another child wasn't in the cards for me.

> We must be willing to let our relationships reveal themselves to us. If we tune into ourselves, trust ourselves, and express ourselves fully and honestly with each other, the relationship will unfold in its own unique and fascinating way. Each relationship is an amazing adventure; you never know exactly where it will lead. (Shakti Gawain)

In November the presidential election between Bush and Dukakis took place. Though I had never voted for a Republican candidate in local, state or national elections, I voted for Bush. Dukakis' style didn't appeal to me. I wasn't a fan of Reagan and his Hollywood sound bites; his "government is the problem" quote would be used by the radical Right to undermine good government for years to come. And, Nixon was, well you know, Tricky Dick, Watergate, and multiple coverups (the extent of his lies concerning the Vietnam War wouldn't be uncovered for years). However, I was willing to go along with Bush's moderate Republican message. On the abortion issue, I was middle of the road; I was pro-choice but not after the fourth month unless for medical reasons. My vote also rattled a couple of friends and their more-liberal-than-thou attitude which I savored.

The drama at work was mostly about sales, or the lack thereof. I was getting despondent until I orchestrated the largest order in company history. On my recommendation, they hired Will, who had become a close friend and fellow astrology aficionado (and still living with my ex, Ann). We had cubicles next to each other. I became acquainted with everyone in the company to some degree or another. Naturally, everyone had their particular dramas. The president was an ex-banking executive who had a gift for the gab and a belief in his bullshit. The vice president was an ex-Marine who was convinced he was God's gift to salesmanship. The accountant was the president's wife. The dynamic between them was less than loving. One of the technicians was a great guy who hadn't discovered the benefit of deodorant. And, there was the administrative assistant Donna, married with a child Layla's age. She was a delightful Sagittarian with a keen sense of humor and a body to die for.

Within a few weeks, Donna and I were exchanging sexual innuendos. During a Christmas party, both of us got lubricated on the punch and had our first overt sexual exchange. I was seated at my desk in my cubicle finishing up some odds and ends before leaving the office for vacation. Donna popped in to wish me well and to tell me that she couldn't stop thinking about a comment I had made earlier that day about enjoying "eating pie" (i.e., cunnilingus). Then I told her that I also liked having my dick sucked at which point I unzipped my pants and pulled it out. Donna proceeded to kiss and suck my dick ever so briefly before explaining that she'd like to continue but couldn't for fear of being caught by someone in the office.

The sexual desire I felt for Donna was beyond anything I had experienced before. Within a month, in addition to daily flirting and petting, we were having sex a couple of times a week in the storage room or in my car with tinted windows at a semi-vacant private parking lot near the office. As you might imagine, this added to the growing sexual frustration with Ruth. I think she suspected something; occasionally she'd comment about how tired or disinterested I was.

You might say I was in a bit of a pickle. I was involved in a torrid sexual affair with a married woman at the office while suffering a deteriorating relationship with the woman I lived with. I was living a lie, but afraid to tell the truth. It was a challenging holiday season punctuated by the death of my dog Raja from old age. Even though I lived elsewhere due to my divorce, I had continued to visit Raja and play our revered Montana/Rice routine. His death was an emotional passage that foreshadowed more endings. I keep a framed picture of him on my wall unit.

I continued studying astrology; each birth chart was a unique stained-glass window illuminated by the One Light. I saw how astrology could help me identify and clarify life lessons that were unfolding. This wasn't determinism nor did I feel fatalistic. It was up to me to discern the meaning and choose a course of action. I discovered transits. They are the past, present, and future positions of outer planets (Jupiter, Saturn, Uranus, Neptune, and Pluto) superimposed on the birth or natal chart. Potential meaning can be ascertained based on angles between the transiting planet and the natal planet. For instance, my natal Venus which represents formation of social and emotional bonds with others was or would be strongly influenced over the next couple of years by the conjunctions of the transits of Neptune, Saturn, and Uranus; an unusual astrological trifecta, if you will.

> The further one gets from the central reality, the more diverse and contradictory life appears. However, as one becomes attuned to that center, to that higher Oneness, one perceives with increasing clarity that the birth chart is a whole, unified, living symbol, that the individual person is not merely a composite of many diverse factors, but is a living unit of divine potential. (Stephen Arroyo)

By May '89 my discontent with the computer peripherals company had become pronounced. The president turned out to be a bigger asshole than I imagined and didn't pay me my full commission which forced my hand. I resigned even though I didn't have another job lined up. I had been working with a recruiter and was confident I'd find a position soon. I had enough savings to tide me over for a few months. I worked part-time at the furniture store to help with the cash flow. And, Donna and I continued to cavort every couple of weeks or so.

Ann and Will broke up in June. Will and I compared notes and found many similarities. He fell in love with Ann for similar reasons including her intelligence, sensuality, and can-do attitude. The reasons he broke up with her were similar as well; the difficulty of dealing with her anger and anxiety. It was a season of relationship woes. My sister and her husband were on the verge of divorce. And, Johnny and Patty got divorced which Patty blamed me in part for instigating. There was some truth to that accusation. A couple of years before, I had brought some LSD with me when I visited Johnny; I figured the potential clarity might help him see how he was making himself unhappy. Torturing himself over a failed marriage wasn't helping matters and, regardless, he would continue being a loving father to his young son.

Later that month Mark informed me that he had AIDS which was pretty much a death sentence. He seemed to be handling the news well which I attributed to his spiritual orientation. He was taking a combination of drugs to combat it. My ignorance of how AIDS was transmitted was highlighted one day when I was visiting him and his friends down at his beach house. As we passed around a joint, I had a fearful thought that I might get AIDS from sharing the joint. I excused myself and went into the kitchen to get a drink of water. However, before I drank from the glass, I wiped the lip of the glass thoroughly.

> Everything perishes. If you don't want to perish go where there isn't anything to perish. Then you find that you are there already. This does put paid to the fear of death. (Douglas Harding)

I started working for HIS at the end of July as a service representative. My responsibilities were to train customers on how to use their information subscription and help keep their subscription up to date. Being on the road was a good fit for me. I worked with three sales representatives that lived in various parts of Florida. Ginny lived in Jacksonville. During our first meeting, we talked for hours mostly about personal matters including our sexual attraction. However, both of us agreed it wouldn't be a good thing to fish off the company pier.

A couple of months later the sexual attraction between Ginny and me became overt. After calling on some customers together, we were relaxing in her living room drinking beer when we started kissing passionately. We backed off and promised not go any further. That lasted a month or so. One night when I was supposedly on the road for business, I spent the night at Ginny's and went fishing. A few weeks later Ruth asked if I had had sex with Ginny (I'm not sure what sparked her suspicions). I confessed with a sense of relief figuring it would initiate the split. Also, it was better to admit to that than tell her about the months-long affair with Donna. It turned out Ruth had her secrets too. Without my permission, she had taken a credit card out in my name and had racked up $1500 in debt which she promised he'd pay off. We agreed to go our separate ways without much more drama; an emotional weight was lifted from my heart. Will helped me move out the end of November.

I had been in some sort of romantic relationship for years; being single, having my own apartment, and not having to negotiate or deal with differences in attitudes, behaviors, and beliefs was a pleasant change. I examined and processed, sometimes restlessly, what had happened in my relationships especially with Ruth. My conclusion was straightforward: premature commitment and ignoring warning signs of incompatibility; an unfortunate tendency

34

I would repeat. Also, I contacted Mary and clumsily tried to make amends. She informed me of her impending graduation and marriage at the end of the year. I wished her well.

Frequently, I found myself disappointed and discouraged because I judged my spiritual progress negatively due to my emotional/mental congestion, a self-reinforcing no-win situation. I kept trying to figure out how to be more spiritual by suppressing the mind. I figured once my mind was contained *then* I'd be enlightened. If I made mistakes, like the relationship with Ruth, I was very hard on myself. I initiated a program of reminding myself to "let go and let God" when I felt disheartened; that is, letting go of the congestion and letting Who I already am shine.

> The state we call Realisation is simply being oneself, not knowing anything or becoming anything. (Ramana Maharshi)

In January Layla turned 9 years old. We had a great relationship; we liked each other. Layla's charm was infectious. I enjoyed her company whether we were shopping or at the beach. Her social life was becoming more peer-centered which meant more dramas. One day when I picked her up at school, she was upset because a friend had unfairly accused her of cheating in a card game. I suggested she move on to other friends. Another curious twist was the "Say No to Drugs" campaign being waged in the school system. I considered it shortsighted and simplistic. Layla and I discussed the campaign one evening. I told her that the biggest danger was alcohol because of its pervasiveness and the dangers of driving under the influence. I mentioned marijuana too; also, dangerous to use when driving. I encouraged her to confide in me when she was older, assuring her of my understanding but knowing chances were slim she would.

I started dating again. Usually, I would have one date and move on. I was leery, to say the least. Ginny set me up with one of her friends from her tennis club because we both had been teachers. It went south quickly when she stipulated that her desire for a child was paramount. I was to be a sperm donor. During my travels due to business, I would meet women as well. I had a few dates with a lady in Melbourne. We had fun but realized there was no sexual chemistry, not for lack of trying. I also had a brief affair with my next-door neighbor. Lucy was a sexy twenty-two-year-old. After a few drinks one night she fessed up to never having had an orgasm. I was happy to solve the problem with some cunnilingus. She was thrilled.

Occasionally I'd hang out with Bert and Mia. I met Bert years before when he worked at a tobacco shop where I purchased my clove cigarettes. Both of them were bright and good-hearted. We'd smoke pot and take walks on the beach. The dynamic between Bert and Mia was a mystery to me. Frequently they talked past each other about different subjects each vying for attention. It was difficult to finish a thought without being interrupted, especially by Bert (Mars in the 1st house). Sometimes I'd encounter Tom when I visited them. Over the last couple of years, Tom and I had become estranged. I don't think he took kindly to my questioning some of his opinions.

> Man is a mix and a flux of two opposing forces. Yin and yang, active and passive, optimistic and pessimistic, extroverted and introverted, beautiful and ugly are a few of the different versions of the dualism. An individual's character and psyche are based on a unique interaction of these contrasting forces. (Sam Reifler; *I Ching*)

Around this time, I purchased my first PC. I was excited by having such power at my fingertips with its speedy 286/16 megahertz processor, 10-megabyte hard drive, and WordPerfect. However, it wasn't portable by any stretch. My journaling changed in some respects; I no longer wrote in a spiral notebook. When I wasn't home, I resorted to scribbling in my day timer on journal ideas which I would transcribe using WordPerfect because of the ease of editing. A few months later I discovered the danger of not backing up when I lost a couple of months' worth of journal entries.

On July 4th my doorbell rang; I thought nothing of it. The man identified himself as some sort of state official. I thought he wanted to talk to me because I was one of Bert's references for reestablishing his driver's license. It turned out he was with Child Protective Services. My neighbor in the apartment below mine had accused me of molesting Layla. She called the 800 number the state had set up for such purposes. She got the idea from hearing me chase Layla around the apartment trying to tickle her as she playfully yelled, "Daddy don't." Besides being shocked and angry, I was disappointed. Our daughters of the same age had played in the pool a couple of times while we chaperoned and chatted. Unfortunately, I was guilty until proven innocent. The state representative had to interview Layla and her mother to clear up the misunderstanding.

My job, for the most part, was going well. I had paid off all my debts. Layla was doing well socially and academically. Ann and I hadn't had a blow up in a while. And, Donna and I continued to rendezvous at my apartment after she got off of work when I was in town. We would chat amicably for a while and then have passionate sex. Sometimes, we'd go on a guilt trip due to her married status and promise not to fuck again but knowing we'd succumb again. Even though she had ample reasons to divorce her husband, Donna wasn't ready to make that decision. I liked the nonexclusive setup and the freedom to date other women.

Kris was my primary contact at one the corporate libraries I called on in Atlanta. Taking customers out to lunch was encouraged by management. I always made a point of asking Kris out for lunch. I found her very attractive; her Aquarius Sun, Taurus Moon, and Scorpio rising didn't hurt. We had a lot in common; we hit it off and started dating. The fact that she was African American and I was European American didn't faze either one of us. However, this wasn't the case with others; we'd get curious stares when we'd enter a restaurant holding hands or being affectionate in some public setting. We dated for a few months but went our separate ways amicably in large part because of the long distance factor.

In December I bought a two-bedroom, two bath condo in one of my favorite parts of town 10 minutes from downtown. I considered it my birthday present to myself for my thirty-eighth year. My view from the balcony was of the pool and deck with a beautiful Florida swamp with

Bald Cypress draped in Spanish Moss as background. This brought up issues with Ann about childcare payment and visitation. Ann and I agreed on a new childcare payment along with allowing Layla to decide for herself when she wanted to stay with me. A new phase in my relationship with Layla had dawned.

At the end of January, my brother and sister-in-law introduced me to Cathy who was recently separated. We met at a restaurant. I found her witty intellect, vivacious sensuality, and beauty very attractive; that would be, Gemini Sun, Libra Moon, and Aquarius Ascendant. We hit it off and ended up making out in her car for a couple of hours. The following evening, we partied hardy at my brother and sister-in-law's home. Quickly, we ascertained that "This isn't a crush, this is a crunch." In the fog of infatuation, the long-distance factor I had just dealt with faded.

Meanwhile back in Jacksonville, circumstances changed when Ginny resigned from HIS because of difficulties with our manager which prompted him to rearrange the territories throughout the region to reduce driving distances. He offered me a promotion and a newly created territory based in Birmingham, Alabama, which I accepted. My primary concern was Layla. I assured her that we'd see each other regularly; she was excited about the notion of visiting a new place (Birmingham was an eight-hour drive from Jacksonville and a three-hour plane trip through Atlanta). Her mother handled it better than I expected. Like me, I think she realized it would put some physical distance between us which would reduce our interactions, potential blowups at any time.

My transfer precipitated the first substantial disagreement with Cathy. She wasn't pleased with my decision to move to Birmingham; our fantasy of my moving to Atlanta was no longer an option. In May we decided to go our separate ways...sort of. Neither one of us wanted to be categorical about not copulating. We got together a couple more times, but it was apparent our "crunch" had no more crackle. Other issues would probably have split us apart; namely, her fundamentalist religious beliefs and difficult daughter. It wasn't lost on me how the numerous relationship changes corresponded with transiting Uranus conjunct my natal Venus; that is, unexpected changes in relationships.

Chapter 6: Multiplication

One light, the light that is one though the lamps be many. (The Incredible String Band)

Mom's mental faculties continued to deteriorate. Dad had moderated his alcohol consumption; he allowed himself a drink or two at a restaurant. He no longer kept alcohol in the home; however, Mom was buying liquor on the sly. It was almost amusing where she hid the empty bottles in drawers, boxes, and shelves. Dad realized he had to restrict her driving privileges as well, a good idea given her compromised abilities. My siblings and I thought Dad should consider a rehabilitation institution. In response to our concerns, Dad wrote us a letter (the paragraph below is part of it).

Ever since we (my sisters, brothers and I) had to support my mother during the last three decades of her life because my diabetic father was unable to, I have thought that it was the duty of parents to so provide for their waning years that the children would not be burdened with that obligation. The old care for the young; the young prepare for their future. I vowed that my kids would never have to help my wife and me, and I still feel that way. Young people have enough of their own; they should not have to take on others. At this time there is no problem. Taking care of Esther is easy. All I do is remind her to do simple things. Unless she gets a lot worse, I can do this forever. I am happy just being near her. Even when her condition worsens, I will care for her until professional care is absolutely required. It is selfish of me, but I want to keep her with me as long as I can. I do not want to live without her—my partner, my lover, my counselor, my wife, my best friend, my children's mother. If it becomes necessary to put her in a nursing home, I would like to go with her. I know that that does not make sense.

In June I started attending services at Unity Church in Birmingham. Having never lived in a town where I didn't know anyone, I needed an avenue to meet people. I had some familiarity with Unity and felt comfortable with the basic philosophy: "There is only One Power and One Presence in the Universe and in my life. God the Good, Omnipotent." My first impression was positive; they even had astrology books in the bookstore! I ended up over the next few years dating a handful of women that I met at Unity.

My dream life was memorable with a couple of recurring dreams. In one I find myself back in school even though I have graduated. However, the teachers don't recognize such, and I have to study for exams. In the next dream, I am walking along when suddenly I get tangled in a spider web with the spider quickly descending upon me. I backtrack as fast as possible. The first dream I felt had to do with lessons I thought I should have already mastered. The second had to do with romantic relationships and getting caught up in a web of difficulties. I also had a dream about Mark, my friend with AIDS. In the dream, he tells me he is doing well. A couple of days later, I called him to share the dream. His partner informed me that Mark had died six months before and that I was the third friend of Mark's to call in the recent past who had a similar dream. Bon voyage, my friend.

Things were working out well in Birmingham. The long-distance factor with my ex, Ann, meant there were far fewer interactions and less chance we'd push each other's buttons. My relationship with Layla was evolving nicely. A lot of credit was due to Layla's initiative and positive attitude. We talked on the phone almost every day. On our bimonthly visits, whether in Birmingham or Jacksonville, we'd go to the mall, view movies, visit natural wonders, and play games. Our favorite was Zilch, a six dice game which is part strategy and part luck.

Layla and I drove to Louisiana to visit Mom and Dad and celebrate Thanksgiving. Within minutes of our arrival, it was apparent Mom's memory and mental capacities had worsened; she asked the same questions repeatedly and had difficulty carrying on a conversation. Dad gracefully redirected the conversation without judgment. The next morning, she proposed making pancakes, my favorite. She got confused and walked away distracted. Layla and I drove back to

Birmingham in a subdued mood; both of us adjusting to the fact that the delightful personality we loved, known as Big Mom or Mom respectively, was dying. Her Alzheimer's disease would be officially diagnosed the following month.

My '92 New Year's resolutions were to quit smoking cigarettes and exercise regularly. I knew the best way to quit smoking was to avoid beer. My beer consumption had become an area concern due to my tendency to overindulge and misbehave. On my next business trip to Atlanta, I stayed at my brother and sister-in-law's home; they were out of town. One evening I got tipsy and made some inappropriate sexual overtures towards their au pair which required an apology a couple days later. Another embarrassing tendency was drunk dialing; that is, calling folks with an alcohol buzz and saying things my sober self wouldn't have said. I was starting to see in full Technicolor how under the influence of alcohol I was more inclined to make stupid decisions; that's why it is called stupid juice!

It so happened, the lady I was dating attended AA meetings. I compared notes with her and noticed a disturbing similarity to what prompted her to join AA: drinking to excess a couple of times a week with accompanying stupid behavior, spotty memories, and hangovers. Per Wikipedia: "Typical symptoms of a hangover may include headache, drowsiness, concentration problems, dry mouth, dizziness, fatigue, gastrointestinal distress (e.g., vomiting), absence of hunger, depression, sweating, nausea, hyper-excitability and anxiety." I decided to investigate AA further. Yep, I did the, "My name is Brian. I'm an alcoholic." I quit drinking and attended AA meetings weekly. And, I joined a gym with a pool and quit smoking.

> Insanity is doing the same thing over and over again and expecting different results. (Albert Einstein)

In April I sold the condo that I had bought the previous year in Jacksonville. Will had temporarily rented it but had to move due to a job transfer to San Antonio. I was glad to get the mortgage off my back. My job was going well; I received Top Ten and the Rookie of the Year awards. In July I received a bonus check for more than what I would've made in three years of teaching. When Tom found out about my good fortune, he asked for a $10K loan to pay off the IRS and banks. I went to the bank to wire him the money. Fortunately, the wiring functions at the bank were closed for the day. By the time I got back home from the bank, I had reconsidered figuring I'd be last to be repaid, if at all. I called him back and informed him of my decision. First, he tried to tell me that he had a job in works that guaranteed him $10K a month and he was good for it. I was dubious of such claims; Tom was known for his grandiose predictions about making money. Then, he tried to guilt trip me based on our friendship from years before. I didn't bite and lost respect for him.

In July of '92, Layla and I went to the Bahamas on the Disney cruise line replete with Mickey Mouse and Goofy characters. I thought Layla would get a kick out of that. She couldn't have cared less. Her fascination was with the one-armed bandits in the casino; curiously, you couldn't get to the children's play area without going through that part of the casino. I figured it was like a Nintendo game for her. As far as I was concerned, I didn't see the harm but the age restriction was 18, and she was 11. Much to her delight, the last night of the cruise she got to play. We saw a friend of hers who was 14 playing; I saw no danger. I gave her permission along with $20. The highlight of our cruise was the snorkeling around the Castaway Cay coral reefs. At first, Layla had a hard time with the concept that she could breathe underwater with the snorkel. She caught on quickly when she saw what awaited underwater. The schools of brightly colored fish and tropical corals were enthralling. We had a blast.

The first time I saw Lynn at a Unity Sunday service I was blown away by her Venusian beauty. I asked her out for a cup of coffee, and we hit it off. She invited me to the Halloween do of '92. She dressed up as a spider (You gotta admit, the Universe has a sense of humor!) and I donned a jelly bean man outfit she provided. We spent the evening dancing and checking out the other couple of hundred folks dressed up for the occasion. Lynn had an intense, almost regal, aura about her with her Capricorn Sun, Libra Moon, Scorpio Ascendant, and Leo Midheaven. After a couple of dates, we became passionate lovers.

During the next few months, Lynn and I spent all our free time together. When I wasn't traveling, I spent nights at her home. We enjoyed working on various home improvement projects. In January we went to Maui for a week; it was a reward trip for my sales numbers. It was an all-expenses-paid trip for two at a five-star hotel with a magnificent view of the Pacific. We got along well. However, at one of the company dinners, one of my workmates got in her face about a snobbish remark she made. That may have been alcohol-fueled; my manager clumsily hitting on her certainly was. Being shutterbugs, we came home with twelve rolls of film each and more pictures of rainbows than was necessary.

Bill Clinton was inaugurated as president in January of '93. I was full of optimism about the "state of the union." I thought a New Age may be dawning because of the fall of communism and the rise of democracies across the globe. However, there were some storms brewing on business, relationship, and political fronts that would have long-term ramifications. Business-wise, my sales numbers took a hit due to a glitch in the networking software which resulted in losing my largest customer to a competitor. And, Lynn's gifts business, which she owned, wasn't doing well either. She was contemplating bankruptcy or selling it. I lent her money to tide her over.

Then the "storm of the century" blew through Birmingham in March. It was a late snowstorm that dumped over half a meter while toppling trees and knocking out the electricity (we still had gas for cooking and heat). I had my first experience of being snowed in. At first, it was fun fucking frequently and reading by candlelight. But, by the third day, we were getting on each other's nerves. She thought I was inconsiderate and I thought she was arrogant. A storm of incompatibilities culminated in us breaking up. And, an unnoticed storm in Arkansas was gaining strength; an independent counsel was authorized to investigate Clinton's real-estate investment in the Whitewater Development Corporation.

Around this time, I stopped attending AA meetings. I was turned off by the coordinators' religious fundamentalism, promotion of AA-as-the-only-way, and the emphasis on being powerless rather than accentuating "a power greater," our true spiritual identity. (Years later I found out that different AA meetings vary in their emphases.) I started to drink beer occasionally figuring I could drink moderately which would prove to be a classic case of personal exceptionalism. That is, thinking I was somehow special; that I could disregard my history of problem drinking. I was ignoring the shadow of excess percolating in my subconscious; justifications or rationalizations that would periodically pester me for years.

Will's job transfer to San Antonio with the data communications company didn't bear fruit as hoped due to unrealistic sales goals set by management. He moved back to Jacksonville and rented a room from Ginny. However, before moving, he met Janet. They dated long distance for a few months until he moved back to San Antonio. Given my break up with Lynn and needing a change of scenery, I drove to Jacksonville to visit Layla, Will, and Ginny. I stayed at Ann's, my old home, which had a surreal feel to it. Ann was staying at her boyfriend's place. Layla and I entertained ourselves with some clothes shopping and perfect beach weather; warm, not hot, with a mild breeze.

The night before my return trip to Birmingham, Will, Ginny, and I got together and partied hardy. Fueled by wine, increasingly my choice in adult beverages, Ginny and I started flirting. Will bowed out. Ginny and I ended up in bed doing the horizontal hump until dawn. On the long drive back with a full-fledged hangover, I decided to patch things up with Lynn including a bouquet of flowers delivered to her home. Lynn and I would break up and reconcile a handful of times over the next year; sometimes initiated by me sometimes by her. The make-up sex almost made up for the emotional roller coaster ride.

> Sometimes the lesson to be learned in a relationship is how to hang in there and try to work things out. Other times, the lesson to be learned is how to exit a situation that doesn't serve. No one can determine for another person what principle applies in what circumstance. (Marianne Williamson; *A Return to Love*)

A week or so after I got back, Layla called me about an explosive disagreement she had with her mother. Practically speaking, Layla was a teenager; officially she was twelve. I realized some upset wasn't unusual between mother and teenage daughter; I grew up with two sisters. However, what worried me was the level of anger being generated. Some of the altercations I had with Ann had left an indelible mark in my memory; I wanted to protect Layla from such. I encouraged Ann and Layla to get relationship counseling. Ann's feedback was negative and defensive; she reminded me of how I once damaged a door with my fist in anger. There wasn't much I could do.

In July '93 a retrogression hypnotist came through town. I had always been curious about past lives; evolutionary astrology is based on such. My first retrogression uncovered an early childhood memory I had completely forgotten. On weekend mornings my brother, sister, and I would wait outside Mom and Dad's room until they gave us the okay; then we'd run in and jump on their bed. Good fun. In the next retrogression, I experienced myself as a little boy with his mother and little sister being herded into a gas chamber. I was holding my mother and sister's hands as I gasped for air before collapsing to the floor. In the last retrogression, I was a local parish priest dying from cold and starvation in a dungeon. Apparently, I was incarcerated for preaching the wrong gospel according to my superiors. These sessions were in first person present tense replete with heavy-duty emotions appropriate to the circumstances (plenty of tissues). I figured even though they weren't actual "real" events, they were worth investigating for subconscious material and astrologically (years later I found them reflected astrologically in my birth chart via the nodal axis).

During one of my breakups with Lynn, I attended a Sunday service at Unity. I had eye contact with a good-looking woman that was hard to ignore. Terry and I ended up chatting after the service in the parking lot followed by lunch. We talked readily about everything, thoroughly enjoying each other's company. We ended up at my apartment where we engaged in enthusiastic sex. We made plans to see each other the following Friday. However, the next day I called and backed out citing my then off, but possibly on, relationship with Lynn. Terry seconded the motion; she was in a similar situation with her boyfriend.

> When an old pattern reappears, it doesn't mean we've been avoiding it or that we're failing; it could mean we're ready to bite off another piece of it. (Gloria Karpinski; *Where Two Worlds Touch*)

Layla and I visited Mom and Dad in their new retirement community in Baton Rouge which eliminated the upkeep of their home and the necessity of cooking. It was a bittersweet stay. Mom's Alzheimer's was worse than before; a growing shadow of incommunicado with a few precious moments of clarity. Dad was gracious as usual both as a caregiver and host. A couple days later, Layla and I drove to New Orleans and stayed at a bed & breakfast on St. Charles near Tulane. We took the trolley to the French Quarter and caught Bourbon Street just before the lunch crowd. I wasn't aware how X-rated it had become. I quickly steered us towards Jackson Square where we feasted on beignets and coffee followed later by shrimp Po'boys.

The long drive to Louisiana and back with Layla provided me time to reflect on the yo-yo relationship with Lynn. It was taking its emotional toll. Lynn was feeling the same. Using Barbara DeAngelis's book *Are You The One For Me?*, we thoroughly analyzed our relationship. We discussed the spiritual/value, mental/intellectual, emotional/feeling, romantic/sexual, physical/appearance, social/recreational, professional/financial, and family/children aspects. No breakthrough occurred. We had given it a good go but decided it best to break up for good.

Terry called and asked me out. She had broken up with her significant other as well. Our first date pretty much picked up where our last rendezvous ended. I made a tasty dinner; for dessert, we copulated copiously. Terry, with her Pisces Sun, Gemini ascendant, and Capricorn Moon, was a pleasant change from the melodrama with Lynn. We wanted to enjoy each other's company without undue deliberations about the future. We agreed to a non-exclusive approach. Due to her two kids and a part-time job we weren't able to spend uninterrupted time together often. However, the more we dated, the more we enjoyed each other's company and, as Terry said, "the sex is great!"

While Terry's kids were living with their step-father for the summer school break, we slept together every night possible. We thought the sexual spontaneity, emotional honesty, and comfortable communication was the best we'd experienced. Terry and I decided to live together and be sexually exclusive. Things were hunky-dory until her two kids returned. I had no idea what living with her two kids entailed. Both were a handful, to say the least. Within a couple of months or so, I knew I had made a mistake. Once again, I had prematurely committed. We started having disagreements; especially if we had been drinking. My enthusiasm faded which angered Terry; she accused me of not trying hard enough to make it work.

In early November I moved out. As I was packing Terry got very angry, almost to the point of getting physical. In a state of shock, I left, staying at a friend's home overnight (my apartment wasn't available until the following day). When I came back the next morning to continue packing, she apologized. I guess to make up for mistreating me, Terry confessed to an office affair with her married boss. My immediate feeling was one of emotional relief coupled with knowing that our separation wasn't entirely my fault. Having cleared the air, so to speak, we engaged in intercourse intermittently as I packed. To our credit, Terry and I remained friends with benefits.

Due to the advent of the internet and electronic delivery, the nature of HIS's business was changing. Information previously sold primarily as a microform subscription was available online, sometimes for free. The job situation with HIS became insecure. Management was now thinking about taking away our smaller accounts ostensibly to allow us more opportunity to prospect. It was a reasonable notion but without merit. I had been prospecting assiduously all along. It meant a reduction in income. For the first time in my six years with HIS, I was considering the prospect of finding another job.

Layla spent Thanksgiving with me. We had a wonderful time clothes shopping, watching movies, and cooking tasty meals. We celebrated my 42nd birthday with Terry and her kids at her place. Her pickup truck served as a backdrop for some excellent photos. A couple weeks later, Will came through Birmingham to conduct some energy work sessions which enabled him to visit. We caught up on our various melodramas including his stormy relationship with Janet who suffered from manic-depression and alcohol abuse. Naturally, we engaged in some astrological shop talk including the evolutionary journey of the soul. We chuckled about the need for seatbelts.

Just before the end of the year, Dad called with some sad news; his prostate cancer from years before had metastasized into bone cancer. Typical of such a dire diagnosis, his window of life expectancy was somewhere between 6 months and 3 years. In a letter that followed he informed me that Mom's Alzheimer's had gotten worse. He ended his letter with these poignant words, "There are times these days when I feel pretty sorry for myself. Then I remember that we have spent 56 wonderful years together. I'll say 'Hasta' on that note. Love ya, Dad." I tasted salty tears on my lips.

Chapter 7: Termination

God grant me the serenity to accept the things I cannot change. Courage to change the things I can, and the wisdom to know the difference. (Reinhold Niebuhr)

For New Year's '95 I drove to Jacksonville to spend time with Layla. As usual, she was a joy to be with. We stayed at a hotel on the beach for an extended weekend. We frequented our favorite restaurants, took long walks on the beach, and saw the movie, *Nell*. Jodie Foster plays an isolated, wild child who is slowly introduced to the larger world she isn't familiar with; an interesting take on the importance of language and socialization. We ended up spending the following day with Frank and his daughter in downtown St. Augustine; a humorous subplot was his unsuccessful attempt to hide his cigarette habit from her.

From Jacksonville, I drove to Pensacola Beach for a rendezvous with Terry at a hotel with a beautiful view of the Gulf. After nibbling on each other along with some snacks, we ended up at a funky bar with pool tables where we dealt with a couple of college-aged pool sharks before retreating to the bar. The bartender was a beautiful woman with blue eyes that didn't quit. After a few minutes of observing her, I told Terry that she was a Pisces. The bartender confirmed my hunch. That was lucky on my part; she could have had prominent Pisces elsewhere in the chart (Moon, ascendant, etc.) and not known it and I would be left empty-handed with an unconfirmed hunch. Then she proposed a threesome with us. That wasn't unusual around Terry; she was bisexual and attracted women of similar persuasion. For reasons I can't recall, we declined which we regretted later.

Astrology is downstream from the Source. Think of it as soul algebra; there are equations with variables that you fill in with planets, signs, and aspects that provide helpful meaning arbitrated by you. These variables or symbols are, as Steven Forrest eloquently states, "…multi-dimensional and are modulated into material and psychic expression by the consciousness of the individual." Case and point were the transits of Jupiter, Saturn, Uranus, Neptune, and Pluto which continued to provide helpful information. It impressed me how they mirrored my psychological and/or biographical experiences; an archetypal description of possibilities and probabilities within my awareness. I was curious to see how the upcoming transit of Pluto (death/rebirth/transformation) conjunct my Sun (primary identity/expression) and sextile my Mars (assertion/courage) would manifest.

Astrology works by reminding you who you are, by warning you about the comforting lies we all tell ourselves, and by illuminating the experiences that trigger your most explosive leaps in awareness. After that, the rest is up to you. (Steven Forrest)

In February I visited Mom and Dad in Baton Rouge. Mom's Alzheimer's had made her memory essentially nonfunctional. And, Dad was suffering from blood clots in his legs which was interfering with his caregiving. Due to these developments, a plan was formulated to move Mom and Dad to Atlanta where they would be closer to my brother and youngest sister. Their new apartment complex offered services which would alleviate Dad of being the sole provider of Mom's care.

In mid-March, I met with my manager. I figured he'd get down on me about my numbers, even though they were close to quota. To my surprise, he asked for my resignation as part of a companywide reduction in force (RIF). I opted to resign at the end of the sales year two months away. HIS was going through reorganization and downsizing due to the dawning of the internet age. My HIS career was concluding; the next chapter was unknown. However, I felt confident figuring my resume spoke well of my skill set. In short order, I interviewed with a company that sold software which went well. The director of sales needed to get the final approval to hire me. I would start in mid-May after I had relocated to Jacksonville. A week before my actual moving date he called and apologetically informed me that the position was no longer available due to lackluster sales company-wide. I was disappointed but not panicked; financially, I was in good shape due to exceeding my sales goal for the year which meant a large commission check. I figured I'd secure a job once I relocated in in Jacksonville where I'd be renting a room from Ginny. She was appreciative of the rental income, and I could use her garage for storage until I found a long-term living arrangement.

Just before moving to Jacksonville I underwent a vasectomy; "a surgical procedure for male sterilization or permanent contraception. During the procedure, the male vas deferens are cut and tied or sealed to prevent sperm from entering into the urethra and thereby prevent fertilization of a female through sexual intercourse." (Wikipedia) I had considered such before dating Lynn and Terry, but pregnancy wasn't a concern due to their tubes being tied. However, a one-night stand a few weeks before with a lady I met on a business trip convinced me to act. I was going to clip any such possibility in the scrotum, so to speak. By the way, watching someone, even if a medical professional, approaching my private parts with a hypodermic needle in hand was unnerving! However, no need to worry, the injection of a local anesthetic called Xylocaine resulted in only a minor prick.

My move to Jacksonville proceeded without a hitch. Terry was a big help packing the U-Haul. We experienced mixed emotions from gladness for our genuine affection for each other and sadness for the prospect of no longer seeing each other regularly. Once I settled into Ginny's spare bedroom, I secured a handful of interviews. I came close to accepting one offer but decided to back off until something better came along. I developed a daily routine of sorts. I'd wake up, meditate, do some yoga stretches, eat breakfast, and take a long walk topped off by a shower. In the afternoon I'd drink beer, smoke cigarettes (yep, I had started smoking again), and sit on the back porch overlooking the lake. Ginny and I interacted occasionally; we weren't involved sexually.

Having not lived in Jacksonville for four years, my social circle needed expansion. I visited a Unity Church nearby but was turned off by the pushiness of the minister. So, I attended the Unity Church near downtown. Before the service, I checked out the bookstore. The first person I saw was Lucy, that sexy young lady who lived next door to me in the apartment complex I mentioned before. She was attractive as ever but married. Then I went to get a cup of coffee in the all-purpose area and ran across Sarah, Will's old girlfriend. We sat next to each other during the service. Afterward, we exchanged stories about what we'd been up to since we last interacted seven years before. She had her own tailoring business and had gone through a few relationship changes. I volunteered to do her chart (Sun and Midheaven in Capricorn, Moon conjunct Ascendant in Aries, etc.). A few days later we got together for dinner to discuss the birth chart; little did we know that this was the beginning of a long-term friendship.

The best part of being back in Jacksonville was hanging out with Layla. We could take a walk on the beach or get a bite to eat with little planning. In the fall she'd be attending high school. I looked forward to seeing her take leaps and bounds in maturation and understanding. Dealing with Ann without the benefit of living in different cities had its definite drawbacks. Her eccentric behavior that irritated me before still did. One day out of the blue she asked me to run a personal errand for her. When I refused, she became angry and accused me of being selfish. I made sure in no uncertain terms she understood my take; the key phrase being, "Go fuck yourself."

The USA has always been a culturally, racially, and religiously diverse society. However, the political landscape was getting very polarized with "cultural wars" **over abortion, recreational drug use, homosexuality, environmentalism, nationalism, and feminism.** The Republican Party was veering sharply to the Right **with military-style smugness.** Their legislative effort to promote fundamentalist Christianity was a violation of the separation of church and state; namely, the 1st Amendment which guarantees freedom of religion (or from religion). And, their distortion of the 2nd Amendment was equally dangerous. Our secular government has the right to sponsor, endorse, and/or enforce the basics; that is, commonly accepted laws concerning murder, theft, rape, safety, health, security, *and* gun control.

> People demand freedom of speech as a compensation for the freedom of thought which they seldom use. (Søren Kierkegaard)

Things were pretty fucked up around the world as well. Tribal warfare and genocide had reared its head again in the Balkans, exacerbated by the ineptitude of the UN. The so-called war on drugs was an ongoing joke. The lure of easy money was corrupting law enforcement and judicial efforts here and abroad. The indictment of ex-federal lawyers and various world leaders was a testament to that reality. In turn, we had created a prison industry based on absurd incarceration rates and procedures. I preached legalization. Drug prohibitions don't work; just like the alcohol prohibition of yesteryear. Making a substance like marijuana (LSD, cocaine, heroin, etc.) or a service like prostitution illegal criminalizes suppliers and users and forces them underground where the lack of quality control is more prevalent and violence more likely. And, there's no collection of sales taxes.

I drove up to Atlanta for a family reunion. My previous phone conversation with Dad left me with the impression that his transition time was coming soon. I was able to hang out with Mom and Dad on two separate occasions. The first day, my brother and I went over to their apartment. Dad was tired. Mom was ornery. The following day Mom and Dad came over to my brother and sister-in-law's for tacos; all my siblings know Mom's recipe by heart. Mom was in a more pleasant mood, and Dad seemed relieved; I think he realized that Mom would be cared for and that he could exit without guilt and/or obligation. He could let go of his noble sense of responsibility for Mom's welfare that had kept him with his body the last few years.

In the meantime, my friendship with Frank had been rekindled. We'd go out to lunch or hang out on the deck of Ginny's home smoking cigarettes, drinking beer or wine, and discussing our relationship dynamics a la *Men are from Mars, Women from Venus*. Frequently, he'd complain about his marriage, and I'd share details about my dating life (i.e., a recently divorced woman I met at Unity with a healthy sexual appetite that had been unfulfilled for years in an unhappy marriage). We had some good laughs.

After six months of unemployment, I accepted a sales job with a local communications company selling network technology, sound systems, and CCTV systems to the educational market. There was a steep learning curve. However, with a job I was able to secure a loan and purchase a home in the old neighborhood where I owned the condo. One of the main reasons I bought the house was the beautiful tropical landscaping including a stand of timber bamboo five stories tall in the backyard. Within short order, I painted the interior and exterior. Home improvement was a guaranteed high.

By January of '96, Mom's Alzheimer's had become so debilitating as to require **round-the-clock care.** I drove up to Atlanta to help my brother move Mom *and* Dad into a special care unit (SCU); memory care units specially designed for Alzheimer's patients. That's right; out of devotion to Mom, Dad was moving in with her as well. After completing the move, my brother had to leave which left Mom, Dad, and me in a small room. In the background, a football game was on TV. Dad and I chatted while Mom ambled restlessly around the room. At one point, she turned and looked at Dad and said clearly, "I love you." Dad looked at her and responded, "And, I love you." That exchange brought a tear to my eye. I lingered a while more before my long drive back to Jacksonville. Dad was seated when I leaned over and kissed him goodbye on the cheek and told him, "I love you." He responded, "I love you too." That was noteworthy. Normally, he would say, "We love you too." I kissed Mom and expressed my love for her as well. That was the last time I saw Dad alive.

The Alzheimer's ward was without compare in my experience; the patients were in various states of mental and physical deterioration that rendered them incapable of doing the most basic things such as feeding, bathing, and toileting themselves. The smell was intense. Apparently, Dad didn't much care for the surroundings; three days later he moved into my brother's home. He let go of Mom knowing she was in a good place for her care. Within a couple days, he entered a coma followed by his death a few days later. At his funeral, I read, through thick tears, a eulogy expressing my appreciation for him being my parent, teacher, and friend. "As a friend, simply put, Dad was fun to be with. His engaging, witty, conversational style helped others feel at ease. His insightful advice was dependable and his generosity never failing. However, above all, what I will remember about Dad was his loving nature. Despite the disagreements we had as I matured, I knew I could count on his unconditional love. But, even more than his love for his children and grandchildren, was his love for Mom. The love Mom and Dad had was a glorious example of a man and woman who truly loved each other. A finer heritage I can't imagine. I will miss him."

The period after Dad's death was another dark night of the soul, a shadowy and dispiriting phase. I started drinking and smoking again after a four-month hiatus. I missed our weekly Sunday afternoon chats on the phone where we'd share what was happening in our lives and pontificate about politics, sports, etc. Because of Mom's Alzheimer's, in a way, I felt like she had died as well. Adding to my emotional distress was dissatisfaction with my job. The networking technology wasn't selling as expected. **The Pluto transit I had expressed curiosity about earlier was plain to see: Pluto (death, transformation) conjunct my Sun (ego, identity) in 4th house (private self, roots) and sextile my Mars (assertiveness) in 6th house (duties, skills).**

A few weeks after the funeral, Regina Donaldson drove up from Melbourne, a 3-hour drive on I-95, for a visit. We connected before the funeral when I called significant family friends to inform them of Dad's death. One of the families I contacted was the Donaldson's (Mr. Donaldson worked for the same oil company as Dad. Like us, they had lived in Puerto Rico and Miami). I called Stan Donaldson, my best friend from high school. We had communicated sporadically since our college days. He was out at sea captaining a commercial fishing boat when I called. His wife recommended I call Regina, his little sister. I had had one brief adult conversation with her fifteen years before when both of us lived in Miami. Regina and I chatted effortlessly; she had fond memories of my father from Puerto Rico. I invited her to visit me in Jacksonville.

Regina and I hit it off immediately. Her dramatic expressiveness matched, maybe even exceeded mine. I found her zest for life and zany humor refreshing. Her Sagittarius Moon and my Sagittarius Sun along with similar Leo ascendants created an agreeable correspondence. And, once she learned to breathe and quiet her mental chatter (Sun, Mercury, and Uranus conjunct), we harmonized sexually. It wasn't long before we fell in love. Over the next handful of months, we visited each other numerous times.

Will's relationship with Janet was failing. The joy of becoming parents had evaporated due to Janet's irrational behavior **complicated by her alcoholism**. The doubts I had before about the viability of the relationship had evolved into the conviction that it was doomed to failure which I kept to myself. All I could do was listen and empathize. At the same time, Terry's once budding relationship with a guy she had met after I left Birmingham was on the rocks as well complicated by physical pain from a car wreck and the less than adequate health care she was receiving.

When Dad was alive, I would occasionally send him books that I thought might appeal to him and spur conversations. One such book was *Life After Life* by Moody. Dad read it and returned it with his feedback written in the margin. Early one morning a dream awoke me. In the dream, I'm observing a group of folks who are milling around after a book club meeting at a community center or such. Upon further observation, I notice that most of them have a copy of *Life After*

Life in their hand. Then I become aware of someone standing to my right side. I turn and realize it is Dad. He looks me in the eye and says, "Brian, you're right. There is life after life." Then he turns and dematerializes a la Star Trek transporter. His inner light (Season 5, episode 25) still lingers in my heart.

As July rolled around Regina and I decided to live together (she could readily transfer with her job selling cosmetics). We rented a U-Haul and moved her belongings, including her dog, up to Jacksonville. It had been a few years since my short-lived fiasco with Terry. Regina's previous live-in situation hadn't worked out well either. It was a leap of faith on both our parts. I figured we had enough similarities, enough friendship that it might work. In some ways, we interacted more like brother and sister. I thought maybe that would be the necessary dynamic for long-term success.

Along with high school comes dating. Being realistic, I knew that natural evolution included Layla. Like many fathers, I hoped she wouldn't date someone like I was at her age. However, like it or not, Layla was no longer that cute little girl that would spontaneously hold my hand. As a typical teenager, she would experience dramas she wouldn't share with me. I hoped she'd be more cautious about alcohol, drugs, and sex than I was in high school. Her mother was initially manic but settled down after a while. And, I'd have to say, I didn't take a shine to her first boyfriend and his lack of social grace. Fortunately, they broke up.

And, after months of frustration trying to sell the network technology, I decided to join a company that sold telephone systems to hotels. Picture me jumping from the frying pan into the fire. My primary customers were predominantly South Asian hotel owners who engaged in manipulative negotiating tactics; they used the bait and switch routine. They'd agree to a contract and then try to weasel various concessions. I figured it was an industry predilection but not to my liking; phone system sales didn't have career potential.

Thankfully, the phone system sales farce didn't last long. A tech startup that sold internet training courses had located their HQ in Jacksonville. I believed it had the potential of being the next internet sensation. I applied for an inside sales position and accepted a job offer in quick order. The CEO was a charismatic fellow who had lined up millions in venture capital. Quickly, I became disillusioned. I was making a shitload of sales calls every day but getting nowhere fast because of poorly conceived course offerings. Also, within short order, the office dynamics became complicated; various egos were in perpetual conflict.

By the end of the year, my relationship with Regina had become complicated as well. Unlike our long-distance relationship, living together was showing us aspects of each other we hadn't seen before. We were no longer willing to keep quiet about certain previously unexpressed feelings and opinions. My complaint was her dark moodiness; Regina's was my work schedule. I was working the 1:00 PM to 9:00 PM shift to cover the West Coast. By the time I'd get home and unwind, she was tired and not in the mood for socializing or sex. Also, she was bothered by my phone friendship with Terry which I wasn't willing to waive because of her insecurities. And,

I embarked on a no smoking (and, thus, no drinking) campaign which Regina showed no interest in joining.

Regina's dark moodiness worsened due to our disagreements and her difficulties work; she sought medical help. The doctor's diagnosis was depression which explained a lot; he recommended Prozac and counseling. I also found out that she hadn't been honest about her economic situation. She had credit card debt up the ass to the tune of almost $20K. I realized she had not entirely supported herself for the last handful of years. She had lived either with her parents or with a boyfriend. And when she couldn't pay for something from her income, she would use credit cards. I recommended she file for bankruptcy.

As I mentioned, the office was peppered with assholes. The lousy sales numbers didn't help. Adding to the toxic brew were frequent rumors that the Jacksonville office would close. Our telephone sales responsibilities had morphed into nothing more than glorified telemarketing. Then came the RIF; six of my fellow "educational consultants" were fired, and a new manager was hired who couldn't have been a worse choice. He lasted only a month. I began looking for another career opportunity.

During Layla's spring break, we drove up to Atlanta to visit my brother, sister, and Mom. The drive provided Layla and me the chance to chat. I probably told her too much about my teenage years (getting laid for the first time in a whorehouse in Old San Juan, smoking pot before my SATs, etc.). However, she reciprocated by disclosing that she'd just broken up with her boyfriend and hadn't told her mother for fear of interrogation. Mom was doing as well as could be expected in the Alzheimer's facility. She couldn't carry on a conversation but upon occasion would make a perfectly clear statement like, "That is a pretty flower." I hope there is a cure in the works soon. Genetically, research indicates my chances are greater to suffer from Alzheimer's. I have a strong preference that not be my fate.

In June of '97, I accepted a job offer with a publisher of academic research material, mostly in microform. My customers were academic libraries such as U of Florida, U of Texas, U of North Carolina, Rice, Emory, Tulane, Duke, etc. My territory included the southeastern and south-central US. The salary and potential commissions were substantially better. Not dealing with office politics and working out of my home was a better fit for me. And, I was traveling again which I really enjoyed.

Regina's depression lightened due to Prozac. However, for me, the relationship prospect had darkened; a chasm had grown that was no longer was passable. I didn't see a future for us as a couple. The sex, friendship, and extensive history with each other's family complicated matters and added to the emotional difficulty of separation. In September she moved out. I found myself alone with some somber doubts about my romantic relationship karma.

> Seeing does not dispense with the need to face the whole of one's past and to undo its knots by exposing them to the light of consciousness. The more analytical work that has been done before seeing, the clearer and steadier the seeing is likely to be.

Nevertheless, such analysis does not itself lead to seeing, nor does neglect of it rule out seeing…Our sole task is just to go on seeing who we are. The necessary situations will then arise, quite naturally, in which we may re-enact the essential aspects of our buried past, so ridding it of its menace. (Douglas Harding; *As I See It*)

One of my favorite TV shows was the sitcom, *Seinfeld*. Occasionally, Layla and I would watch it together. After one episode where George lied about something to take the easy way out, Layla and I discussed how we had done likewise. We shared various scenarios where we had lied, typically trivial, unnecessary lies. She blamed the predilection on me, and I blamed it on Mom who told me when I was a kid it was okay to tell a white lie to protect someone's feelings. It was amusing and one of those interactions that make parenting a joy.

Due to my love of ping-pong, I purchased a table for the garage which could be folded up when not in use. Bert and Frank came over regularly, two or three times a week when I wasn't on the road. We'd play for hours, frequently fueled by weed and beer. Notably, we never kept score; we agreed that it minimized the egotism; each point was played with conviction and concentration. Our level of play was skillful based on Frank's amateur ranking.

The midwinter national library conference of '98 was in New Orleans which meant booth duty; meeting and greeting and standing for hours. Once again, my New Year's resolution was breaking my cigarette addiction. I had quit a handful of times over the last few years; once for close to six months only to succumb to some tempting rationalization. I was also concerned about my alcohol consumption; I was drinking to excess more often. I knew breaking my cigarette addiction meant avoiding any type of alcohol. So, when my fellow sales mates went to the French Quarter to party on the company dime, I stayed in my hotel room reading and writing. For the next six months, I didn't drink to assure myself that my cigarette habit was no longer. It worked. I haven't smoked since. Not smoking proved to be shadow boxing compared to my upcoming bout with booze.

Under the category, "What was I thinking?!," I started dating again. I put an ad in the local entertainment paper: "Compatibility means going well together spiritually, intellectually, emotionally & physically. Looking to share the joy & woe of life. WDM, 44, 6'1'', 200lbs, walking, beach, movies, gardening, cooking, travel, etc." I received a handful of responses. One lady seemed really promising; we exchanged pictures via email and planned a rendezvous at a local restaurant for dinner. When I saw her seated at the bar, I was disappointed; she looked nothing like her photo. She admitted the photo was taken ten years before. While we ate dinner, I informed her with as much sensitivity as I could muster that another date wasn't going to happen. I dated a couple more women before I withdrew my ad. Ascertaining the necessary chemistry online was next to impossible.

Frank and Bert were gun aficionados. Both had tried to talk me into buying a gun for years. I had mixed feelings about such; I enjoyed target practice at the range, but couldn't justify the purchase for home security reasons. According to a couple of cops I had spoken to previously, an alarm system or a dog was a better choice. However, one day while eating lunch with Frank,

I spontaneously said, "Let's go buy a gun!" Frank was delighted. He had the type of license which allowed him to buy guns on demand. I have used it twice since at a range. It's safely stowed in a closet. The idea of walking around carrying a gun or living in a society where that is commonplace is repulsive to me.

Then the shit hit the fan between Layla and her mother who proceeded to lose any semblance of composure. In a clumsy and sad attempt to get attention, Ann asked Bert if Layla could live with him. Layla had carte blanche to live with me as long as I wasn't out of town traveling. I blasted Ann in a letter for "actively disavowing any responsibility" for her actions. When the dust settled, I was able to get her and Layla to agree to meet with a counselor. Layla attended her session first. Ann broke her promise and never attended her meeting. Later, Layla confided in me that the counselor told her that she was the adult in the situation and that Ann was behaving like a hurt child.

My flight through the Newark hub to Hartford for our August sales meeting was on time, an unusual occurrence. One of the attendees was Carol from the UK; she was the marketing manager and lived outside of London. I found her attractive but thought it impractical to pursue. Nonetheless, in the spirit of friendliness, I invited her out one evening for drinks. We carried on famously. So well that the last day of her stay, we went out to dinner again where we discussed visiting each other on either side of "the pond." In October she visited me in Jacksonville. We got along quite well; I liked her uncomplicated nature and frank sexuality. The only glitch was her desire for a baby; she hoped I'd reverse my vasectomy and I hoped she'd drop the fantasy.

My trip to England to visit Carol resulted in my becoming an Anglophile within minutes of landing at Heathrow. Her tour started with a couple of near panic attacks on my part; I wasn't used to driving on the left side of the road. My arrhythmia became a distant memory as we cruised through some beautiful rural areas and quaint villages. Oxford proved to be my favorite town. We also visited London twice; a big city with its famous landmarks such as Trafalgar Square and the giant Ferris wheel on the River Thames, the London Eye. We went to a play in the theatre district which was quite good, at least what I saw of it. The theatre was uncomfortably warm which lead to some sleepy moments. The second time in London we took a two-hour double-decker bus tour. Carol, who grew up in London, admitted that she learned things about London she didn't know.

Carol and I got along smashingly until the last night which was anti-climactic (after some very climactic sex, I might add). She wanted me to commit to a long-term relationship. I refused based on the long distance and the short time we had known each other. She became upset and terminated our relationship. Carol's Leonian temper would cool. A couple months later we rendezvoused in Atlanta for a family reunion followed by a trek to Amicalola Falls at the southern end of the Appalachian Trail. I had made reservations at the hotel situated at the top of a hill at the entrance to the trail. When we got to the base of the hill, I told her that we had to hike up the hill to our accommodations. In disbelief, she started to drag her luggage up the hill until I told her I was kidding. We had a good laugh as she chased me around the car.

However, her desire for a child would prove paramount, so we went our separate ways romantically. We've remained friends, exchanging an occasional email. She is now married and the mother of two.

My original optimism about Clinton administration was in tatters in part because of his extra-marital affair with Monica Lewinsky. The Whitewater investigation had morphed into a major scandal consummated by a blowjob and a blue dress. It was big news, seemingly the only news which Clinton made worse because he lied about it (and the way he lied about it). I'm not sure his misbehavior required impeachment, and I had my suspicions about the motivations of the star inquisitor. Little did I know that Clinton's facile fabrications would pale in comparison to future executive falsehoods.

The relationship between Will and Janet continued its inexorable deterioration. Janet, who had been on the wagon for just over a year, was bingeing again. She'd take off in the car, destination unknown, with their son and not have the decency to communicate with Will. To say the least, he was concerned for his son's welfare but was financially strapped, so his options were limited. I used some of my frequent flyer points and bought him a round trip ticket so he could visit in January and decompress a bit.

Chapter 8: Maturation

What we are looking for is what is looking. (St. Francis of Assisi)

Ginny accepted my invitation to New Year's Eve dinner. She was no longer angry with me for moving out of her place a few years back. Over poached salmon and many glasses of wine, we caught up on each other's melodramas; she was in a bit of tight spot with her mortgage. Dessert consisted of kissing and caressing. In the midst of the passion, I told her she could move in with me if she needed to. The next morning, I woke up hungover *and* without any recollection of her reply, if any, to my preposterous proposal. Alarmed that Ginny might have replied in the affirmative, I called her and apologetically rescinded my offer. I explained it was wine induced which didn't go over well with her.

It was a season of unexpected relationship challenges, not just romantic. This was reflected astrologically with transiting Uranus moving through my 7th house of relationships. Robert Hand in his book, *Transits,* put it succinctly: "Relationships, in general, will be a significant challenge, and you won't even be able to take the old reliable ones for granted." Business relationships were demanding too. SMP online publications weren't selling well, and microform sales were iffy, subject to fiscal year-end discretionary spending. Librarians who had been longtime customers refused to consider microform anymore. SMP sales representatives were quitting on a regular basis. Within two years, I had become the senior member tenure-wise on the sales force. I started wondering if it wasn't time to look for a different opportunity.

My annual medical in May included a treadmill stress test which provided a good laugh. I started out with a cocky attitude. As the speed of the treadmill was raised my cockiness changed to confidence, then determination, then concern, and finally, while barely hanging on outright supplication. My blood work indicated, as expected, high cholesterol which runs in the family. The doctor advised me to lose some weight which I had gained after quitting cigarettes as well as a low-fat, no alcohol diet and exercise. For exercise, I continued to play ping-pong with Frank and Bert. And, based on a TV ad, I purchased an exercise machine called a Gazelle which I took to readily unlike the low-fat, no alcohol diet.

Late that summer a significant milestone was reached. Layla moved to Gainesville to attend the University of Florida for the fall semester. I was proud of her; she had graduated with honors from high school which meant skipping her freshman year of college because of AP credits. Her mother and I agreed that she should live in a dormitory. Her roommate was her best friend, and by lottery or by design, in the same dorm and on the same floor as my freshman year! It looked no more comfortable than when I lived there. However, she enjoyed reasonable visitation rules; marijuana was still prohibited which defied rationality.

A couple weeks later Wayne Dyer came through town on a nationwide tour. His lecture was laced with humor and spiritual insights. While sitting in the auditorium during his talk, I had a brief peak experience. I saw a magnificent blue pearl; it is a breathtakingly beautiful dot of bluish-white light that sometimes appears in meditation, sometimes in other circumstances. It was an inspiring evening, a needed tonic that removed an accumulation of cynicism. Oh, at some point in his talk Dyer recommended Nisargadatta's, *I Am That*. The quote below is one of my favorites. A copy of it is on my refrigerator door.

> Wisdom tells me I am nothing.
> Love tells me I am everything.
> Between the two my life flows.
> (Nisargadatta; *I Am That*)

During Thanksgiving vacation, Layla and I smoked weed together for the first time. We were sitting in my living room when I asked her, "How would you like to smoke some weed?" She agreed enthusiastically. I went to the kitchen to get my stash. By the time I got back, she had her pipe packed with her own weed and ready to smoke. We had good fun, so much so that we partook a couple more times over the vacation. **Synchronistically**, there was an article in the *USA Today* a few days later about being honest with mature children about smoking pot. I enjoyed marijuana and wasn't going to lie to my child about such when the time was right. Layla was a freshman in college and the time was right.

As was our tradition, we drove up to Atlanta for the Thanksgiving celebration at my brother and sister-in-law's home which drew quite a crowd due to all the nieces and nephews. It was fun to see how much they had matured, distinctly unique yet similar to their mother and/or father. The Thanksgiving meal was mouthwateringly delicious. The creamed cauliflower retook top honors. Layla and I were on the road early Sunday morning to beat the traffic clusterfuck Atlanta was famous for especially during holidays.

Then I turned around and drove to Tallahassee to visit Johnny who was in town for a short stay. He lived in Paris with his girlfriend. From what I could gather, things weren't going well in Paris with her or work. Back in Tallahassee, things were testy; his sisters were criticizing him because of his tax situation and delinquent child care payments. On my way back to Jacksonville, I had a phone conversation with Jess, Regina's sister. She was concerned about Regina's well-being as was I. However, there was a delicate complication. Regina and I saw each other occasionally on a sexual basis; that is, fuck buddies. Regina had shared some stories of our sexual escapades which had been misconstrued. It was embarrassing explaining to Jess that S&M played no part; sometimes a dildo is just a dildo.

> No matter what your sexual beliefs, fantasies, kink or persuasion...nothing beats a good backrub. (*The Guide To Getting It On*)

Will flew in from San Antonio for a visit over the holidays. As usual, we picked up where we left off. We had fun discussing current events and reminiscing. He was happier than I had seen in a long time. That's not to say things were hunky-dory. His girlfriend was emotionally unstable and drinking morning, noon, and night. In the past, I would always call Ginny when Will came to town. I decided against such based on our previous encounter last New Year's. Well, the Universe had other plans. We went to our favorite breakfast spot down at the beach. Ginny and her girlfriend walked in shortly after we were seated. We shot the shit for a while and went our separate ways. Ginny stopped by the next day for a short, pleasant visit. Little did I know it would be our last visit. I left a few voicemails over the following weeks and never heard back.

Cheryl Mendelson's *Home Comforts* was my Christmas gift for family members that year. Her take on housekeeping jibed with mine.

> ...housekeeping actually offers more opportunities for savoring achievement than almost any other work I can think of. Each of its regular routines brings satisfaction when it is completed. These routines echo the rhythm of life, and the housekeeping rhythm is the rhythm of the body. You get satisfaction not only from the sense of order, cleanliness, freshness, peace and plenty restores, but from the knowledge that you and those you care about are going to enjoy these benefits. (Cheryl Mendelson; *Home Comforts*)

2000 started with a bang. In spite of my doubts, I ended up making sales quota which translated into a handsome commission check. One of my goals was to limit my debt as much as possible, so I paid off my car loan. Next was a European vacation with Layla. Once again, she proved to be a great travel companion. First, we flew to Amsterdam where we quickly availed ourselves of the famed coffee houses where they openly sell marijuana. I wanted Layla to witness how folks could enjoy marijuana sensibly, if so inclined. We also enjoyed the Van Gogh museum; I saw paintings that had stood out in my memory since I had last seen them twenty-five years before when I was a student in Utrecht (I love his Japanese inspired period). Also, we walked about town sightseeing and shopping. Then we traveled first class by high-speed train, another sensible option, through Belgium before taking a right turn through the Chunnel to London.

London was as grand as before. We walked about enjoying the sights enhanced by the crystal clear skies with a nip in the air. Our favorite was the Piccadilly Circus area. One afternoon we both had Tarot card readings for fun. Layla's reading accented her frustration with deciding what course of study to major in; a resolution was forecast. My reading highlighted career, travel, and, curiously, no mention of a romantic relationship. We also toured the new British Library which was most impressive. Having visited the Library of Congress a few weeks before, I felt it was an appropriate accompaniment. Worth noting, many of the collections I sold to academic research libraries on microfilm were sourced from the British Library.

On the trip, my feet ached and burned especially after a day of walking about. Upon my return home, the discomfort continued particularly after playing ping-pong. The podiatrist's diagnosis was plantar fasciitis, and his prescription was orthotics which helped. Along with greying hair, the signs of ageing were becoming apparent. According to the Cleveland Clinic, "The greatest challenge facing us as we age is the prevention of physical disability and the extension of active life expectancy…Illnesses like diabetes, congestive heart failure, and some forms of dementia can be delayed or even prevented." I had a strong preference to prevent such illnesses. Thankfully, remembering that I am Aware Space helps and is always available.

> Getting old isn't easy for a lot of us. Neither is living, neither is dying. We struggle against the inevitable and we all suffer because of it. We have been trying to find another way to look at the whole process of being born, growing old, changing, and dying, some kind of perspective that might allow us to deal with what we perceive as big obstacles without having to be dragged through the drama of misery. Understanding that we have something - that we are something - that's unchangeable, beautiful, completely aware, and that continues no matter what, really helps. (Ram Dass; *Still Here*)

The November '00 election was a frequent topic of conversation with friends and acquaintances. I knew I couldn't vote for Bush because of the religious Right's influence which smacked of intolerance and intransigence. I favored Gore, not the most riveting speaker, but intelligent and sincere. I watched all three debates and was disappointed; policy differences weren't analyzed thoroughly. There was actually very little debate, mostly canned responses; the sound bite was paramount. Also, they refused to be honest about their past, including drug use; discussion of such could have contributed to a constructive analysis of the current prohibition. Little did I know this situation would worsen hundredfold in years to come.

My sales year ended on a positive note; I reached my quota. In addition to a substantial commission check, it meant a reward trip to the Cayman Islands. Selling my home and upgrading to a nicer one entered the mix. I loved the yard, but the neighborhood hadn't become the magnet I thought it would with its central location not far from downtown. I was favoring a townhouse or condo. I wanted a pleasant view along with some amenities like a pool. The idea of not having to maintain the exterior since it was covered by HOA was attractive as well.

Layla had decided to major in education. I understood; teaching was in many ways the most satisfying career I had had. However, her mother was advocating business administration courses. She explained to her mother that she found them boring. I helped her study for a macroeconomics test...boring. Given her math aptitude, I suggested she look into getting a math degree and teach at the high school level. She liked that idea. Above all, I encouraged her to continue taking courses. If the teaching angle didn't work something else would grab her interest.

Due to Layla's part-time job at the university, she was staying in Gainesville for the Christmas holidays. In the spirit of the holiday season, her mother and I agreed to meet Layla at her home. From there we planned on driving to the Universal Temple for their holiday service (it's where her mother and I exchanged marriage vows 24 years before). Within minutes, Ann copped an attitude and refused to go because Layla wanted to drive with me on the way there (I hadn't planned on returning to Gainesville). Layla and I ended up going by ourselves which worked out better than either one of us imagined.

The next challenge was finding the Temple. It had been over twenty years since I had been to the Temple and had only a faint idea of how to get there. The landscape had changed quite a bit as well. After some trial and error, we found it in time to hear the teacher's lesson; it was about letting go and letting God! We ducked out of the service a little early and drove to Great American Outdoors in High Springs where we enjoyed their excellent oatmeal pancakes. Moral of the story: Let go and, sometimes, you can have your pancakes and eat them too!

> Your true Nature is the Paradox to take care of all paradoxes: there is nothing that is not you and nothing that is you; the Aware Space is and isn't its contents; you care and don't care; you control things and they just happen. This may sound silly, but in fact it is the perfection of wisdom. (Douglas Harding)

A month later I was back in Gainesville to call on the library at UF. They were some of my favorite librarians because of their friendly, laid-back professionalism (some academic libraries were stuffed with ego). This also gave me the opportunity to meet Layla's boyfriend, Brad. They had started dating back in June. Brad had long dreadlocks and looked a bit like Bob Marley; his birth father was African American and his mother European American. It was obvious he had a good heart and a sharp mind. It was a real delight to see them together, being considerate and affectionate with each other. On a similar note, Bert and Ellie were talking marriage. Bert had broken up with Mia a few years before and had been single until he met Ellie.

My sales reward trip to Grand Cayman was enhanced by Layla's companionship; her poise around my workmates was most impressive. Besides a few formal business meetings and group activities, our time was spent enjoying the beautiful weather and scenery. I did a couple of firsts: rode a wave runner and parasailed. The parasailing was exceptional. I imagined it would be very windy and that I would be buffeted by such. It turned out to be very calm and quiet. We also snorkeled at the famous Stingray City where you can feed stingrays which is quite a rush when they approach you with an open mouth. The beauty of the coral reefs didn't fail to enchant; the cornucopia of color from cyan to cinnabar was spectacular.

The Ground of Being is a given; enlightenment already is. Peak spiritual experiences, on the other hand, come and go (and frustrating if chased). Sometimes these experiences were rather surprising. On one particular occasion, I was at my local grocery store checking out the chicken selection and trying to decide whether to buy chicken breasts or legs when effervescent waves of elation rippled through my Being, leaving me in tears. Thankfully, the store was close to empty, and I could enjoy the peak experience without feeling self-conscious.

> Enlightenment is quite free and available instantly. However desirable, spiritual maturity is not an essential prerequisite: we don't have to remodel our human nature before we are capable of seeing our real Nature. Nevertheless dedicated practice, sooner or later, is indispensable. (Douglas Harding; *As I See It*)

For reasons unknown, Frank and I had a falling out. We planned on meeting for dinner, but he never responded to my voice mails. He may have taken offense to an inquiry I had made a few weeks before when we were playing ping-pong. He was telling me about a new home he planned on building. I asked him why if he was so unhappy in his marriage; a frequent topic of conversation. That may have struck a nerve; if so, that was my bad. I tried a few times over the years to get in touch without success. His opting for a passive-aggressive ending to our friendship was a big disappointment.

My sales numbers were substantially ahead of my goal. I was making more money than I ever imagined I would. However, there were some developments with the mother company that concerned me. Upper sales management rearranged who sold what which resulted in cross-channel conflict; that is where different sales channels step on each other's toes and get into spats about who gets sales credit (i.e., the sales credit shit hits the fan). It was short-term thinking on the part of sales management that disregarded long-term consequences. I lost thousands of dollars in commission as a result. It reminded me of the bullshit I went through at HIS years before.

Pluto transits are not for the faint of heart, not that there's a choice. At the risk of getting knee deep in the astrologese, transiting Pluto had moved on from the conjunction with my Sun and, after a brief breather, was conjunct my Mercury *and* square my Moon. I sensed I was in store for an emotional/intellectual purging; call it a Plutonian roto-rooter. Beliefs, reactions, and attitudes would be questioned and, in some cases, jettisoned.

One of the notions being questioned was being *in* my body. Based on present evidence I saw my body and the world with associated thoughts and feelings in me; that is, in ordinary, non-conceptual Awareness. Look for yourself. Are you in your hand or your arm or chest? You might think you're in your brain. Do you see a brain? I don't. Do you see a head? I don't; I see all sort of things, from toes to elbows, from planes to trains, arising and disappearing in an emptiness that is aware of itself.

> Only I am in a position to report on what's here. A kind of alert naivety is what I need. It takes an innocent eye and an empty head (not to mention a stout heart) to admit their own perfect emptiness. (Douglas Harding)

Will and Janet were no longer living together. Janet's emotional/mental problems complicated by alcohol abuse had ruptured their relationship beyond repair. I flew to San Antonio in July for a weekend visit. Will was in a much better place both emotionally and financially. His part-time job had evolved into a career; basically, he was running an insurance business. San Antonio is the Orlando of Texas, peppered with amusement parks. So, along with his son, we braved the heat and attended Sea World. A good time was had by all.

Later that summer I had the pleasure of hanging out with Ron, my college buddy; he came through town on his way to visit family. Since our college days, we had talked on the phone only a few times. He was a CPA living in Mid-Atlantic with his wife and two kids. We met at a restaurant on the beach and chatted for over two hours; the passage of time had no bearing on our friendship. His Sagittarius Sun, Libra Moon, and Gemini ascendant sparkled as usual. We reminisced about Muktananda, college, and discussed the subtleties and difficulties of marriage.

Chapter 9: Recognition

> It's never too late to have a marvellous childhood. True maturity is that second childhood which I still call alert idiocy. (Douglas Harding)

Fortunately, I wasn't traveling on Tuesday morning, September 11th, 2001. I was in my home office going through a stack of email when Angela called and told me to turn on the TV. A plane had crashed into one of the two World Trade Center towers which I had admired a couple of weeks before from a regional turboprop flying down the Hudson River from Hartford to Newark. The news was indefinite as to the type of plane or why it crashed. I figured a small plane had mistakenly flown into one of the towers; there'd be a handful of fatalities with minimal damage. I left the TV on and went back to my home office. Not two minutes later I heard excited but scared voices screaming about another plane. I ran into the living room and watched in shock the video replay of a large commercial airliner purposely fly into the other tower. I watched the replay repeatedly. In the meantime, another commercial airplane crashed into the Pentagon and another into a rural field in Pennsylvania. Then I remembered my brother, a commercial airline pilot, was flying at that very moment the type of plane favored by the terrorists. I called his wife, but the line was busy. I kept trying until all airline flights were suspended. I found out later he was in route from Orlando to Detroit at the time of the attacks when he was told to land ASAP. The next day I went to the local hardware store and purchased an American flag to display on the front of my house.

The videos of the destruction were disorienting, almost dreamlike. The interviews with family and relatives of the victims were gut-wrenching. I reflected on how my parents might have felt after Pearl Harbor. I remember telling Layla that I was sorry for her generation. I grew up with the Cold War and Vietnam. Her generation would have to deal with terrorism which wasn't like traditional war with invasions and occupying territory (or so I thought). The terrorists were a hateful, violent, self-righteous minority faction of Islam with pockets of supporters scattered throughout the world. They were an entirely different kind of enemy; they didn't represent a country but a religiously based value system. The attacks killed 2,996 people, injured thousands, and caused roughly $10 billion in damage.

My scheduled trip to Europe on 9/13 had to be rearranged. I wasn't going to let the terrorists discourage me. I rescheduled for 9/18. I spent ten days in Europe, visiting France and Switzerland for the first time. My first stop was Johnny and Leann's small flat on the outskirts of Paris in Vincennes. It was a bittersweet stay. Paris was as touted: tres super. Just outside their apartment building was a metro entrance and shops to satisfy one's every need; an urban setting that only major cities can offer. I found the Parisians quite friendly and not averse to speaking English if they could. However, the relationship between Johnny and Leann left a lot to be desired. He would go out of his way to please her as she acted in an entitled fashion.

Three days later I took a TGV train to Zurich which afforded me beautiful vistas of the French and Swiss countryside. The most dramatic sight was the mountains partially hidden by misty clouds with Lake Zug in the foreground. The workshop with Douglas Harding and his wife, Catherine, occupied my days. As expected, the workshop offered a cornucopia of reminders; experiments designed to point out my True Nature. The invitation to be my own authority and to trust the non-verbal Aware Capacity was accepted; That I am.

The finishing touch was sharing biscuits and tea with Douglas and Catherine after the workshop was over. We sat around a small dinette table discussing the efficacy and simplicity of face to no-face. He questioned me about what I had done since I took my first workshop in 1974. I gave him a brief overview of my "seeking peak experiences." At one point, Douglas looked at me casually and said, "You get it." He was right, I got it, but often, out of habit, I forgot. As Harding states in *Look for Yourself,* "If you want to be Real, you must break the habit of continually leaping out of yourself in the effort to see yourself from out there as others see you, and cultivate the habit of sitting at Home and seeing yourself as you see yourself."

After my stay in Zug, I returned to Zurich and hopped on a plane to Amsterdam. I wandered around a bit until I found a bar. Later, with a substantial wine/weed buzz and feeling horny, I ambled across the street to one of the legal red-light establishments. After negotiating a price, I entered her apartment. As she proceeded to undress me my swagger wavered; the thought of having intercourse became less than attractive. I opted for a hand job and left feeling dusty.

> I came out alone on my way to my tryst. But who is this me in the dark?
> I move aside to avoid his presence but I escape him not.
> He makes the dust rise form the earth with his swagger;
> he adds his loud voice to every word I utter.
> He is my own little self, my lord, he knows no shame;
> but I am ashamed to come to thy door in his company.
> (Rabindranath Tagore)

The Thanksgiving '01 in Atlanta was a nice celebration along with some delicious delights. With the passing of the years, Thanksgiving had become my favorite holiday, not complicated by gift giving or tedious religious references. As usual, traveling with Layla was a charm. She was about to turn twenty-one; adulthood was almost official with its pleasant surprises and inevitable disappointments. We stayed at my sister's home the last night of our trip. Looking through her albums, I ran across one of my favorite albums of all time, *All Things Must Pass* by George Harrison. A couple of songs drifted through my mind accompanied by memories of seeing him in concert with Ravi Shankar in 1974 in Atlanta with my friend Ron. The following week, on November 30, George Harrison died from cancer. He was a beautiful soul that will be missed. Indeed, all things must pass.

Because everyone had New Year's plans, I decided to celebrate New Year early with a party the day before. I enlisted Sarah to help me, a guru of hosting social functions. The party was a success. There were about 20 folks with nice mix of ages from 20 to 50 something; some of whom I didn't know that Sarah invited. Layla and Brad attended as did my ex, Ann, who stopped by for a few minutes. And to my delight, Debbie showed up. Sarah had introduced us the week before at a party she hosted. We hit it off which resulted in her inviting me to her New Year's party the following evening where our attraction was reinforced.

A couple days later I was in Connecticut for a company sales meeting. SMP was becoming a subsidiary of a larger company which meant a loss of our autonomy. However, the larger company believed in incentive trips like Grand Cayman the previous year. Because of 9/11, sales management decided that being within 5% of the quota was sufficient to qualify for the incentive trip. That meant I was going to the big island, Hawai'i, all-expenses-paid. Part of the reward package included bringing a guest, be it family or friend. Layla couldn't accompany me as she had on the Cayman trip. I thought about asking Debbie, but it was too early in our relationship, so withheld inviting her.

The romantic dance with Debbie was intoxicating; her good looks and sexual energy were hard to deny. She was smokin' hot. Yet, there was a disconcerting emotional edge to her.

Nonetheless, I proceeded to court her. A week later was our first date, a romantic evening with dinner and drinks in St. Augustine. She wasn't dressed when I arrived which was a promising start. While sipping wine, we picked out her outfit starting with her panties. Both of us enjoyed our entrees topped off by a cappuccino which must have had triple shots of espresso along with a couple of martinis. Yep, you heard right, martinis. Vodka martinis...Russian firewater with a splash of vermouth; a tasty but dangerous concoction. Then we drove back to her place passionately kissing while managing not to wreck the car. With a coffee and alcohol buzz, we fucked on and off the rest of the night.

The next weekend we attended a circus. There were clowns, elephants, acrobats, and uncomfortable communication; it felt like a first date again. When we got back to my place I hoped that we might share our feelings and, if things flowed, end up in bed. She bolted as soon as she saw an opening. A couple of days later Sarah told me about a card she had received the previous week from Debbie thanking her for introducing us. I called Debbie to express my appreciation for sending the card. She was rude and crabby. A "thank you for calling but I'm busy" would have sufficed. The flickering flame of affection I felt for her died. I broke up with her shortly after that. I was glad I hadn't invited her to Hawai'i trip—it would have complicated matters.

Alas, my all-expenses-paid trip to the big island of Hawai'i would not be graced by feminine companionship. After a twelve-hour journey through numerous time zones, my longing was lightened by a splendid five-star hotel with spectacular tropical foliage and a sensational view of the Pacific. I rented a car and thoroughly investigated the island including an attempt to reach the summit of Mauna Kea which was blocked due to snow! The most memorable part was the helicopter tour of the island with my boss, Ben. The view of the volcano spewing magma was without compare; Earth giving birth. Then we flew over the ocean before turning and entering a canyon opening along the eastern shore north of Hilo with a twenty story tall waterfall whispering into the air. I got some great photos with my new digital camera.

The end of February '02 I flew to Los Angeles to attend a Headless Way workshop with Douglas and Catherine and sightsee a bit. My first evening I met a couple for dinner I'd known when they lived in Jacksonville; we enjoyed reminiscing over some delicious Mexican food near where I was staying at Marina del Rey. The next morning, I woke up intent on seeing more of coastal Southern California. I jumped in the rental car and proceeded north on the Pacific Coast Highway. At one point I stopped to get my feet wet in the Pacific near Topanga Beach. I was surprised by the smell apparently because of the kelp, not common to the Atlantic. Near Pepperdine University I took a right on Malibu Canyon Road to the 101 freeway and back to LA. As I approached the urban sprawl, the infamous LA traffic seemed manageable. However, that assessment quickly changed; LA traffic was as advertised. When I got to Venice Beach, I took a walk along the boardwalk, a human menagerie of sorts. Synchronistically, there was a wall mural on a nearby building with the message "turn your attention around 180 degrees."

The workshop was attended by fifty folks or so at a community center in a beautiful Hollywood Hills neighborhood with the aroma of citrus flowers in the air. Douglas and Catherine stepped us through various experiments which required paying attention to the present, nonverbal experience. Instead of habitually imagining a face, I saw boundless, timeless space that is simultaneously capacity for everything and "the joy that casts no shadow." Worth noting, a portion of Douglas' talk was about pain being an integral part of the mystery of Being. We can't get rid of pain; an inseparable part of the polarity with pleasure.

I tried online dating again. My first date was a fiasco; the chemistry wasn't right from the get-go. My next date was better. Lynn was a teacher with two kids. We met at a restaurant. After a few beers and some snacks, we went back to her place for more drinks. We chatted comfortably before ending up horizontally. We dated a couple more times before I realized she was still hankering for her previous lover. We went our separate ways amicably. I decided to back off the online dating scene…again. The adage "once bitten, twice shy" regained relevance.

I ran across this cute joke via email: A man walking along a California beach was deep in prayer. Suddenly, he said out loud, "Lord, grant me one wish." Suddenly the sky clouded above his head, and in a booming voice the Lord said, "Because you have tried to be faithful to me in all ways, I will grant you one wish." The man said, "Build a bridge to Hawai'i so I can drive over anytime I want to." The Lord said, "Your request is very materialistic. Think of the logistics of that kind of undertaking. The supports required to reach the bottom of the Pacific! The concrete and steel it would take! I can do it, but it is hard for me to justify your desire for worldly things. Take a little more time and think of another wish, a wish you think would honor and glorify me." The man thought about it for a long time. Finally, he said "Lord, I wish that I could understand women. I want to know how they feel inside, what they think when they give me the silent treatment, why they cry, what they mean when they say 'nothing,' and how I can make a woman truly happy." After a few minutes, God said, "You want two lanes or four on that bridge?"

My faith or confidence in our economic and, by extension, our political system, reached a new low with the Enron and Merrill Lynch debacles. The Enron/Anderson meltdown was an outrageous violation of commonly accepted and needed business practices. The Merrill Lynch situation, where analysts recommended purchasing stocks they knew were not performing well, was another violation of trust. And on top of that, the CEOs responsible for the unethical behavior were canned but handsomely compensated. Once again, this airing of dirty laundry was represented by the world transits of Pluto (purging) and Saturn (responsibilities), this time opposing each other.

In August '02 I decided to purchase a condo a few blocks from the beach. My home sold the first day it was listed for twice what I paid for it. I looked at the purchase as an investment; beach area property values were exploding. I wasn't sure about the condo lifestyle, and the monthly HOA fee gave me heartburn as it tripled in price within a few months. My financial indigestion was soothed somewhat by figuring it was a fee for maintenance, insurance, and country club dues for the pool, workout facility, etc. As it ended up, I rarely used the facilities. I exercised my green thumb by puttering around with potted plants and small touches about the condo grounds.

The first-year anniversary of the WTC terrorism highlighted how much the tragedy still weighed on folks. The actual footage of the planes flying into the towers and the heart-wrenching interviews with friends and family were still regular fare on TV. The depravity terrorists were willing to engage in had been reinforced by more savagery. The terrorists' value system was vastly different from ours; theirs was Dark Age coding, so to speak, where democracy, women's rights, religious plurality, and freedom of speech were forbidden. It was a sobering realization that religious fundamentalism was as real a threat to present day civilization as it was in the past, maybe even more. So much for that New Age, I once thought possible.

> All religions,
> All this singing,
> Is one song.
> The differences are just
> illusion and vanity.
> The sun's light looks a little different
> On this wall than it does on that wall…
> But it's still one light. (Jalāl ad-Dīn Muhammad Rūmī)

My spiritual lessons continued; that is, another problem wrapped in pain. I had enjoyed good health and average athletic ability throughout my childhood and adulthood. My most notable athletic feat over the last few years was learning to play ping pong decently. However, I had an arrogant disregard for my body and age-related limitations. Plantar fasciitis had knocked my cockiness down a couple of notches. Then I started experiencing a tingling, burning sensation along with numbness mainly in the toes. I sought medical advice from my GP. He recommended a neurologist who diagnosed my condition as neuropathy. Thankfully, additional tests indicated no diabetes. Nonetheless, my conceit was knocked down a couple more notches. I had no choice but to surrender to the unpredictable pain in life. I reminded myself that clinging to what was and resisting what is wasn't helpful.

All along I continued to take my anti-cholesterol medicine as prescribed. However, in frustration, I did some research on the web and found out that one of the possible adverse effects of statins was neuropathy! I was angry and disappointed that both my doctors, the GP and neurologist, didn't bring this up. I sent them a copy of the research and asked for feedback. The neurologist grudgingly acknowledged that my adverse effect did occur in a small percentage of patients which, in effect, minimized my experience. I decided to stop taking the medication. My trust in the medical/pharmaceutical complex, along with government agencies not exercising necessary oversight, was substantially diminished. I realized that one must be vigilant in today's profit-driven health care system.

Per tradition, Layla and I drove up to Atlanta to celebrate Thanksgiving '02 which gave us a chance to catch up. The celebration at my brother and sister-in-law's home along with my sister and all the nieces and nephews was a lighthearted affair. The next day before our return trip to Jacksonville, Layla and I visited Mom at the Alzheimer's facility. She seemed genuinely pleased to see us, babbling like a happy one-year-old while fondly clutching her doll. After our visit, we went shopping. Layla had the hots for the store, Lululemon, which was located only in major cities like Atlanta. Layla found what she was looking for and, in a shop next door, I ran across some home décor stuff right up my alley.

On the job front, my boss, Ben, was struggling with his boss who was threatening to fire him again if the sales team didn't make quota. We already knew we wouldn't make quota because she had increased our goal arbitrarily by 40% mid-year with no new product to sell. Library budgets had been reduced, drastically in some cases, by the recession. This wasn't the first time his boss had acted like an asshole; she was famous for her contemptible behavior which was made worse by her belief that her shit didn't stink. Ben wasn't fired, and I ended up making quota due to a large order that I hadn't forecast until the following year. That also meant I'd qualify for the Caribbean cruise incentive trip and reap a substantial commission. I treated myself to a new PDA phone that included calendar and contacts functions. What would they think of next!?

Over the previous few years, my friendship with Sarah had grown. We'd get together for dinner and chat, mostly about relationships and spirituality. She was dating a guy who lived in Orlando that she suspected of cheating on her. I stopped by to see how she was handling the drama. Her daughter, Stella, happened to stop by as well. Stella proceeded to verbally list Sarah's shortcomings in raising her. At first, it was funny; Sarah didn't take offense. Most parents will readily admit to not having been perfect parents. Stella's listing became a long-winded rant. Eventually, I reminded her that the statute of limitations on parental crimes is over at age 30. Stella was over 30.

During Layla's holiday break between the fall and spring semesters, we met at Ragtime, one of our favorite restaurants with a Cajun theme in Neptune Beach. She gave me the rundown on their plan to get married the following December which would coincide with her graduation from college, a dual degree in psychology and statistics. Brad had graduated and was working on his masters. The ceremony would be conducted at a nondenominational chapel and the reception held at a faculty lounge on the UF campus. Layla had even picked out the color of flowers she wanted. Her Capricorn Sun and Virgo ascendant were in full bloom.

Chapter 10: Dispersion

I live my life in widening circles that reach out across the world. (Rainer Maria Rilke)

During one of my road trips, I listened to an article on NPR about the drug, Neurontin, which my neurologist had prescribed for the neuropathy in my toes. Much to my chagrin, via the article, I found out that Neurontin wasn't approved for that use. The article went on to say that

Neurontin was approved for the treatment of epileptic seizures. However, it was being marketed for unapproved uses, a practice known as off-label marketing which meant I was taking a drug for a condition it was not tested for which struck me as questionable, if not dangerous. I decided to stop taking the drug and severed my relationships with the neurologist and GP.

Towards the end of '02 as part of my typical sales routine, I called on a librarian at Houston University library. I hadn't been able to connect with her via email or phone which wasn't unusual; most librarians were either resistant to sales calls or too overwhelmed to be responsive. Beth had purchased collections from SMP before so there wasn't a question of applicability. While making small talk, an unmistakable romantic exchange occurred. That evening, in whatever hotel room I was staying, I sent her an email expressing my attraction. Beth reciprocated.

After a couple of weeks of multiple phone calls on a daily basis, I spent the weekend with Beth. Her Scorpio Sun, Capricorn Moon, and Capricorn ascendant along with her intelligence, good looks, and down-to-earth sexuality delighted me. My preferred airline at the time was Continental. Its major hub, IAH, was in Houston which made it easy to plan my business trips so that I could spend time with Beth on weekends when she didn't have her son. I had to chuckle; once again I had fallen in love with a woman with a prominent Capricorn signature (I am told it has to do with my Venus in Capricorn). She accepted my invitation to be my guest on the Caribbean cruise.

The Caribbean cruise provided us with many tropical delights. The ports of call were Key West, Cozumel, and Costa Maya. I hadn't been to Key West in a couple of decades; it didn't disappoint. However, it wasn't as quaint as it used to be with thousands of cruise ship passengers roaming the streets. In Cozumel, we went to a state park and enjoyed swimming in the Caribbean and walking through a tropical jungle. Our last port of call was Costa Maya, the least developed tourist-wise, included some impressive Mayan ruins near Belize.

Beth and I spent every moment of the 6 days and 5 nights together. Only once did I get irritated with her when she made a derisive remark about my spiritual orientation which I let slide. I was just beginning to understand the extent of her Catholic devotion and question the implications of such in regards to our relationship. However, there was no question about our sexual compatibility; we fucked frequently.

> Because gratification of a desire leads to the temporary stilling of the mind and the experience of the peaceful, joyful Self it's no wonder that we get hooked on thinking that happiness comes from the satisfaction of desires. This is the meaning of the old adage, "Joy is not in things, it is in us." (Joan Borysenko)

The last weekend of April, I spent time with Beth's son for the first time. He was an energetic boy with a good vocabulary and a pronounced stubborn streak. I rediscovered some parenting muscles I hadn't used in a while. Beth took us on a tour of the countryside outside of Houston where we enjoyed the bluebonnets and Indian paintbrush. Being a good sport, I attended a Catholic Church service with her which reminded me of an Episcopalian service I witnessed a decade before with the numerous rites and rituals. Much to my surprise, we started talking about marriage which meant selling my condo and moving to Houston.

For Father's Day weekend Beth flew in Jacksonville. My tour accented the beach and St. Johns River along with introducing her to Layla and Brad who had driven up from Gainesville for a visit. A month or so later we flew to Beth's old hometown to visit her mother, brother, and some high school friends. We stayed in her old room in the attic where we had fun trying fuck without making too much noise. On the last afternoon of our visit, Beth's mother asked me if I was ready to be a stepfather after her grandson had thrown several temper tantrums. I responded unenthusiastically, "I think so." It was becoming apparent to me that in addition to Beth's devout Catholicism, the other potential deal breaker was her son.

A professional deal breaker of sorts arose due to depressed sales. Ben and I were "put on plan." The plan stated that if sales didn't improve in forty-five days, our jobs were on the line. Ben's boss, the aforementioned asshole, blamed the sales force for weak sales as if we preferred making less money (there was an industry-wide downturn due to slashed library budgets). Ben and I felt the goal was unrealistic, if not impossible to achieve. I treated it like a termination notice and started investigating other job opportunities in the library market. I figured it was a good six-year run with the company; I had made some decent money and, most importantly, I had a good friend, Ben.

To get a different astrological take, I consulted the Vedic astrologer I last used when I was married to Ann. Without any prompting on my part with questions, he started with my career situation followed by a concise statement, "You won't suffer much." He saw things gradually improving throughout the rest of the year. However, I did ask him about my relationship with Beth and the projected move to Houston. He recommended that I not get married before the end of the following June of '04. And then in passing, to my surprise, he said that the next few years would be favorable for writing.

In August '03 my condo sold for the asking price which meant I was breaking even given realtor commission. While calling on UTK with Ben, I landed a sizable sale. We figured it delayed our termination a few months. And, it gave me a nice financial cushion for my move to Houston. A week before the movers packed my furniture I had another dream with a spider, however, without the web. The spider was situated in an undesirable place, so I sprayed it with insecticide. The spider got angry and lunged towards me as its body turned red. I continued to spray it, eventually overwhelming it with pesticide. I woke up with an unsettled feeling. If it was a subconscious message, it wasn't positive.

The movers performed as contracted. However, I was disappointed with the apartment Beth had selected; it was within a block of Interstate 610. The highway noise was always in the background. Also, I found myself getting bothered by Beth's expectations concerning religion; she was praying that I'd get baptized! From her point of view, I was not guaranteed salvation without undergoing a religious ritual which I found foreign and fanciful, to say the least. So, there I was, new to Houston and with Pluto (transformation, power) traversing my 4th house (home, roots), conjunct my Mercury (communication, perception), and square my Moon (mood, subjectivity). Fill in the variables; you get the equation.

The job situation was no better; the disingenuousness on the part of upper management had reached new lows. Even though I had exceeded quota, they kept me "on plan." Our best-selling microfilm collection had been electronically converted and was available online for purchase. Management asked us to train the electronic delivery sales team on how to sell it; commissions would be shared. Then they reversed course and refused to pay us commissions which amounted to tens of thousands of dollars. Meanwhile, my first interview with another publisher had gone well. My second interview would be at an upcoming library conference in San Diego.

One day while wandering around the net, I happened along Ken Wilber's web site. He introduced me to two new concepts, Boomeritis and Spiral Dynamics. Boomeritis is Wilber's critique of my generation, the baby-boomers. The major obstacle for baby-boomers is "a disease of egocentrism and narcissism." Damn, I thought I was special! Spiral Dynamics is a model of cultural/psychological development via memes, kind of like genes; that is, worldviews with differing characteristics and qualities that societies and individuals inherit, exhibit, and/or evolve through.

> Transcend and include... this is the self-transcending drive of the Kosmos—to go beyond what went before and yet include what went before... to open into the very heart of Spirit-in-action. (Ken Wilber, *A Brief History of Everything*)

Layla and Brad's wedding plans were unfolding in an orderly fashion. Remarkably, Ann and I agreed without rancor to give them equal amounts of cash to cover the cost. Layla was the wedding planner; early in the process, her mother had bowed out. However, towards the end, Ann started to make demands which Layla rightly dismissed. Layla sent her an email: "We want it to be simple. We don't want an open bar. We want there to be a couple choices. We want everyone to have a good time but not go overboard. If any of the guests want to start taking shots, then they can take a cab to their hotel. I don't want to provide transportation for everyone. We do not have an endless budget. That's something that is excessive, not necessary. I'm rephrasing and reiterating all of these ideas over and over so that you understand what I want. I don't think it's unreasonable. I want you to have a fabulous time; the best night all year but I also want me and Brad to make the decisions. Please let me go at my own pace, and I'll come to you when I need help. If you'd still like to come with me to see the wedding coordinator, then that would be helpful. You do probably have more questions than me, and your insight would be helpful. It's not that I don't appreciate your help, but I just need it in smaller doses. Do you understand where I'm coming from?"

Back in Houston, Beth's lease on her apartment came to an end, so she moved into the vacant apartment across from mine. It was larger, more convenient, and gives us a better idea of what it would be like living together, especially with her son. Other issues surfaced immediately;

namely, my TV viewing habits. As a child, Beth felt that TV dominated her family's evening time thus she didn't want us to do likewise. I liked the entertainment and relaxation that TV offered; I appreciated news, sitcoms, and sports. Also, there were issues with her ex-husband's irresponsible parenting along with our own difficulties at work. The one area that didn't suffer was our sex life.

Layla and Brad's wedding ceremony and reception went off without hitch. The chapel nestled along a lake with majestic live oaks was aesthetically pleasing and the faculty lounge provided an august touch with ample room for entertaining. Brad looked great in his tuxedo and Layla was breathtaking in her lovely white gown. My brother and family along with my two sisters attended; it was a family reunion of sorts. Brad's mother, stepfather, and stepbrother attended along with his grandparents, uncle, and aunt from his biological father's side (who wasn't in attendance). The bridesmaids and groomsmen were in fine form; their intelligence and grace gave me a sense of optimism about our future.

Ann was amiable and not overly eccentric unless you think her inviting a cross-dresser friend qualifies. Unfortunately, he looked like a beat-up linebacker in fishnet stockings who crossed the line by taking part in the bouquet toss. Ann's mother and brother were in attendance as well; her mother was gracious as usual, and her brother was quirky as usual. Before returning to Houston, the last night in our B & B room, Beth and I had a disagreement, fueled by copious amounts of wine, over some forgotten observation I made about the ceremony. I fell asleep with an uneasy feeling about our relationship. Another dark night of the soul was looming.

January '04 I attended a library conference in San Diego. For us, the SMP crew, booth duty was a struggle due to management's lack of appreciation for all we had accomplished over the years. Their accommodation was placing more of us "on plan." It was a deliberate attempt to get us to quit rather than going through a RIF and the HR complications. My second interview with the other publisher's president and vice president resulted in them offering me a field sales position. I would be selling digital research collections to the same libraries I already called on. With mixed emotions, I submitted my resignation to Ben. Over the years I had grown very fond of him and would miss working with him. Yet, I was glad to be moving on to another career opportunity.

Friday evening, February 13th, 2004, my sister called and informed me that Mom's condition had taken a turn for the worse because she had aspirated some food. I had already planned on visiting her the following Monday, the 16th, to take advantage of it being a vacation day, Presidents' Day (the rest of the week I had scheduled sales calls with my boss, the vice president, in the Atlanta area). I told my sister I'd be there as planned. I arrived at the Alzheimer's facility just after lunch. My sisters were already there; my brother couldn't make it due to his flight schedule. As soon as I saw and heard her, I knew death was imminent; I felt she had waited for me. Her breathing was shallow but steady and her eyes non-responsive. Tearfully, I asked the Universe to help her let go. Over the next couple of hours, her breathing became quieter and softer; much like can happen in meditation. She died peacefully around 4:30 PM. Her last exhale had a sparkling substance to it.

What can I say? If Dad was my head, she was my heart. I have many fond memories of her. One of my favorites was listening to her whistle as she prepared delicious concoctions; her pancakes, tacos, gumbo, beans and rice were legendary. Or, how she would alternately purse and pucker her lips when she was engaged in some creative effort; her homes were aesthetic delights. Or, how she would affectionately kiss me on the lips for any number of reasons; she loved being loving. Or, how she and Dad would banter with each other; they were a lot of fun to be around. She was a beautiful, caring, witty woman. I will miss her dearly.

Layla, Brad, Beth, and I rendezvoused at the New Orleans airport to attend the funeral in Baton Rouge. All my siblings were present along with 9 of 10 grandchildren and 2 of 3 great-grandchildren. We, the siblings, opted for a closed casket with numerous pictures of Mom and Dad. The funeral was simple but diminished by the minister's overreach. He was hired by the funeral home to give a benediction which turned out to be nothing more than preaching to attendees about being "saved." I wasn't there to be preached at. The eulogies given by my sister and nephew were quite touching. The ceremony at the cemetery was peaceful; the partly cloudy skies fit the mood. Mom was buried next to Dad which is in the same area where numerous other relatives are buried. After the funeral, we went back to the hotel where we sat around and partied a bit. The following morning, we met for breakfast and went our separate ways.

At Beth's prompting, we started the South Beach diet. Both of us lost 5 pounds in the first week. Within two weeks I had lost 12 pounds. For me, the South Beach diet was the solution to my diet confusion I had struggled with for years. The confusion was the result of a mix mash of old vegetarian ideas that had morphed into a diet based on minimal proteins, large quantities of carbohydrates (rice, pasta, and potato), and too many refined sugar products (cookies, ice cream, chocolate, etc.). I would eventually lose 30 pounds.

Unfortunately, my relationship with Beth's son was floundering. His annoying behavior which he engaged in deliberately had become burdensome. Upon Will's suggestion, we introduced the *123 Magic* techniques which helped. However, no number of timeouts was going to overcome his resentment of me. There wasn't much I could do about that. I found myself limiting my time around him when possible. Beth wanted a more committed approach. I couldn't oblige her. Beth was gracious; she acknowledged my attempt to embrace the stepfather role which helped me feel less like a shit for initiating the split (which I was trying to accomplish as considerately as possible).

I decided to move; living across the breezeway from each other in the apartment complex was no longer viable. I considered Austin, Atlanta, and Jacksonville. A few factors tipped the scale in Austin's favor. One, it was close to San Antonio where Will lived. Two, it had an excellent reputation. And, three, it had good transportation options with nonstop flights to many of my business destinations. I sent Beth an email about my moving plans. Her reply was much appreciated. "Thanks for keeping me posted. I am here to help you pack; just let me know what you need. I'm so sorry that things didn't work out as we had hoped. I thank you for taking the chance though. You have given so much to me, in so many ways, and I feel I can never fully repay you for that, but know that I am grateful. As always, I will continue to hope and pray for your happiness as well as mine."

I also received some positive feedback from my boss, Ellen: "You are a mover and shaker. It's no surprise you're successful in sales. Your driving was another indication. Also, the way you grabbed biscuits from the buffet in College Station. All of this should be on your resume." The most humorous feedback was from my buddy Johnny: "Sure about this brother? Gee, takes a woman cheating on me, lying, forgetting my birthday and not making love with me for four years before I even consider breaking up! Even then, I think, gee, are you sure about this! I love you."

11: Gravitation

Gravity can not be held responsible for people falling in love. (Albert Einstein)

Early May '04 I signed a six-month lease on a two-bedroom apartment in Austin and moved in the following week. I immediately started shopping for a home in part to invest the inheritance I received from Mom's passing. Two weeks later I signed a purchase contract on the perfect sized home that would be built within six months: 1720 square feet, 3 bedrooms, 2 ½ baths, loft, small yard, and HOA. Watching the house being built was very satisfying from the laying of the foundation to the framing, especially when the rafters were crowned by the roof. The finishing nail, I mean touch, was choosing the various design elements including tile, cabinets, appliances, fans, carpet, and fixtures.

My new job was progressing as well. My boss, Ellen, thought highly of my sales skill set. We worked together on a couple of trips calling on academic research libraries; taking advantage of the relationships I had established over the years. We stirred up some good business. However, it started to dawn on me that she was a curious bird; behind her chirpiness was pushiness and one-upmanship. Regardless, by the end of the year, the overall sales numbers were the best in company history. My performance review was glowing. I looked forward to our new sales year.

However, on the political front, things were retrogressing. The election season was warming up and, once again, I was going to vote Democrat as a vote against the increasingly radical GOP. In my opinion, they had gone off the deep end. They were reveling in misinformation and appealing to the inner demons of our nature. Another reason I was going to vote Democrat was to register my disapproval of the blatant dishonesty of the Bush administration concerning WMD before military intervention in Iraq. A war that had devolved into an unwinnable religious, tribal, civil war that should have been avoided like a biblical plague. The Middle East was a stockpile of historical strains, spitefulness, and savage violence wrapped in an ongoing geopolitical chess game with shifty players; there were Israelis, Arabs, Turks, Persians, Saudis,

Egyptians, Jordanians, Syrians, Lebanese, Kurds, Russians, British, French, and Americans. Don't forget the medieval spat between Shia and Sunni. I wasn't optimistic about the prospects for peace.

Being new to Austin, I needed to expand my social circle. I checked out a Unity Church nearby but felt it was too cliquish. However, a real estate agent I met while shopping for my home was quite friendly. Our first date exceeded expectations. Sheila was down to earth, expressive, beautiful, and affectionate (Libra Sun and Venus, Capricorn Moon and Ascendant; notice that Capricorn again!). Her spiritual orientation was Christian. She was raised Southern Baptist, migrated to Catholicism, which had morphed into "nondenominational." She didn't express any reservations about my spiritual orientation. On our third date, we discovered our sexual compatibility. One drawback was her menstrual bleeding; it was as if she had a non-stop period. That didn't stop us from fornicating frequently and making a mess of the sheets repeatedly. We fell in love.

As July rolled around, I realized our most significant difference was our spiritual beliefs. It turned out Sheila's "nondenominational" approach was more fundamentalist than I had initially thought. One morning Sheila and I were in her kitchen drinking coffee. She was paying bills; one of them was from the 700 Club. My beliefs and opinions differed substantially from Pat Robertson's religious fundamentalism and parochial politics. I shared my concern hoping to avoid "compatibility bomb" where differences aren't acknowledged only to blow up later. Sheila assured me there wasn't a problem; she appreciated my spiritual alignment. I figured we had put the potential issue to rest. Time flew by. We discussed marriage and shopped for a diamond ring (something I never imagined I'd do). The idea was to give her a ring when I proposed on our seven-day eastern Caribbean cruise in January.

> There is no God external to life. God, rather, is the inescapable depth and center of all that is. God is not a being superior to all other beings. God is the Ground of Being itself. (Bishop Jack Spong; *Here I Stand*)

We had our first substantial disagreement while watching TV. During one of the advertising breaks, I decided to share some concerns hoping to spur some sort of discussion. The major obstacle in discussing relationship dynamics with Sheila was her belief that our falling in love was God's answer to her prayers. It wasn't up for discussion. In my opinion, not doing so was dangerous. For Sheila, it meant lack of faith on my part which I resented. She thought I was trying to back out of the relationship and told me to leave. Seeking clarification when I got home, I called and left a voicemail. Three days later she called back and acted as if nothing had transpired. I thought our relationship was over. Supposedly, she had sent me an email a couple of days before telling me that she loved me and that she needed some time alone. I never received it and doubted her explanation as to why.

As I mentioned before, Sheila wasn't inclined towards discussing issues which were reinforced by her disconcerting anti-intellectualism based on belief in biblical infallibility. Her supplemental reading consisted of apocalyptic claptrap. I started having trouble sleeping through the night waking up at various times chewing on our differences. I felt like I was mired in an emotional minefield camouflaged by romantic delusion. In other words, transiting Uranus was squaring my Sun, transiting Neptune was opposing my Ascendant, and my progressed Moon was conjunct Mars.

> The more I reflected on these matters, the more I began to see that the authors of the New Testament were very much like the scribes who would later transmit those authors' writings. The authors too were human beings with needs, beliefs, worldviews, opinions, loves, hates, longings, desires, situations, problems—and surely all these things affected what they wrote. (Bart Erhman; *Misquoting Jesus*)

The job situation at PAS was disturbing my sleep as well. The problem was dealing with my immediate boss, Ellen, as you might have suspected. She had some strange, almost prudish, notions about interpersonal relations. During my last performance review, she raised objections about my interaction with fellow sales reps. She felt I was too touchy and engaged in sexually inappropriate talk. I was the only male in the field sales group. I checked with my female counterparts, and they didn't agree. Heck, sometimes they were the ones that initiated the flirtatious bantering. She also had an inflated view of her sales skills which translated into inflexibility and conceit. Once again, another manager who didn't think her shit smelled.

Pretty much right on schedule, my house was ready for occupancy. I was thrilled to have my own place again where I could engage in creative home improvement projects. My existing living room furniture was now in the loft which meant I had no furniture for the living room. I ended up buying a merlot colored leather couch and love seat with some end tables. Due to space considerations, I also planned on buying one of those new flat screen TVs that were the rage. Naturally, the yard beckoned for some TLC and dirty fingernails.

> A garden is always a series of losses set against a few triumphs, like life itself. (May Sarton)

And, finally, the election season was over (there should be a Constitutional amendment limiting campaign periods, advertisement, and financing). Bush won more decisively than I expected. I found it bewildering that most conservative Christians voted for him because of so-called moral issues such as gay marriage but didn't consider the multi-trillion-dollar mess in Iraq a moral issue. While advertising themselves as "people of faith" they advocated political initiatives entangled with intolerance and arrogance. The harassment of religious minorities by fundamentalist Christians at the US Air Force Academy was an example of such.

Sheila decided to get a partial hysterectomy before Thanksgiving; she was tired of feeling fatigued along with frequent cramping and bleeding. There would be a six-week recuperative period. I took Sheila to the outpatient surgery facility for her pre-surgery preparation. At her request, the pastor from her church stopped by for prayer. His delivery was purposely loud enough so everyone else in the pre-operation room could hear him. And, his prayer was laced with condemnation of Catholics and "non-believers" which shocked me. I understood why the Bible advises praying in a closet.

> This clean light, which tastes of Paradise, is beyond all pride, beyond comment, beyond proprietorship, beyond solitude. It is in all, and for all. It is the true light that shines in everyone, in "every man coming into this world." It is the light of Christ, "Who stands in the midst of us and we know Him not." (Thomas Merton)

After the surgery, Sheila slept most of the day. I sat around and read until early evening when I returned to Sheila's home. I got a bite to eat and fell asleep. The next morning, I picked Sheila up at 6:30 as planned. We went back to her home where I fixed breakfast; afterward, she went back to bed. I worked remotely from my laptop for the rest of the morning. However, to complete various business transactions, I needed to go home. After fixing lunch, I informed Sheila of my plans. Her two daughters, who lived nearby, would assist in my absence. Sheila accused me of acting inconvenienced. I told her that wasn't the case; what she was sensing was my recognition of our irreconcilable spiritual orientations highlighted by the minister's performance the day before. I saw confusion across her brow; she had no idea why I found her pastor's behavior objectionable.

I left Sheila a voice mail that evening inquiring about her welfare. The ball was in her court, so to speak. She returned my call three days later. Without any explanation of why she hadn't returned my call until then, she accused me of letting her down. I was tempted to counter but decided I wasn't going to play that game. Our romantic rapture had ruptured without a doubt. I terminated our relationship.

> Not getting what you want is sometimes a wonderful stroke of luck. (Dalai Lama)

I spent Thanksgiving with my brother and sister-in-law which provided a diversion for my aching heart. Once again, I had underestimated the role religion can play in a romantic relationship. The celebration included all five of their kids along with my youngest sister and her two kids. Layla and Brad were able to make it as well; they seemed to be thriving in their academic pursuits. Layla was working on her master's degree and Brad was working on his dissertation. The delicious feast and festivities reminded me of the goodness of family; a comfortable space where one's personality/ego with its contradictions and quirks are accepted or at least put up with.

A month later I flew to Jacksonville to celebrate the holidays with friends and family. The family part fizzled when Layla and Brad's plans changed which meant that I'd miss them. I visited Regina and Sarah as planned. Regina and I checked out a new restaurant and seasoned the steaks with good humor. We ended up back in my hotel room for some romance. However, both of us drank too much and passed out. A couple of days later I met with Sarah. She had accepted my invitation to the non-cancellable Caribbean cruise in place of Sheila, so we had plenty to discuss including the possibility of us having sex. Both of us agreed we didn't want sex to fuck up our friendship.

I'm not proud of the way I am, nor am I ashamed. This is who I am, and I've learned to accept myself as I am and not try to fix myself...When I'm able to be fully responsible for the way I am, without justification or rationalization, new possibilities for being come into existence. I find myself growing naturally, without effort. (Werner Erhard)

The seven-day Caribbean cruise with Sarah was a luxurious treat. We had a living room and bedroom with a private balcony overlooking the ocean that allowed for nude sunbathing. The highlight for both of us was the island of St. Maarten. We took an excursion on a Rhino Rider; a two-seater watercraft with a small outboard engine that is difficult to roll over (thus the Rhino designation). After a half hour journey through some choppy seas, we snorkeled around some coral reefs decorated with breathtaking fauna and flora. Then we returned via the same choppy waters. I had the pedal to the metal on the way back. Good fun. The low point of the cruise was some minor seasickness. Oh, we ended up having sex every day.

The first week of February '05 I was fired which I accepted without hesitation and with relief. Just before the holidays, my compensation plan had been downgraded, so I knew it was only a matter of time before I moved on to another opportunity. I wasn't worried about finances nor was I concerned about landing another job even though I didn't have any job prospects at the time. One day in a reflective mood I wrote: As I go through the dance called life, or better yet, as the dance of life unfolds within me, the more I trust the process, the more I trust my Self, the less I suffer. From this space of clarity, an awesome play of Sun and shadow unfolds.

Living in south Austin meant I was within an hour or so driving time from Will's home in San Antonio. We visited each other often. Will was an avid golfer and was selling me on the benefits. I had grown up around golf and watched my fair share on TV. My father tried to teach me the basics in late elementary school, but it didn't take. However, Will found the rough, if you will, when he was diagnosed with heart disease. Due to some chest pains, he consulted his cardiologist who determined he was on the verge of a heart attack. A quick trip to the hospital and an angiogram indicated the need for the installation of stints. Besides some discomfort, everything went well. He realized he would have to make some lifestyle changes from watching his diet to giving up cigars. Mortal self was knocking on the door, a reminder of the Immortal.

Being unemployed meant I had time on my hands. I decided to create this memoir, *The Play of Sun and Shadow*. With years of momentum behind me, I wrote up to 10 hours a day. The first fifteen years of my journals were in longhand in spiral notebooks which were hard to decipher at times. A few events were hard to reconstruct because I had no journal entries or incomplete ones which meant relying mostly on memory (most of the Initiation chapter). It was an invigorating experience; however, not without some distressing moments remembering some of the difficult dramas. After finishing the rough draft, editing proved more trying than I anticipated. The spelling and typos were one thing, but the grammar and syntax were enough to make me despair (an editor I am not). Thankfully, my home improvement and gardening projects helped lift my spirits.

As May rolled around, I still hadn't landed a job. With no immediate prospects, I took a short trip to Jacksonville to visit Sarah. We pretty much picked up where we left off after the cruise. We didn't see us becoming a couple in the traditional sense. We were friends first; fucking was optional. We visited Washington Oaks State Park which is one of the prettiest beaches in NE Florida along with the gardens across A1A highway. The citrus trees were blooming; a fragrance that has to be in my top ten. Shortly after that, I flew to NYC for a job interview with a large publisher. The interview went well, but the job required relocation, which I declined despite my strong preference for securing employment. All I could do was embrace the process; that is, continue my job search and let go of FUD (fear, uncertainty, doubt) as it arose. My transits and progressions reflected this approach as well.

Chapter 12: Predestination

> I believe we are free, within limits, and yet there is an unseen hand, a guiding angel, that somehow, like a submerged propeller, drives us on. (Rabindranath Tagore)

Just before the holidays, I followed up on an attraction to a lady that worked at Macy's in the local mall. Gabriella and I went out a couple of times before I asked her over to my place for dining, wining, and romance. A dance enhanced by her Capricorn Sun, Aquarius Moon, and Libra rising (need I mention the presence of Capricorn again?!). Gabriella's sister had purchased a home that was in the midst of being built. When completed in a couple of months or so, Gabriella planned on living there to help with the mortgage. However, her living conditions at the time were subpar, so I invited her to live with me. I didn't intend it to be a long-term commitment, pero el sexo fue sublime y, para mi sorpresa, nos enamoramos.

We pleased each other without trying. Naturally, there were some differences; you guessed it, religion. Gabriella was Catholic, but unlike Beth, a mellower, non-defensive version; maybe because she was Mexican and Catholicism is somewhat a given. In light of my previous two relationships, I made sure she understood I had no interest in religion. There were amusing peculiarities as well; shopping—she loved to lollygag; I swear, she considered food labels pleasure reading. I was predisposed to a more perfunctory approach which sometimes meant purchasing the wrong item. When the Unmoved Mover was distributing patience, I was preoccupied playing in the sand pile.

As I settled into my new home, I became disillusioned with my backdoor neighbor. His dogs, collies, were barking a lot, day and night (2 AM, 4 AM, etc.). A collie's bark can pierce tank armor. Doing the neighborly thing, I asked him nicely if he could do something about his dogs' barking in the middle of the night. He brushed me off. That left me with no option but to contact the city department that deals with such and file a complaint. The problem with barking dogs became a hot issue on the Yahoo group site for the neighborhood. Astonishingly, some dog caregivers didn't understand that a barking dog was an inconsiderate imposition, especially at night when others, including other dogs, are trying to sleep.

I succumbed to Will's persuasion and bought a set of golf clubs. We started playing a couple times a month. Initially, I hit the ball well. Then I started overthinking my swing, and things got ugly...real ugly. I got so frustrated I considered giving up. I was humbled by golf; it had to be one of the most challenging sports to play decently. Even though the ball was still when struck, not moving like baseball or ping pong, the number of unintended results was disheartening. There were too damn many variables to consider from wind to wind up.

Nick and I may have been a bit obsessive, not an uncommon trait on the links, in our approach to golf. One Saturday morning in San Antonio we woke up to the sound of thunder and very heavy rain, a drought buster. Unfazed, we maintained an optimistic attitude that the rain would stop, preserving our 10:45 tee time. Soon after we arrived, it stopped raining, and a bit later the course was opened. We were the first to tee off which meant there was no one ahead of us. Soon we realized we weren't going to be pressured from behind either. This enabled us to take second shots and experiment with clubs; namely, my newly acquired 3 and 5 wood. It was without a doubt the best day of golf either one of us had ever experienced.

> Go Gators! Bravo! In Europe they have a way to hail transcendent performances, whether they take place in an opera house or a sports arena. So, bravo, Joakim. Bravo, Oh-Fours. And bravo, Gators. You are the 2006 national champions, and there's nothing fake about that." (*Sports Illustrated*, April 10, 2006)

My new field sales job at DCP left me wanting. Some of the online databases in political science and history sold quite well, but other equally fine databases didn't because some of the data, not the presentation or ease of access, was available on the internet for free. I was making my monthly goals but wasn't confident I could attain the yearly goal. And, there was ferment in management ranks which didn't bode well. The manager who hired me left suddenly for another job. I kept my ear attuned to other job opportunities.

With the advent of spring, Gabriella and I took a road trip to Port Aransas to visit the beach. The scenery reminded me of Fernandina Beach, Florida, with wide beaches and small-town atmosphere. A few weeks later Brad and Layla came into town for a short visit. The steam train tour through the Hill Country was the highlight. As anticipated Gabriella's multi-month living arrangement with me came to an end; she moved into her sister's home. We continued seeing each other, but only a couple nights a week. One night after an erotic opera climaxing in vocal arias, she casually inquired about my feelings concerning marriage. I told her it wasn't a realistic option for me. It wasn't what she wanted to hear which added to our drifting apart. I didn't see the whirlwind in the distance.

One day at my local grocery store I used their blood pressure monitor. The high reading prompted me to schedule my yearly physical. My GP confirmed the high blood pressure and recommended changes to my diet and more exercise. He also took some blood and said he would get back with me in a week or so with the numbers. A week later he requested I meet with him again. I figured the cholesterol numbers were worse than expected. However, our discussion had nothing to do with LDL or HDL; it was about my PSA number and my prostate. The prostate is a walnut-sized gland next to the bladder and urethra that helps make semen and acts as a carrier for the sperm which is part of the ejaculate. He recommended I consult a urologist because the PSA reading was above 4.0.

During my first consultation, the urologist used digital technology; that's a finger up the ass in case you're wondering. He found no apparent cause for alarm. However, he performed an additional procedure, a biopsy, just to make sure. If the biopsy showed no signs of malignancy, I would have another checkup in four months. If it did, I'd cross that bridge when I got to it. A couple weeks later I crossed that bridge. The urologist informed me that one of the sample tissues from the biopsy was cancerous. He explained the options: surgery or radiation. I conducted a thorough search via the internet on the pros and cons and spoke in depth with my brother's friend who had recently undergone radiation treatment. I decided if the PSA number continued to rise, I'd opt for radiation treatment rather than surgery. Naturally, my most significant concern was quality of life issues below the waist: urination, defecation, and erection. The survival rate from prostate cancer was 90% plus—so I wasn't worried about death. Call it a faint knock of mortal self, if you will.

Worth noting, there were some significant astrological transits at play. Transiting Saturn was conjunct natal Pluto and ascendant *and* transiting Pluto was sextile natal Saturn. Here's what Steven Forrest had to say in his *SkyLog* interpretation: "To succeed, there is first a need to face reality squarely, even if it's unsavory. Then to make a hard choice...that is, to reach an emotional bottom line and not be crippled by your awareness of the ambiguities in your situation...When sober-minded Saturn gets involved with dark-hearted Pluto, you'll have little patience for fluffy, frilly superficiality. This is a serious moment, something of a day of reckoning. Truths must be recognized and told...You are ready. The situation is pressing. It will not go away or improve of its own accord. Take responsibility, move decisively, and do what must be done." You gotta admit; that's spot on.

Along with these medical considerations was a possible job change. The manager who hired me was now the national sales manager for another publisher which specialized in government contact information and was interested in hiring me. I was willing to consider his offer because of better money, better territory, and hopefully a better run organization. The only negative was the database look and feel; we were told it was being reworked. While mulling over his offer, I had to fly to DC to attend a sales meeting. My connecting flight through Houston was delayed due to thunder storms. While waiting at the gate, I noticed a good-looking flight attendant waiting as well. I got to check her out at my leisure. Four hours later while boarding, I made small talk with her; I liked how she responded. After another brief exchange, I decided to ask her out. But how? Then, I saw my chance; I slipped her my business card as she came by picking up trash. I noticed her name tag read Maya. Just before landing, I heard Maya asking in Spanish a frightened lady seated behind me if she wanted gum. I added in my well accented Spanish that I wanted a piece as well. She left me a message a week later. We had several phone conversations over the next couple weeks covering many topics. I looked forward to our first date.

By the end of August, after a few whirlwind weekends of whoopee, Maya and I had fallen in love. It was effortless and lighthearted. Her beauty, sensuality, sense of humor, and positive attitude were a pleasure to be around. Oh, I almost forgot...once again, a lady with Capricorn accented; that is, four planets including Sun in Capricorn! I looked forward to spending as much time as possible with her. We even talked about her moving in at the beginning of the year. However, one glitch reared its head: her financial debt. Due to credit card debt and expenses, Maya was falling further behind every month. At my urging, she declared bankruptcy which I paid for.

I was pleased that Layla and I still talked on a regular basis. I wasn't sure that'd be the case after she got married. In August, Layla visited without Brad. We took several walks: U of Texas campus, Hamilton Pool, Pedernales River, and downtown Gruene where we met Will and his son. We ate lunch at the Gristmill restaurant overlooking the lovely Guadalupe River; the local trout was quite tasty. Layla seemed more relaxed; she had earned her MA and already had some job leads. However, where she would eventually settle would depend on Brad's job offers; UT was one of the possibilities.

My next blood test showed an increased PSA number which meant the prostate cancer was growing. I decided to bite the bullet and undergo radiation treatment. As I mentioned before, my primary concern was the adverse effects south of the waist; due to my new sexual relationship with Maya, erection was in first place. One night while sleeping next to her, I woke up after having a dream about transiting Saturn and its impending square to my Sun. From previous experience with that transit, I knew it could **correspond with reduced physical vitality.** I figured it might not be the best combination with radiation treatments. I got up and checked my ephemeris; my radiation procedure was scheduled after the square. There is no double-blind study data about the effects of Saturn transits (it would be next to impossible to conduct because of the numerous variables). **Regardless,** it was a heads-up prompted by a dream in the language of astrology.

> A knowledge of astrological principles reveals the laws of energy and polarity active in all of life—yin/yang, positive/negative, male/female, Sun/Moon, Venus/Mars, and so on. And a keener awareness of the implications of the polarities and the paradoxes of life allow one to step back and see the whole picture and the whole person. (Stephen Arroyo; *Person-to-Person Astrology*)

To avoid working reserve, Maya was working international flights to Europe out of the airline hub in Newark. Some of Maya's trips were two weeks long so she wouldn't have to commute as often; we relied on texting when she was overseas. That didn't stop us from traveling for pleasure. We flew to San Jose, CA, for a short visit to nearby Monterey. I had to attend a conference, so my travel and hotel costs weren't a factor, and Maya flew non-rev. We had a delightful time; the affection flowed freely between us. The Monterey Bay Aquarium's jellyfish

79

display was a sight to behold and Domenico's on the Wharf pawn pesto a taste to treasure with playful sea lions frolicking in the marina as entertainment. Our tour by car from Santa Cruz to Carmel included many spectacular views that required a photo or two (call that a shutterbug rationalization but I'm clicking to it). We got crabby only once after a very long day in traffic on Highway 1. The library conference was worthwhile as well.

The mess in Iraq had turned into a civil war as many feared it would; we had a catastrophic clusterfuck lubricated by more fabrication a la Bush & Company. I hoped there'd be some significant changes in the upcoming elections; first, we had to weather the political primaries and their slew of negative ads. It has been said that politics is a necessary evil. The French poet, writer, and politician Alphonse de Lamartine (1790-1869) once wrote: "The more I see of the representatives of the people, the more I admire my dogs." The same can be said about most religious leaders as well; in fact, many are politicians in disguise. They share a similar tendency which is probably genetic--they obfuscate and they lie. The homosexual scandal a few months back with the evangelical minister was a classic case. During his day job, he preached against homosexuality while on the side he was screwing a male prostitute fueled by meth.

Pessimism was tempering my optimism; you can't have one without the other. In addition to the increasing political polarization, the news was awash with stories about warfare, global warming, pollution, epidemics, nuclear proliferation, and religious stupidity. We were up to our knees in shit, you might say. To ameliorate these problems would require international cooperation which was in short supply due to political, cultural, religious, and economic forces throughout the world. In the US these problems were ignored or downplayed by various industrial complexes, the Republican Party, Fox News, the religious Right, and radio rabble-rousers. As Pogo said from his home in the Okefenokee Swamp near my old stomping grounds, "We have met the enemy, and he is us."

> Thus, because we are rapidly advancing along this non-sustainable course, the world's environmental problems will get resolved, in one way or another, within the lifetimes of the children and young adults alive today. The only question is whether they will become resolved in pleasant ways of our own choice, or in unpleasant ways not of our choice, such as warfare, genocide, starvation, disease epidemics, and collapses of societies. While all of those grim phenomena have been endemic to humanity throughout our history, their frequency increases with environmental degradation, population pressure, and the resulting poverty and political instability. (Jared Diamond; *Collapse, How Societies Choose to Fail or Succeed*)

Even though it had been only a few months, I was increasingly concerned about my job. The database I was tasked with selling wasn't catching on as anticipated. I started checking around for other sales jobs in the library market. The timing was tricky due to my upcoming radiation treatment which was being covered by company supplied health insurance. The lack of a universal health care system meant my insurance didn't follow me should I get fired or laid off. Companies shouldn't be tasked with providing health insurance for employees; it isn't part of their business mission. Secondly, company-provided for-profit health insurance was increasingly non-sustainable with insurance premiums rising astronomically for workers and employers. Those without company-provided insurance were more than likely unable to afford such. In some countries, the health care system is entirely government-run while in other countries it is coordinated with private companies. Research conclusively proves the universal health care approach improves well-being while decreasing costs.

My brother and sister-in-law's hospitality, elegant but unpretentious, once again provided the setting for Thanksgiving. Due to balmy weather, nobody's travel was delayed; Maya, Layla, and Brad made it in time for the festivities. My sister and significant other along with all the nieces and nephews that live in Atlanta were present at one time or another (due to divorces many of them have more than one celebration to attend). And, the food...where do I begin? I gained at least five pounds. Layla and Brad gave me a birthday card for my 54th with a touching note: "I'm glad that we get to spend this birthday with you. It makes it that much more special (at least for us). You're a wonderful father and friend. Birthdays are a time to remind you how much we appreciate everything about you—your humor, candidness, silliness, easygoing and loving nature. You're the best!"

In mid-December, I drove to Houston to meet Maya and a couple of her friends for dinner. We ate at an Indian fusion restaurant (i.e., chicken pot pie Indian style which was scrumptious). While Maya was in the bathroom, her friends expressed their pleasure about Maya meeting me and moving to Austin (and away from her family complications). My doubts about us living together had subsided as had my concerns about her finances. Her bankruptcy had been finalized which would allow her to pay off her debts to IRS, dentist, and friends. In astrology, there are twelve houses in the natal chart representing different areas of life. It's worth noting, Maya had five planets transiting the second house which has to do with financial security issues.

The radiation treatments proceeded as scheduled: 9:00 AM, five days a week. I usually got to the radiation center a few minutes early. This allowed me time to help assemble a giant jigsaw puzzle, something I hadn't done since I was a kid, and interact with fellow patients; some of whom were gruesomely disfigured. One guy was missing most of his ears and nose due to skin cancer. In my third week, the first side effects of radiation appeared: frequent urination and lessened quality of sleep. The doctor prescribed sleep aids. A positive side effect, if you will, was my growing bond with my brother. We talked, texted, or emailed frequently, to see how things were going. Often, we pontificated, another genetic trait, about issues of the day.

Douglas Harding died on January 11, 2007. Without a doubt, Douglas was a great spiritual teacher who didn't seek the trappings often associated with such. Through his extensive writings and numerous workshops given around the world, he shared the "meditation for the marketplace." That is, headless seeing; a highly practical Way that is always accessible. He devised various experiments like face to no-face that remind us of this naked simplicity frequently overlooked out of habit. "All I need to do to see into my Essential Nature is to turn around the arrow of my attention at this very moment and see that I am looking out of nothing whatever, and certainly not out of a small, opaque, coloured, complicated thing."

Chapter 13: Expectation

> To see myself in everybody and everybody in myself most certainly is love.
> (Nisargadatta)

Maya's move to Austin wasn't without some complication. When I arrived with the U-Haul ready to pack her stuff it was obvious her packing efforts had been minimal at best which made me angry. Then I saw the filth in her home which added doubt to the disturbance. I started thinking that living with her would be a mistake. I considered calling it quits; instead, I shared my feelings with Maya which helped diffuse them. The rest of the move was accomplished without more drama. We settled into living together and Maya continued commuting to the airline base in Newark to work international flights in order not to fly reserve.

The beginning of February brought an end to my radiation treatments. Besides a radioactive glow, the side effects were minimal...at first. I felt fortunate; the radiation oncology staff provided excellent customer service. The worst ass-pect was the painful bowel movements (think giving birth to pine cones) along with frequent urination, but systems south of my belly button were still working properly. The next step in my prostate cancer treatment was the insertion of radioactive seeds later in the month.

Before that step, I flew to Seattle to man a booth at a library conference; something I had done dozens of times. I was the sole company representative which I preferred. On my way to the bathroom, I ran across an old business acquaintance at a booth selling a learning software/hardware package for children. He mentioned that they were looking for sales representatives. Coincidentally, I had been discussing the opportunity with a recruiter. I ended up interviewing with the president of WAS at lunch.

The insertion of the high-intensity radioactive seeds was performed under general anesthesia. Seeds the size of rice were injected into the prostate through the skin between the scrotum and anus. The logistics were professionally managed. My experience with anesthesia was remarkable; the best sleep I had in weeks. Most bothersome was the muscular discomfort due to lying prone for two days and the open season on viewing my genitals by every Tom, Dick, and Mary that came by to check out my condition. I should have charged admission.

I was touched by the sympathy friends and family expressed. Layla and Brad sent me a vase of flowers and, my ex sent me a plant. Maya brought me some balloons and a get-well card with an electronic ditty by Julie Andrews, *A Spoonful of Sugar.* She also included a book by Fred Rogers, *The World According to Mister Rogers*, which was apropos. I frequently used a telephone greeting based on Mister Rogers', "It's a wonderful day in the neighborhood." Mine was, "It's a wonderful day in the Universe."

> When you combine your own intuition with sensitivity to other people's feelings and
> moods, you may be close to the origins of valuable human attributes such as generosity,

altruism, compassion, sympathy, and empathy. (Fred Rogers; *The World According to Mister Rogers*)

Ben, my friend and ex-boss, who had retired from SMP a few years back, burned some of his frequent flier miles with a visit to Austin. Even though he hadn't played in 10 years, Ben was agreeable to playing golf. The cold and windy conditions added to the adventure. The following day we went to the UT/Iowa State basketball game along with Will and his son. UT won readily with the help of Kevin Durant, their great forward. The rest of our time was spent watching TV and movies along with feasting on some delicious food from Mexican to Cuban. As usual, hanging out with Ben was easy.

After Ben's visit, Maya and I had our first substantial argument since living together. She didn't trust my warning about a sleazy sycophant visiting the neighbors next door. Maya encouraged him by being engaging which pissed me off. She finally understood later in the evening when he showed up at the front door requesting a massage. I told him to fuck off and slammed the door in his face. He was gone the next day. I asked my next-door neighbors why they allowed him to stay at their place. They shrugged their shoulders and said he had conned them.

At the end of February, I accepted a field sales job offer from WAS selling the children's learning software/hardware package (based on my interview the previous month at the conference). That meant resigning from my current position; I would miss working with them. I was quite fond of the whole bunch...decent folks. My WAS territory was public libraries from Texas to Florida, familiar selling grounds. Basically, the country was split into equal parts population wise. As part of my orientation for WAS, I took the Caliper Profile Evaluation/Sales Dynamics Profile. Like the MBTI, it's a credible profile but inherently limited due to being self-administered. Compared to astrology, it lacked the depth and nuance and none of the developmental or evolutionary insight.

> He seems assertive, comfortable communicating directly, and unlikely to be easily deterred by setbacks and criticism. Furthermore, he shows the interpersonal dynamics to be at ease networking and reaching out to others within the community, and he should be supportive without overextending himself. He is apt to be an attentive listener who could adapt to different personality types. He tends to be quite independent, and while this trait may be an asset, we would recommend gaining his initial buy-in to company guidelines and procedures. He also might need to have greater patience for handling routine administrative matters, since he is inclined to be impatient with such tasks. Similarly, he may rush when making decisions, and if his impulsiveness is not tempered somewhat, he may make occasional errors due to oversight. (Caliper Profile Evaluation/Sales Dynamics Profile)

It's probably not surprising that I became a Barack Obama fan. His obvious intelligence, considered opinions, and sense of humor appealed to me, especially as expressed in his informal interviews a la Jon Stewart. We needed some hope, some light, after what we have been through with the Bush administration. Bush's right-wing supporters tried vainly to portray themselves as the moral standard but had been exposed as a vindictive, vitriolic vanguard of intolerance.

After a month or so, I secured my first orders for the children's learning software/hardware package which I knew was going to be a big hit. It was a welcome change from the difficult to sell database with the previous publisher. My first two conferences in Oklahoma City and San Antonio resulted in immediate sales and numerous leads. Selling was a thrill; however, most sales training courses characterize selling as hunting or something along those lines. I found that approach limiting; it suggested the prospect was prey which was the opposite of the consultative relationship I wanted with my customers.

Maya's two weeks on the road and one week at home schedule continued. Coupled with my travel schedule, it meant sometimes we didn't see each other for three weeks. This was difficult to deal with at times; however, I was determined to make it work. Up to that point, my romantic life had been like a round of golf with numerous blow-up holes. Jim Carrey put it another way when asked about his relationship with Jenny McCarthy and whether it would have worked before. "No, not at all. I went through a lot of relationships that I believe were meant to define what I don't want in another person and in myself, and it refocused me on what I do want."

And, the debate raged on about the extent of humankind's negative impact on Earth; this is, climate change and global warming. Per NASA: "Global warming: the increase in Earth's average surface temperature due to rising levels of greenhouse gases. Climate change: a long-term change in the Earth's climate, or of a region on Earth." The signs of global warming were everywhere from glacier melt to coral bleaching. My two cents worth: regardless of how much global warming and resulting climate change is man-made, it behooves us to pay attention due to the immediate quality of life issues. Namely, we need clean air, water, and food. It isn't clean in many places, especially in the developing world. Doing something about it will, by default, help with global warming and climate change. The continuing breach in our stewardship is non-sustainable and will be catastrophic.

The April 16th mass shooting at Virginia Tech, a lovely campus I visited back in my SMP days, was hard to fathom. Apparently, the mentally deranged killer didn't like rich kids or women, so he decided to kill a bunch of innocent folks. The question of gun control arose, as it should. Gun violence in this country is a disgrace. The Second Amendment was written when there were muzzleloaders, not automatic weapons. I'd dispose of my gun gladly if there were a nationwide effort. In England, which instituted meaningful gun control after a mass shooting, the number of gun-related crimes is less than one-tenth of what NYC's has with seven times the population. But that's England, not the Wild West, where even the mention of background checks fuels the NRA's delusions of persecution riddled with hallucinations of black helicopters.

Maya and I continued passing each other at the airport, so to speak, due to our travel schedules. It was sort of like a long-distance relationship. Regardless, we started talking about marriage which surprised me given my reluctance in my previous relationship with Gabriella.

Somehow, it felt destined. Via astrological interaspects, aspects between the two natal charts, I sensed a past life connection. One night while Maya and I were hashing out the differences in our wedding plans, I lashed out at her. I don't remember the details, but my wine infused orneriness disappointed me. Such barking was unusual; however, what was increasingly common was waking up in the middle of the night covered in a wine-induced sweat while gnawing on my problem drinking.

> The function of problems is to direct you to their solution at the Center. Having some problems is very helpful. (Douglas Harding)

My regular check-up with my urologist indicated a declining PSA number, much to my relief. However, the urologist behaved like a dick on occasion. He was still smarting from my not opting for surgery which he would have performed. His customer service was lacking because he couldn't get his ego out of the way. Speaking of dicks, mine wasn't working as well. I figured it was the combination of factors: the result of the prostate radiation treatment and a natural decrease in libido due to age. However, my priorities had been rearranged, my primary concern was more fundamental, urination.

On the job front, I traveled extensively throughout the territory visiting libraries and demonstrating the children's software/hardware package; basically, a PC with learning software for kids ages 2 to 12. These sales efforts were creating a substantial buzz in libraryland. It was a pleasure selling product public librarians wanted; whether they could afford it was another question. Typically, public library budgets were very lean which meant securing funds through grants, donations, raffles, etc.

Back at company HQ, the primary difficulty was getting along with the president and vice president who behaved like self-absorbed jerks at times. However, I was comfortable with the company's direction financially and product development wise. The salary was okay and the promise of substantial commissions to my liking (I lived on my salary; commissions were gravy). I liked working out of my home even though it was lonely at times; a much better environment than the politics and egos of an office setting.

Over the years, I have made no apologies for my appreciation of astrology in spite of occasional condescension, usually based on religious or scientific bias. I have found most folks are open-minded even though they have no idea what astrology encompasses. One paragraph Sun sign horoscopes in newspapers and magazines can be uncanny (Rob Breznsy's Free Will Astrology); however, what I'm talking about is much more in depth. In addition to one's Sun sign, there is the ascendant or rising sign, Moon sign, Mercury sign, Venus sign, etc. Then there are astronomically measured angles between these planets, all of which adds significant definition and meaning. However, for me, the most intriguing insights were provided by transits and progressions, a psychological/biographical report *and* forecast.

Maya and I squabbled more. Things came to a head during Layla's visit in September. We took Layla to Manuel's to sample the flan we had raved about. While paying the bill, I imitated our waiter's surfer demeanor. Maya took exception to my imitation even though the waiter didn't hear me. I countered her objection which ended up with us yelling at each other outside the restaurant. After Layla left, we had a much needed discussion about our relationship. We shared our frustrations with the frequency of travel and sex and our doubts about sustaining such. We decided to postpone our marriage plans for December.

My urologist never informed me that one of the potential side effects of radiation treatment for prostate cancer is the inflammation and scarring of the urethra. "The urethra is a tube that connects the urinary bladder to the urinary meatus for the removal of urine from the body. In males, the urethra travels through the penis and also carries semen." (Wikipedia) This side effect got my attention when my urine turned red from blood amplified by the passing of blood clots. Another visceral reminder was a stinging sensation in the urethra when I urinated; that is, a sharp, burning sensation that would bring me to my knees in pain (and worse when coupled with wine). My urologist did explain that fatigue was par for the course in part due to waking up more often because of increased frequency of urination. Sometimes I had a hard time falling back to sleep so I'd read.

Alexander Hamilton, a biography by Ron Chernow, was a captivating read. All I knew about Hamilton was the famous deadly duel with Aaron Burr. He was a genius. We can thank him for much of the way our government functions; that is, liberal capitalism. I favored Hamilton's view of a strong central government; that included vigorous checks and balances among the branches, international trade, national military and bank. I would have preferred the Federalist/Hamiltonian ticket vs. Republican/Jeffersonian if I had had to choose. Jefferson's apologetic stance about the French Revolution and its violent excesses wasn't to my liking. I also thought his preference for a weak central government with an agrarian-based economy based on slavery was wrong; a moral/ethical failure that undermined the unity of the new nation from the beginning and foreshadowed the Civil War.

> Men are rather reasoning than reasonable animals, for the most part governed by the impulse of passion. (Alexander Hamilton; Letter of April 16, 1802)

It was worth noting, the party politics during the post-Revolutionary days (1800-1840) were quite acrimonious with some sad parallels to today including accusations of not being patriotic, faithful, etc. Also, something the religious Right conveniently forgets, there was a diversity of religious beliefs among the Founding Fathers; some weren't religious at all.

If you look at the political spectrum from Left to Right, on the far Left you have communism, and on the far Right you have fascism; both require excessive and oppressive government. The Bush administration was as far Right as I had seen. Appealing to anger and fear, they decided that undocumented immigrants were the new bogeyman. Rounding up and returning the 10 million or so undocumented immigrants to their home country would require a police state. The Right was also courting controversy and confrontation between religions; it was both sad and absurd. There is but One...Spirit. End of discussion. There are many religions, faiths, and belief systems; to each his own. Personal preference rules especially in matters of religion, politics, and sexuality. Ultimately, and thankfully, quite simply, I Am...my own authority.

The mismanagement at work was becoming difficult to stomach at times. During a conference call, I objected vocally to the president's disparagement a fellow salesperson's comments. Along with the vice president's boorish behavior, it was discouraging. They were getting peevish because we hadn't been able to penetrate the education market based on imaginary sales projections. All the while, our actual sales in the library market were robust with plenty of room to grow. Not surprisingly there were occasions where I wanted to yell, "Get fucking real!" Oh, transiting Uranus was square my natal Mercury and progressed Moon was trine my natal Uranus. The basic meaning was: individuation, impatience, and dissent; a vintage I would become increasingly familiar with.

> Everybody works, except for a very few independently wealthy people. Work targets basic needs and puts us in touch with very primal feelings. Survival, our public identity, power, money, politics, it is all there. Work is a very ripe domain for people to play out their worst neuroses. (Fred Kofman, founder of Axialent)

Time magazine had an article on Steve Martin's memoir, *Born Standing Up: A Life*. Memoirs, autobiographies, and biographies have piqued my interest since I was a kid. The first biography I read was about Thomas Edison in third grade. After learning that he would tug his eyebrow when he brainstormed, I imitated such for a while; however, no inventions appeared, so I decided to save my eyebrows from further damage. I downloaded Steve Martin's memoir and devoured it in short order. He nailed it about the fear of writing a memoir, "My biggest fear was that when you're writing about yourself, you're writing about yourself. It could come off like an ego trip." However, in his favor are obvious intelligence, talent, and fame.

A few days later a newspaper headline caught my attention: Dan Fogelberg, a pop/folk/country singer, died of prostate cancer. I recognized his name and remembered his tune, *Longer*. His cancer wasn't diagnosed until the late stages. He was my age. Once again, mortal self was knocking on the door, a reminder of the Immortal.

My sleep continued to be fitful, and my urethra still stung like a son of a bitch when I pissed. I minimized certain diuretics such as coffee and wine. I was also dealing with a decreasing flow; I tried various OTC drugs to no avail. Desperate for relief, I went to the urologist. It turned out I had an obstruction in the urethra due to scar material. He performed a telescopic procedure, a roto-rooter of my urethra, which was one of the most painful experiences of my life but effective.

Maya also had her medical challenges as well. One of her breast implants sprang a leak while she was working a flight. Initially, she considered removal of both implants but opted for replacement a la encouragement of the plastic surgeon, a beautiful woman with a bodacious set of ta-tas (I guess it goes with the profession). Her replacement operation went without a hitch albeit with a stitch or two.

My quest for a beautiful garden (the yard was gradually being minimized) continued in spurts including a cement stepping stone path off the back porch that added a nice touch. Along with gardening, another love was astrology which I trust you've already figured out. As I said before, a transit/progression report is similar to a weather forecast; high and low-pressure systems are tracked and precipitation, or lack thereof, is predicted. The report is specific to your chart. However, due to unique psychological, familial, cultural, and/or political circumstances, multiple interpretations within an archetypal range are necessary. How could it be otherwise? 360,000 babies are born each day. Outer planet transits don't move very fast, and progressions of inner planets move slowly. It is safe to say a couple of million folks have similar transits and progressions. It's up to you to decide whether to bring an umbrella or not.

> ...the proper use of astrological information and techniques is to further one's depth of understanding in order to live more consciously. Astrology should not be used to evade personal responsibility or to foster illusions of perfect solutions or ultimate bliss. Rather, astrology provides us with an extremely useful and reliable tool for understanding human nature as well as for tuning in on the essence of specific interpersonal dynamics. It allows us to gain perspective, objectivity, and insight. (Stephen Arroyo; *Person-to-Person Astrology*)

Again, because I was waking up at various times of night and not readily falling back asleep, I read. I finished reading the biography of *Aldous Huxley* by Sybille Bedford with Dad's notations in various places. I had given it to Dad back in college, having only read a bit of it, thinking he would appreciate reading about an intellectual, not unlike himself. As hoped, it had spurred discussions between Dad and me about Huxley's LSD use and mysticism. Huxley's *The Perennial Philosophy* was my first formal introduction to "tat twam asi" or "that thou art." I appreciated his basic conviction: "...in spite of Pain, in spite of Death, in spite of Horror, the universe is in some way All Right, capital A, capital R..."

Since our blowout a few months back, Maya and I were getting along better. As I have mentioned, our sexual frequency had dropped substantially. Maya assured me she was okay with the situation. My acceptance was partially based on my hope there would be an uptick in my dick when the side effects of radiation and medication subsided. Maya's financial issues had improved since declaring bankruptcy and paying off her IRS debt. However, indicative of her financial values, Maya wanted to spend her profit sharing on some additional plastic surgery. I disagreed thinking she should pay off the rest of her debts ASAP. Eventually, she agreed with me.

In Austin, January and February is cedar fever season. Cedar fever is an allergic reaction to the Mountain Juniper tree pollen which they spew voluminously. It has all the symptoms of the flu without, ironically, the fever. Maya was especially susceptible and suffered considerably to the point of becoming bedridden. It was so bad that one of two courses of action would eventually have to be taken. One, go to an allergist and go through a treatment procedure that according to most folks didn't work. Or, two, move from the Central Texas area.

Toward the end of February '08, Maya and I flew to Veracruz, Mexico, to visit her father. It was a journey full of vistas both in outer and inner, both pleasant and unpleasant. Veracruz was a viaje, a trip, down memory lane for me. The whole sensory array reminded me of Caracas, Venezuela. Just as folks say that American cities look alike to some degree, the same can be said of Latin American cities with the cinder block construction, walled yards, and littered, dusty streets with vendors hawking everything from snow cones to designer jeans.

Maya's father and mother-in-law gave us a tour of the city and surrounding countryside including some impressive ruins from an Aztec era tribe. The visit afforded me the chance to formulate an impression of Maya's father. To some degree or another, most of us have issues with our mother and/or father; it is the nature of an imperfect relationship. I could see why Maya had issues with him. He was a friendly man with a nasty temper and stubborn disposition, possibly with a Napoleon complex. The relationship with his adopted teenage daughter provided painful reminders for Maya.

Political discussions with my brother and sister were increasing in frequency. They were fed up with Bush & Company as well. We were up to our necks in a Middle East quagmire, cities ravaged by gang violence, inadequate infrastructure, busted educational systems, and a tax code for special interests. I had become a full-fledged Obama fan but was cautiously optimistic about his prospects. I didn't trust the power broker billionaires, special interests, and industrial complexes that pulled the levers at the expense of the average American regardless of who is president or which party controlled Congress. They had been buying Congress off for a long time, and I doubted it would change quickly. However, I thought Obama represented a fundamental desire of a majority of people to improve the system. ¡Si se puede!

> America was given great gifts, this ideal form of government, this most improved form of self-government that has ever come along up until that time, and we squandered it. And once again, on the same two things: gizmos and toys and gadgets -- goods, property, possessions -- and also this country is far too religious for its own good. (George Carlin; interview by Heather Havrilesky in *Salon*).

At the end of March, I attended a library conference in Minneapolis which was exceptional. The software/hardware package for kids was making significant inroads in the public library market. The booth attendance was the best I'd experienced at a vendor's exhibit. Frequently, librarians who were customers stopped by the booth and thanked us for the product. As you might imagine, this impressed the potential customers I was talking to when they heard such.

My flight back to Austin proved to be out of the ordinary as well. About twenty minutes after we took off from MSP, one of the passengers had a heart attack. The flight attendant and a couple of passengers, who happened to be doctors, tried to revive him with CPR while the man's wife became distraught. The flight was diverted to Omaha. After the quickest descent and taxi I had ever experienced, we were met at the passenger boarding bridge by EMT. They confirmed his death and dragged him down the regional jet aisle on a blanket because it was too narrow for the gurney. His wife tagged along in tears. It would have been more respectful had they let us deplane first.

My next reading adventure was *The Tipping Point* by Malcolm Gladwell. He described how positive and negative changes cross a threshold and spread because of a small number of influential people (i.e., our behavior is strongly influenced by our environment). I had seen this first hand in my business. Gladwell used the terms connector, maven, and salesperson to describe agents of change. I am obviously a salesman. Heck, I will try to sell you on the avocados at Costco even though I'm not on commission. My friend Johnny is definitely a connector. He knows lots of folks all over the world and connects readily. I think my brother has strong elements of maven with his knowledge and expertise in many areas.

> ...human beings invariably make the mistake of overestimating the importance of fundamental character traits and underestimate the importance of situation and context. We will always reach for a "dispositional" explanation for events, as opposed to a contextual explanation...Character is more like a bundle of habits and tendencies and interests, loosely bound together and dependent, at certain times, on circumstances and context. (Malcolm Gladwell; *The Tipping Point*)

One of the reasons I purchased my home in the particular neighborhood in Austin was because it had an HOA. I figured it would lessen the problems I had encountered in previous neighborhoods where some folks didn't care about the appearance of their homes and city covenants lacked teeth. I attended the HOA meetings regularly along with 5% or so of the other homeowners. The usual issues about litter, lawn care, and walking trail/park maintenance were addressed. Then the discussion, to my surprise, moved on to gang activity at the park. Gangs had found our neighborhood park to be a **convenient** place to conduct their drug business (another good reason to legalize). We decided to contact the police department and set up a crime watch program.

Taking advantage of the beautiful spring weather, Chuy the Chow, Maya, and I drove down to Port Aransas for a mini vacation. It was a celebration of our engagement. We had changed our minds about getting married. The ceremony would be held on December 13th, the midpoint between our birth dates. This would be the second marriage for both of us, a "triumph of hope over experience." An unexpected bonus was Sandfest; a weekend extravaganza where sand artists from all over the world descend on a given beach that has the necessary quality of sand for sculptures that are impressive works of art. Chuy didn't take to the ocean or the beach and was unimpressed with the sand sculptures.

Will's insurance business was hemorrhaging. I invited him to Austin for some rest and recreation. We had fun hanging out; the movie *Charlie Wilson's War* was a big hit. Saturday, we played golf at one of our favorites, a links course; even though there were few trees to contend with, the rolling fairways always proved challenging. I realized my golf game wasn't going to improve without devoting more time, especially at the range, which I wasn't willing to do. So, the challenge was to accept my mediocre level of play without becoming disagreeable. I enjoyed the round without letting myself get frustrated. Well, there was one chip shot that scooted across the green and landed in a worse spot than the previous lie that prompted some cussing. All it took was one good shot, and I was hooked again. Or was it sliced again?

Douglas Harding once said, "the loss of one's head issues in the finding of one's heart – a heart so tender that it is mortally wounded by the world's appalling suffering." Online or via TV the news was frequently about suffering from natural disasters in Myanmar and China to wars in the Middle East and Africa; horrifying, heartbreaking stories and pictures of parents trying to protect and save their children. Suffering, an indecipherable burden we all bear; alleviating such, to whatever degree possible, a goal we all must share.

Chapter 14: Repetition

You cannot change the cards you are dealt, just how you play the hand. (Randy Pausch; *Last Lecturer*)

I was thrilled with the results of my blood work; I had lowered my LDL 40 points or so with the use of herbal alternatives and diet. My GP was a buzz kill; he told me I needed to get it lower and that I should consider taking a statin. At that point, it dawned on me that he was nothing more than a marketing representative for Big Pharma. I reminded him of the adverse effect, neuropathy, I suffered because of statins. He could barely hide his contempt as if it was my fault. Fuck him, I changed doctors.

Cholesterol is essential for the normal functioning of cells, especially the brain and nervous system. An Institutes of Health study "confirmed that long-term treatment with statins caused a clinically silent but still definite damage to peripheral nerves when the treatment lasts longer than 2 years." The medical/pharma complex has effectively demonized cholesterol. They want everyone taking statins; it's more profitable than a decent diet and sensible exercise. The combination of health care and the profit motive is a slippery slope.

Life continued to be peppered with problems which I knew was par for the program. The best way to handle problems according to developmental psychologist, Abraham Maslow, was to engage in self-actualization. He described self-actualizers as folks who "embrace the facts and realities of the world (including themselves) rather than denying or avoiding them. They are spontaneous in their ideas and actions. They are creative. They are interested in solving problems; this often includes the problems of others. Solving these problems is often a key focus in their lives".

The upcoming WAS sales meeting in July was a potential problem; to a large degree, it depended on the demeanor of the president and vice president. Thankfully, the meeting was without incident. Overall sales were robust; my fellow sales reps were all having banner years. After the sales meeting was the annual library conference in Anaheim with booth duty which resulted in more leads. As usual, one of the highlights of attending conferences was running across friends from previous companies I had worked for and librarians I had called on over the years. During off hours I read *Clapton*, Eric Clapton's autobiography. It was an easy, engaging read highlighting his musical growth with the resulting fame and fortune, his various romantic relationships, and his account of addiction initially to heroin followed by alcohol and eventual sobriety.

> The last ten years have been the best of my life. They have been filled with love and deep sense of satisfaction, not because of what I feel I have achieved, but more because of what has been bestowed on me. I have a loving family at my side, a past I am no longer ashamed of, and a future that promises to be full of love and laughter. (Eric Clapton; *Clapton*)

After I got back from Anaheim, Maya and I flew to Atlanta to attend a family reunion at my brother and sister-in-law's home. It was quite a gathering topped off by the 4th of July fireworks which was held across the street on a golf fairway. For the first time in months I drank wine but backed off again due to stinging sensation in urethra; I started wondering if my urinary track would ever be normal. The reunion allowed Maya to see similarities among my siblings. All of us prefer cleaning the kitchen as we prepare a meal which we inherited from Mom, a silly streak which we inherited from Dad, and sticklers for being on time we inherited from both.

The next day we drove to Durham with Layla and Brad. We mostly hung out with Layla. Brad was busy with his dissertation. Layla took us to Duke Gardens where we were blown away by the bodacious bamboo stands. Also, I got to play with my new digital camera that allowed for some nice close-ups of flowers as well as some spectacular scenery photos. The flight back home was before dawn, but we managed; our luggage didn't. Somehow it was lost between RDU and IAH. We figured it would be a few days before they found it. After a couple of weeks, it was determined to be lost permanently. The airline refunded us fairly; however, the articles of clothing, some being our favorites, were non-replaceable including my toiletry kit which would have made a Boy Scout proud.

My reading extravaganza continued due to not sleeping through the night. The next biography I read was Walter Isaacson's *Einstein, His Life and Universe*. I guess like most folks, I had a superficial idea of his life and times; he was a multi-faceted genius. During time off from his job at a patent office, he came up with the theory of relativity, one of the most significant intellectual achievements of the modern era. He went on to prove that gravity is "geometric property of spacetime". And, something which we all know emotionally, time slows down as gravity increases. He was a Zionist, a socialist, a musician, and an agnostic or "deeply religious nonbeliever". Also, he campaigned for the civil rights of African Americans considering the virulent racism in America as its "worst disease".

The most beautiful emotion we can experience is the mysterious. It is the fundamental emotion that stands at the cradle of all true art and science. He to whom this emotion is a stranger, who can no longer wonder and stand rapt in awe, is a good as dead, a snuffed-out candle. To sense that behind anything that can be experienced there is something that our minds cannot grasp, whose beauty and sublimity reaches us only indirectly: this is religiousness. In this sense, and in this sense only, I am a devoutly religious man. (Albert Einstein)

My next read was Jodie Forrest's astrology book, *Ascendants*. It provided a clear explanation of the ascendant or rising sign (the sign on the eastern horizon at birth which changes every two hours). The ascendant is your mask or persona. Often, it is the sign others guess you are if they are familiar with astrology; it colors your appearance and demeanor. Add the Sun and Moon, and you get 1728 possible combinations and a pretty good picture of the personality. Frequently, this triad captures contradictions that most of us entertain. For instance, Maya's intense Scorpio ascendant mixes well with her goal-oriented Capricorn Sun. However, the two signs are substantially different from her spontaneous, verbal Gemini Moon. My variance is empathetic Pisces Moon in contrast to expressive Leo ascendant and enthusiastic Sag Sun.

An astrological birth chart is an archetypal x-ray of one's life lessons along with a course of instruction, primarily via the transits and progressions. The coincident family, gender, culture, and history are important factors as well, *not* to be discounted. Think about it; you are a woman with first house Mars-Uranus energy bursting with the need for expression but born in a repressive, fundamentalist Wahhabi family in Saudi Arabia. I see frustration and a possible fatwa or two. Astrology encourages self-acceptance, especially aspects of the personality that have been discounted or disparaged by family or society. It's a spiritual aid, not necessary but beneficial and a whole lot of fun when sharing anecdotes with other astrology aficionados.

On Facebook and eventually via phone, I reconnected with an old friend from my senior year in prep school; he was a gifted visual artist living in Miami. Our conversations consisted of catching up on individual biographies. Eventually, we ended up talking about astrology which he was well versed in. We discussed the various polarities between signs such as Aries and Libra or Taurus and Scorpio and the inherent contradictions all of us exhibit. We went back and forth about determinism and free will. My take was that we are more determined than we care to admit; free will is invariably conditioned or limited by family, gender, culture, meme, and history. Our conversations, fueled by copious alcohol consumption, eventually lost the required combustion to continue.

Carl Hiaasen's *Downhill Lie* was a smooth read with numerous laugh-out-loud moments about how he improved his golf game. As I mentioned, my goal in golf was to accept my mediocrity without becoming a volatile depressive. Will and I favored the old UT course because the fairways were forgiving and fun to play. For me, that meant the usual handful of blowup holes and the propensity, given my Leo ascendant, to go theatrical at any given moment. Will, with his Virgo ascendant, wasn't prone to outbursts. Towards the end of one round, he put two drives out of bounds in a row which was unusual. His only comment was a very controlled, "I haven't been this frustrated playing golf in a long time". That's it?!

Play to your strengths and try not to get too wrapped up in the outcome. (Willie Nelson)

Unlike my golf handicap, my PSA number continued to decrease which was good news. However, the urinary discomfort still haunted me and, according to my urologist, could do so indefinitely. I asked him about my ebbing eroticism and erection. He assured me that wasn't unusual either. He gave me a prescription for erectile dysfunction which I was familiar with from recreational use in the past. It helped but had some unpleasant side effects. The popular Zen-like adage "it is what it is" was applicable; bitching didn't help.

In preparation for marriage, I started doing research on prenuptial agreements. AARP and my insurance company recommended that someone with my financial circumstances should have a prenuptial agreement; especially with Maya's credit history. Maya wasn't buying it until I told her it was a deal breaker. An example, in my opinion, of how romantic relationships or marriages are a mix of unconditional love and conditional realism (i.e., there may be good reasons in the future for separation or divorce). Don't get me wrong, romantic love is sweet but not necessarily practical; I speak from experience. Commitment isn't self-denial. I've been told that's my Venus in Capricorn opposed Uranus talking.

Gardening was a reliable source of felicity. For reasons beyond my understanding a bloom or a bud, a flower or a frond was all it took to delight in the play of Sun and shadow. On the north side of the house, against a brick wall, was some variegated bamboo (yes, I'm bananas about bamboo). I figured some variegated ginger in front of it would look spectacular. I also added a cedar deck to the back patio which opened the backyard to more hanging out. Even though it was hot in Austin, it was breezier and drier than Florida which meant a lack of mosquitoes who have an uncanny knack for finding me. However, it was not so dry as to prohibit the growth of Spanish moss which draped the live oak in the backyard. In fact, Spanish moss' westward range is the Texas Hill Country (the southern extension is Central America and the northern reach is the south-east Virginia coast). It favors large trees such as the live oak or bald cypress.

> To see a world in a grain of sand
> And heaven in a wild flower
> Hold infinity in the palm of your hand
> And eternity in an hour.
> (William Blake, *Auguries of Innocence*)

The difference between patriotism and nationalism was on display throughout the political campaign. Patriotism is pride in one's country and the willingness to consider deficiencies as well as strengths. Patriots actively defend their country but avoid unnecessary aggression. Nationalism, on the other hand, is based on rivalry and feelings of superiority or inferiority; behaving contemptuously toward other nations. Nationalists are prone to aggressive behavior; favoring war over diplomacy. Unfortunately, certain political and religious figures were fomenting nationalism in "the name of God". Religion should have nothing to do with nationalism and be very careful with patriotism.

Johnny and Phoebe's wedding ceremony and reception were held at a boutique hotel in downtown Chicago on 8/8/8; it was a grand gala. Their artistic bent was on display from the table arrangements to the music. Everyone was given a CD with a beautiful collection of songs including one of my favorites, Van Morrison's *I'm with You,* along with an unfamiliar tune from Donovan, *St. Valentine's Song.* Earlier in the day, before the wedding ceremony, Maya and I took a boat tour of Chicago architecture which was impressive. I learned about the difference between modernism and post-modernism architecture. Then we ate at La Frontera Mexican restaurant. The owner/chef is Rick Bayless, TV personality. Overall, we rated the chips, salsa, guacamole, and main course an A; however, the flan was a B; not as good as Manuel's in Austin. Maya and I came away with some good ideas on how to proceed with our wedding which wouldn't be as elaborate or expensive but still aesthetically pleasing.

During one of our phone conversations, Layla mentioned *Eat, Pray, Love* by Elizabeth Gilbert and that part of the plot took place in the ashram in India where I lived for three weeks. It was a best seller, so I figured it would be entertaining and professionally crafted. It started off with her divorce and the subsequent journey of psychological healing and spiritual enlightenment. Italy was her first destination; her description of eating pizza in Naples had my mouth watering. Then I got to the second section of the book which took place in the ashram in India. Her toeing the company line about various shoulds and shouldn'ts was disappointing. I stopped reading the book.

In early September, I realized it had been an unusual number of days since Layla and I had communicated. I suspected something was amiss. The basis of my suspicion was a conversation we had the previous month in which she mentioned an ongoing disagreement with Brad about having children. Brad wanted nothing to do with parenthood. I figured there were other motivating factors. Possibly because he was young and starting his career, he didn't want the added responsibility of children.

A few days later Layla tearfully told me they were separating. That was followed by news of Brad's infidelity. Layla was emotionally devastated. I felt for her knowing how gut-wrenching divorce can be. I looked at her planetary transits. No surprise; they reflected the changes: transiting Uranus (sudden changes) and transiting Saturn (hard decisions) squaring Venus (relationships)! Here's a taste from Steven Forrest's *Skylog*: "When Venusian energies unite with Uranian ones, the unexpected (Uranus) makes itself felt in the intimate sphere (Venus). Improbable encounters occur. Warp-speed evolutions unfold in love, friendship, and working relationships. Behind the fireworks, what is happening is that you are rapidly disentangling your real essence from your polite, conventional, socially-programmed "personality." When that happens, inevitably all interpersonal contracts come up for review". Ya gotta admit; that's spot on!

As the year progressed, my sales numbers improved. I was going to surpass quota which would result in a hefty commission. I had found a real nice groove; I was soft selling a product which appealed to public librarians because it benefited their young patrons. Also, I found a way of handling my discontent with management; I approached it on a quarter-year basis. If I didn't like what was going on after a particular quarter, I'd start shopping for another job. Once again, these changes corresponded astrologically; transiting Jupiter (expansion) trine my Midheaven/Jupiter conjunction (career).

By the end of September, the financial meltdown and madness were beyond anything anticipated by most financial experts. My faith in our economic system had been replaced by disgust and dismay. I thought the guys on the corporate side, namely Wall Street, and on the government side, namely Treasury, were smart. It turns out they were greedy and stupid, respectively. Hopefully, some of the significant Wall Street players would be spending time in jail for their Ponzi like schemes. However, I had no choice but to stick with my stock portfolio until I recouped some of my losses; then get the hell out if practical.

> Every day brings another financial horror show, as if Stephen King were channeling Alan Greenspan to produce scary stories full of negative numbers. *(Time* Magazine; By Andy Serwer and Allan Sloan)

As October rolled around, Maya and I started getting cold feet about having a formal wedding ceremony. We considered skipping the rigamarole and getting married in Reno. Eventually, we overcame our hesitancy figuring it would be a good excuse for folks to get together. Both of us invited family and friends; one of my invitees included Terry, ex-lover from Birmingham, and her husband, Leo, which was cool with Maya. Much to her credit, Maya wasn't the jealous type.

Early one morning, around 4:00 AM, I woke up to urinate but couldn't manage even a drop. I called my urologist's office and set an appointment for as soon as the office opened. I knew I was in store for some severe pain but needed to pee something fierce. Once again, my urologist stuck a tube up my penis to break through the scar tissue that had constricted my urethra. I fainted from the pain. To say the least, I wasn't pleased with his lack of pain management. Later, when comparing notes with others who had gone through a similar procedure, I discovered his lack of pain management was the exception. I kept my ear open for a new urologist.

Back to the procedure...after the roto-rooter procedure, the urologist inserted a catheter along with a plastic bag strapped to my thigh for urine collection. As instructed, after four days I returned to urologist's office to have the catheter removed. That was uneventful enough. However, I left with another catheter in hand! Yep, for the near future, I had to administer my own catheter twice a day to assure I was voiding my bladder. Mind you, I liked playing with my dick as much as the next guy, but this was a bit much. The previous year my brother had told me about a copilot he flew with that had to do likewise. I remember thinking at the time that I rather die than do such; curious how my opinion on that changed.

As the election approached, I had to step back to avoid the barrage of political ads and treat politics like I treated most sports; I watched the highlights. In my opinion, Obama was the superior candidate due to his political platform, educational background, temperament, and sense of humor. The tone of the election was going down-hill fast. I read a news article about some preacher at a McCain rally praying for Obama's defeat. That struck me as absurd; that is, praying to a capricious deity who might intervene on behalf of his political candidate. Unfortunately, this was becoming a somewhat common occurrence at Republican rallies. The GOP platform was a convoluted, contradictory mix of capitalism, libertarianism, nationalism, provincialism, and Christian fundamentalism. They were against social security, public education, public health insurance, environmental protection, birth control, and gun control.

Before a product demonstration at the Huntsville, AL, public library system, I had time to peruse their library book sale (libraries raise funds by selling donated books from folks like you and me). One book stood out, *How We Die*, by Sherwin Nuland. He intended to demythologize the process of dying by pulling the rug out underneath the "death with dignity" fantasy. Death is "all too frequently a series of destructive events that involve by the very nature the disintegration of the dying person's humanity. I have not often seen much dignity in the process by which we die". My recent prostate cancer episode brought dying closer to home, so to speak. Given a terminal illness, I should have the right to end my own life via voluntary euthanasia and certainly by refusing life-prolonging treatment.

The following week Johnny sent me the URL to a NY Times article by Dana Jennings titled, *The Good Cancer?* Dana hit the nail on the head about prostate cancer being dismissed as the "good cancer". His prostate cancer was aggressive and had spread beyond the prostate, unlike mine. The "twin shadows" of incontinence and/or impotence loomed. Dana captures the essence of having prostate cancer concisely in one sentence: "Prostate cancer isn't just about surgery, treatment and survival — it's also about relationships, sex, self-esteem, embarrassment, hope and fear."

Meditations on maturation and mortality gained momentum; mind you, nothing morbid, just musings. No doubt, maturity had its dividend, a delectable detachment from delusions and dreams deemed no longer doable. A couple of weeks before, *USA Today* had an article about the various celebrities turning fifty. I liked what Jamie Lee Curtis had to say about getting older: "means paring yourself down to an essential version of yourself". I, too, saw room for paring down; namely, my wine consumption which had undergone significant expansion minus the urinary irritation.

Obama won! McCain's concession speech was commendable for its grace; the lack of diversity in the crowd spoke volumes. The USA is diverse; it's time to embrace it. Obama's victory speech was understatedly eloquent yet inspiring. In many ways, Obama symbolized the changes we needed in this country. This was our chance to change certain aspects of the government operating system. I felt optimistic about our political landscape for the first time since the early Clinton years; a luminosity that hopefully would help disperse the shadows of racism, regression, repression, and religious fundamentalism.

After eight years of misgovernance, it has lost some of its global swagger ... but also some of its arrogance. It may no longer be as dominant, economically or diplomatically, as it once was. But it is younger, more optimistic, less cynical. It is a country that retains its ability to startle the world - and in a good way, with our freedom. It is a place, finally, where the content of our President's character is more important than the color of his skin. (Joe Klein; *Time*)

Maya and I celebrated my 56th birthday by getting our marriage license. Then we ate at Houston's which had a grilled chicken salad we favored. The apple cobbler with a scoop of vanilla ice cream and one candle served as my birthday cake. Delicious! Then we got the necessary signatures to make our prenup official. In the process of filling out the required financial information, both of us realized that we could have a comfortable retirement given our pensions and Social Security. For me, retirement was an increasingly attractive notion. If I could recoup the losses in my IRA that I sustained, maybe I could retire early. Of course, as Benjamin Franklin cautioned, "Gain may be temporary and uncertain, but ever while you live, expense is constant and certain".

My last round of golf for the year with Will and his son was the typical roller coaster ride. I had some superb shots and some frustrating flubs. It was my first round with my new Taylor Made driver (same model as Will's). There was no magical transformation of my game. It was just a better driver for me. However, I'd be remiss not to mention the #3 hybrid. I discovered its groove during the round having only used it sporadically before. It quickly became my indispensable club. After finishing the round, we ate at Macaroni Grill. Their bread and spiced olive oil were so good that by the time the main course arrived, I was stuffed or, if you will, breaded. That didn't stop me from eating every bit of the lasagna.

On December 13th, 2008, Maya and I were officially married. The wedding ceremony was a celebration, a public expression of thankfulness for our relationship. The setting at Chapel Dulcinea in the Texas Hill Country was aesthetically pleasing and graced by partly cloudy conditions with a breezy nip in the air. The minister, a Sharon Stone look-alike and flight attendant friend of Maya's, officiated with tenderness and humor. The reception at home was comfortable with a variety of delicious finger foods with a French theme. There was a wide variety of alcohol and weed for those who cared to partake. Thirty-five friends and family enjoyed pleasant conversation and laughter.

> You don't marry one person; you marry three: the person you think they are, the person they are, and the person they are going to become as a result of being married to you. (Richard Needham)

For Maya's birthday, we ate lunch at our favorite Lebanese restaurant followed by shopping at Macy's. After seeing what she was generally checking out, I picked out a few dresses. I'm proud to say, one of the dresses I chose ended up being her choice. She referred to it as an A-line. All I know is it looked great on her. Later in the day we prepared an excellent dinner of stir-fried shrimp and watched a touching movie, *Autumn Hearts*, with Susan Sarandon, Gabriel Byrne, Christopher Plummer, and Max von Sydow. It was a beautifully photographed, poignant story of two children who survived a Holocaust concentration camp in France during WWII. The themes of grief, growth, and grace were prominent.

Chapter 15: Expedition

> What you see and hear depends a good deal on where you are standing; it also depends on what kind of a person you are. (C.S. Lewis)

Living in Austin means becoming, if not already, a Willie Nelson fan for good reason. He's a gifted singer/songwriter who exudes warmth and wisdom. He's also co-chair of the advisory board of the National Organization for the Reform of Marijuana Laws (NORML) and the founder of the TeaPot party; "Tax it, regulate it and legalize it!" He's noted for his Farm Aid benefit concerts that raise money for farmers struggling with mortgage debt. His song *Crazy* is one of my favorites whether sung by him, Patsy Cline, Linda Ronstadt, or Norah Jones.

A week into 2009 I attended a company sales meeting in Philadelphia. Fortunately, the previous year's numbers were better than expected given the recession; however, the rodeo wasn't without fireworks. The president and vice president, two Type A bulls, would sporadically snort and butt heads in the conference room while the rest of us ducked under the table. Bereft of de-horning, the sales force had to put up as best as possible with their insufficient emotional quotient. Unfortunately, the recession was adversely affecting a couple of friends' businesses. Johnny was self-employed as a home improvement carpenter/contractor. His clientele list had dried up. Will's insurance auditing business was slowly dying due to the loss of some significant customers.

> A recession is when your neighbor loses his job; a depression is when you lose yours. (Anonymous)

On Tuesday, January 20th, Barack Obama was inaugurated; it was one of the most viewed events ever around the world. His speech emphasized the themes of renewal and unity via a phrase from the Gettysburg Address, "A New Birth of Freedom." Finally, the Bush adminstration was exiting stage right. It was responsible for the disastrous Iraq war, the worldwide economic meltdown, and The No Child Left Behind Act (a noble attempt to help disadvantaged students and support standards-based education reform). It seemed like the time was ripe to "choose our better history". I assumed the American public and their representatives in Congress would gladly agree.

In the midst of the greatest economic crisis since the Great Depression, Wall Street's idea of choosing our better history meant distributing more than $18 billion in bonuses, after getting $125 billion in taxpayer bailouts. Bailouts designed to keep another economic depression from happening because of the stupidity and greed of various financial firms. Obama criticized this behavior; calling it "the height of irresponsibility." I think the Spanish statement "sin verguenza" or without shame is a more accurate description. Wall Street glorifies wolves, psychopaths with no conscience, that don't care about the repercussions of their culture of greed. Intermittent greed obfuscates; constant greed blinds.

Unrelated but just down the street was the "Miracle on the Hudson." A USAir pilot performed a controlled ditching of his passenger plane in the Hudson River which had been disabled by geese. My brother's take on the crash reflected his pilot training and experience. He said it was rare for both engines to be disabled by birds; then added that it was very fortunate that it was a river landing and not on land, and that the crash landing was during the day, not at night. Think about it.

The national mid-winter library conference was held in lively downtown Denver. The WAS president and I arrived a day early which allowed us to dine together a couple of times. We had some engaging exchanges about topics ranging from healthcare to the importance of customer-centric thinking. As I mentioned, he was a Type A...with a twist; occasionally, he was sympathetic. With my encouragement, he rehired a sales rep that had been fired by the sales manager. However, his bullish demeanor was easily stirred. One night he lost his temper when the beeper we were given at the restaurant didn't work, and our table was given to someone else. Curiously, he seemed unconcerned by his cantankerous conduct. The waiting staff quickly accommodated us.

Life, the play of Sun and shadow, continued to astound and confound. Acknowledging one's shadows is an often-neglected part of the maturation process based on observations of myself and others. These often-denied aspects of one's personality can be personal (addiction, anger, greed, etc.) and/or cultural (racial prejudice, xenophobia, etc.); frequently both. A couple of my shadows were impatience and intemperance. As I mentioned, minus the inhibiting stinging experienced with urination, my wine consumption had climbed. I was binge drinking once or twice a week and waking up with a hangover; that is, foggy memories, headache, and shakiness. I should have invested in Bayer, owner of Alka-Seltzer.

> ...you can be at different levels of development in different lines of development. People excel in some multiple intelligences, but not in others. You might be highly developed in some lines (e.g., cognitive), medium in others (e.g., emotional), and low in yet others (e.g., moral). (Ken Wilber)

Maya and I started mulling over the idea of moving to Houston. She had grown concerned about the quality of her mother's care at her sister's home in Houston. I weighed the pros and cons. One part of me saw the value of moving to Houston because it would eliminate Maya's commute to the Houston airline base and help her mother. However, another part of me saw the value of maintaining distance from her family melodrama by living in Austin. I desired to be helpful but not entangled. When thinking about issues like these, I found it beneficial to work up a sweat gardening. After which I'd shower and settle in my favorite seat and read *Time*. I had read it on and off since I was in junior high. It had the advantage of week-at-a-time perspective along with cogent, sometimes humorous, writing.

Whenever possible Will and I played golf on weekends. We figured out how to make golf, the most emotionally taxing and capricious game ever invented by man, more enjoyable: don't keep score and skip holes if crowded. Golf provided us a chance to talk about our various triumphs and tribulations; business was a frequent topic of conversation. Will was shutting down his office. His brother and sister-in-law who lived out of state were incorporating the business. Will would work out of his home. Will and I had found an old course with reasonable fees and shorter fairways. I could have shot even lower if my putting was better. Par exemple of the clever golf adage: if ifs and buts were birdie putts, I'd be on the tour.

Along with everyone else, the internet and Facebook had opened up new horizons for communicating with family and friends. I reconnected with Donna which led to phone calls. We reminisced and chuckled about our office affair. She had finally gotten divorced and was unhappily married again. I also exchanged notes with Maria, my junior high prom date in San Juan, about long lost friends and children. After while our conversation simply petered out. I was surprised when Nora, the student that had a big-time crush on me that I wrote about earlier in this story, contacted me. Nora lived in California; a divorced mother with a six-year-old who still had a crush on me which I found fascinating and flattering.

I have been a fan of bamboo ever since I was a kid. I love "boo" because of its gorgeous, geometrical look and the way it soothingly sways in a breeze. Spotting bamboo stands is one of my favorite sports as I drive around town or on a trip. To this day, some stands make my knees quiver when I bring them to my mind's eye: Duke Gardens (Durham), Fairchild Tropical Botanic Garden (Miami), Birmingham Botanical Gardens (Alabama), and Zilker Botanical Gardens (Austin). In Asia bamboo is, and has been, revered for its many uses including utensils, furniture, boats, building, tools, art, and food. The problem in the USA is the negative attitude some folks entertain based on a couple of varieties that thrive along highways. If you are in this camp, please reconsider; numerous clumping varieties don't spread.

> Unlike cotton, bamboo doesn't require pesticides to flourish. It needs modest amounts of water to thrive — some species rise a foot a day during growing season — and its root system can help stabilize hillsides and prevent erosion. When you harvest some of a stand's canes, the underground rhizomes survive and continue to quickly produce mature culms, unlike trees that die when chopped down. The woody grass grows on every continent except at the poles. (Paula Bock; *Pacific Northwest Magazine*)

Insomnia continued to provide reading time. I read Isaacson's biography, *Benjamin Franklin; An American Life*. He was a fluid diplomat, fabled scientist, and a flawed Founding Father. His *Poor Richards Almanack* included proverbs and aphorisms that are in use today such as, "There are no gains without pains." And some that should be added minus the sexism, "Women and wine, game and deceit make the wealth small and the wants great." If I had assimilated his opinion about opinions, I'd have saved myself some grief; he considered opinions fallible, subject to change, *and* not necessarily under our command. "They are formed and governed much by circumstances that are often inexplicable as they are irresistible."

One of my earliest memories was in Amuay, Venezuela, a refinery town, watching an oil terminal fire light up the night sky a few kilometers away while being held in Dad's arms. My father was an oil company marketing executive. His expert explanations of the industry gave me some familiarity; for instance, how many liters or gallons a gas station sold and why the location was important. To this day, when I drive by gas stations, it's not unusual for me to mentally critique their location and their upkeep. My seventh-grade science fair project was on oil exploration including a flimsy balsa wood oil rig I constructed. I made a point of reading about the petroleum industry. When I saw the interview with Daniel Yergin on CNN about the global petroleum industry, I promptly bought and read his book, *The Prize--The Epic Quest for Oil, Money & Power* (and later *The Quest*). From its first industrial development before the Civil War in Pennsylvania, oil has strongly influenced national and international economics and politics and will continue to do so because of its extensive impact and importance

Oil and its close cousin, natural gas, are integral to our modern lifestyle; products include fuel, plastics, tires, cosmetics, clothes, asphalt, paint, *and* electricity generation. I'm not discounting the environmental effects; they're huge. Hopefully, with more technological innovation and alternative sources, the environmental impact will become negligible. However, the social, political, and economic effect on oil-rich countries hasn't been negligible nor necessarily a blessing. Venezuela, with the largest oil reserves in the world, has been beset by dictators (Chavez, Maduro, etc.) for decades who dispense with the rule of law and legislate according to their whims.

The economic crisis was getting worse. The housing bubble had burst; greed and financial stupidity were the culprits. A dangerous lack of confidence was threatening not only financial institutions but the very solvency of the economy. The federal government's purchase of ginormous chunks of bank debt and outright infusions of cash was controversial. Predictably, critics were crying socialism. I wondered if they'd have similar complaints waiting in a soup line. It turns out significant Wall Street players were corrupt to the core and had engaged in flagrant fraud. Once again, this airing of dirty laundry was represented by the world transits of Pluto (purging) and Saturn (responsibilities), this time squaring each other.

> They should have taken the CEO out and hung him up by his fucking testicles. Instead they sold the company and the CEO made a hundred million dollars. (Steve Eisman; Money Manager)

In anticipation of moving to Houston, I put the house on the market. It was a bit saddening considering all the home improvements I had made, especially painting and landscaping. I justified the move because of the decreased commute for Maya along with giving her mother a better environment. Houston had an undeserved bad reputation. I had lived there before; I knew what I was getting into. There were pluses as well as minuses which could be said for any major metro area. The Houston metro area was the fourth largest with close to 6 million folks; neck in neck with the Dallas/Metroplex and Atlanta metro area. We were favoring a suburb convenient to the airport, located in the county north of Houston proper with lower property taxes (Texas compensates for no income taxes with hefty property taxes).

The religious and ideological Right continued to foam at the mouth about anything and everything Obama tried or even suggested. It was the most vitriolic political climate I had witnessed. It was almost funny the way they would portray him as a communist or a fascist depending on the issue. I suspect some didn't understand the difference while others were just mean-spirited. Opponents had a slim argument for calling him a socialist with the recent bailouts of banks, thus partial government ownership. However, there was no wholesale movement on the part of the government to control industries across the board. Our economy was alive, but not well. Hopefully, the government bailouts were the necessary tonic.

With all the comings and goings, the endings and beginnings, occasionally I would pen a line or two about such. For instance: Life is a mix of pain and pleasure punctuated by disease, death, war, and economic misfortune. None of us are spared or special. Yet, sages through the ages have in one way or another told us about a way or path that makes things easier: remembering one's essential identity as ever present, ever new Aware Space.

> This does not involve the cessation of suffering, but of the sorrow, the anxiety, the bitterness of suffering. (Madame Guyon)

One of the benefits of business travel was it afforded me the occasion to check out houses and neighborhoods where I had lived (Miami, Fort Lauderdale, Gainesville, Baton Rouge, Tallahassee, Birmingham, Jacksonville, and Houston). Some looked better and some not. The first house my ex and I bought in Miami looked worse but was on the market for seven times more than we sold it for! From Palm Beach to South Beach real estate prices had risen astronomically. The house I purchased after my divorce in Jacksonville looked worse as well yet was still valued at what I sold it for. I bought it thinking the neighborhood would undergo a rebirth; not enough other buyers concurred. "Location, location, location" was a familiar mantra, but still pertinent.

Members of all three branches of the government, executive, legislative, and judicial, have been guilty of unethical behavior including paid vacations, campaign favors, and other advantages over the years. Scandals such as the Whiskey Ring of 1876 where federal agents helped distillers evade federal taxes have racked the executive branch throughout the years. Congress, the two chambers of commerce, was purchased long ago; oligarchs, large corporations, and/or special interests have dictated to both sides of the aisle since the beginning of the republic. I was surprised they hadn't sold branding rights for the Capitol building in tandem with sports stadiums. However, I believed, in spite of ample evidence to the contrary, that the Supreme Court was above political motivations and our political process.

Gore v. Bush obliterated that misconception. The Supreme Court was a mix of religious and ideological partisanship. Bias and questionable reasoning were to be expected; for instance, the expansion of corporate rights under the guise of free-speech rights.

> ...the Court is a product of a democracy and represents, with sometimes chilling precision, the best and worst of the people. We can expect nothing more, and nothing less, than the Court we deserve...The justices of the Supreme Court are selected by the president and confirmed by the Senate because they are part of the grand political design that is our Constitution. (Jeffrey Tobin; *The Nine*)

Due to a bill I received for $2000, healthcare and insurance came into focus again. It was an ambulance charge for my back and forth trip across a two-lane street amounting to 100 meters from recovery to the operating room at $1000 per trip! My prostate procedure cost upwards of $60,000 of which company issued insurance covered all but a few thousand dollars. I had no idea how much of that total was insurers and providers taking advantage like the ambulance service. I did know the medical/insurance/pharma complex was out of cost control; we needed a universal health care system...period.

The sales meeting was a mixed emotions expedition. The economic downturn had negatively impacted library budgets due to lower local tax receipts. The behavior of the president and vice president ranged from discouraging to downright deplorable. Probably even more disappointing was the acquiescence on the part of my two sales managers. They made fools of themselves trying to outdo each other in the brownnosing department. On the positive side, it was a pleasure interacting with fellow sales reps that I didn't see often. Usually, the flight home was uneventful. However, on this trip, I was asked to give up my seat so a mother and child could sit together. I did so **unhesitatingly**. I was to take the seat of a fellow who was getting bumped up to first class. Out of appreciation for what I did, he gave me his first-class seat; what goes around comes around.

> True wisdom is learning to wish that each thing should come to pass as it does. (Epictetus)

In July my home sold; I broke even after factoring in the realtor's commission. Then I turned around and purchased a home in a suburb north of Houston as planned. Probably because of the stress of moving, Maya and I squabbled more. I got angry when she asked me to be careful about my marijuana use around her mother who'd be living with us. Being told how to behave in my own home didn't go over well with me; neither did my telling her to get her own place go over well with her. And, to top it off, Maya's car needed repair work that cost more than the car was worth which meant purchasing a replacement and, because of her recent bankruptcy, cosigning the financing.

Chapter 16: Opposition

All journeys have secret destinations of which the traveler is unaware. (Martin Buber)

The move to Houston went as planned despite the rain. Due to the unusual floor plan, furnishings didn't fit as well as they did in Austin. The fun part was considering the various options for window treatments, carpet, paint and countertop colors. While setting up my home office, I experienced a powerful déjà vu; however, the scene I saw was unrecognizable (stay tuned). To alleviate the stress of moving, Maya and I introduced some lightheartedness by referring to each other as "the German" and "the Mexican". Admittedly, I had a strong preference for order and being on time was next to godliness thus I was "the German" and Lupe with her more laid-back demeanor was the "the Mexican".

Layla, Maya, and I planned on meeting for sushi dinner on the last weekend of September. However, it depended on Layla and Maya's flights arriving on time. Layla started in RDU and was routed through ORD. Maya worked a round trip to EWR. O'Hare and Newark were notorious for delays. Remarkably, their flights were on time. We ordered our sushi favorites with a new twist: brown rice. At first, we weren't impressed but eventually took to the change in taste. The extended weekend unfolded in a carefree manner enhanced by Layla's charming expressiveness and accommodating nature.

It looked like we were climbing out of the recession in large part because of the federal government intervention. Considering that, I found it confounding that many conservatives insisted that the government shouldn't regulate financial institutions. They conveniently forgot history. Banks, Wall Street, credit bureaus (Equifax, etc.), and insurance companies (AIG) had royally fucked up because of greed and stupidity. Related to regulation was government intervention, another hot topic. The local pet store going out of business was one thing; watching an entire industry die was another. Bailing out the car companies was a good move. Not letting some of the "too big to fail" banks fail was debatable and the watering down of Glass-Steagall possibly a mistake. I'd like to think smart folks were making those decisions; however, recent history suggested otherwise.

> The first truth is that the liberty of a democracy is not safe if the people tolerate the growth of private power to a point where it becomes stronger than their democratic state itself. That, in its essence, is fascism—ownership of government by an individual, by a group, or by any other controlling private power. (Franklin Delano Roosevelt)

During Maya's two-week-long trips, Nora and I started emailing each other. After a while, we combined our emails with phone calls. Initially, our conversations were friendly but, after a few more calls, became flirtatious. A few weeks later, lubricated by wine, the flirting became suggestive; eventually, climaxing in phone sex. It was stimulating and startling; I was having an extramarital affair. After a few more episodes, we agreed to back off on communication frequency and sexual content. Regardless, a foreshadowing of things to come had dawned.

When Maya moved in with me, Chuy came along for the ride; he was Chow mutt with a stubborn streak but non-demanding. Unfortunately, he was diagnosed with cancer; tumors were popping up throughout his chest and neck. He underwent an extensive operation to remove the tumors. The result wasn't promising; the vet gave him a couple months. He was in obvious pain, and within a week his condition had deteriorated substantially; he could barely stand up. Maya was out of town when I decided he had suffered enough. I took him to the vet to be euthanized. Maya handled his passing with more equanimity than I anticipated. It still brings a tear to my eye when I think about it.

It had been over a year since my last physical. Per Big Pharma propaganda, my new GP preached lowering cholesterol via statins (based on blood work done the previous week). When I mentioned my adverse reaction, he suggested other varieties of statins which I vetoed for the same reason (duh!). Grudgingly, as if I was inconveniencing him which I found annoying, he acknowledged my predicament and suggested exercise and the Mediterranean diet. On the positive side, my blood pressure was lower than it had been in years. Go figure, I thought it would be higher with all the stress in my life. Anyway, I instituted a walking routine around the neighborhood trails. The diet favored flavors from other parts of the world with Mexican (on every block in Texas), Middle Eastern, and Indian populating the plate. Houston was blessed with ethnic diversity and a wide variety of restaurants.

I was hooked on watching *Mad Men*, the TV series in the same vein as *Six Feet Under* and *Dexter*. *Mad Men* took place in New York City during the early '60s. It revolved around the lives of advertising executives, both professionally and domestically, in an era when my parents were not much older. The clothes, cars, décor, and appliances were vivid reminders. As I watched, memories of my parent's parties along with the smell of cigarettes, scotch, and bourbon came to mind along with the treatment of women as second-class citizens (I remember my sister's objections to the inequity). It also highlighted the Kennedy/Nixon election which was my political initiation. Mom voted for Kennedy and Dad for Nixon.

In October 2009, Maya and I attended the *U2* concert with another couple, friends visiting from The Valley. It was held at Reliant Stadium where the NFL team, Texans, played; it had a capacity of over 70,000. There were 40,000 plus in attendance. The stage and special effects were outstanding and, being *U2*, there was a spiritual accent including a couple verses of *Amazing Grace*. One notable takeaway was seeing everyone hold up their cell phone flashlights instead of Bic lighters when directed by Bono; a testament to how times had changed. Once the concert was over, we planned to take a taxi back to our parked car a few miles away to avoid the parking lot traffic jam. The plan didn't work as expected. We had to wait over an hour in a line to get a taxi. A TV news video crew was interviewing some of the folks waiting in line. I volunteered Maya which she handled with assurance. A friend of hers saw the video clip on TV the next day.

> When I die, please don't play *Amazing Grace*. Not even last. That'll piss me off. Because I'm not a wretched sinner. (Carlos Santana)

WAS sales metrics continued to be depressed; management became obsessed. Our weekly teleconferences were difficult to stomach. Instead of acknowledging the marketplace facts, they thought it best to beat the sales force up figuratively. I had seen this happen before at other companies when numbers were down. A part of me wanted to quit. However, I didn't want to be unemployed. Based on a couple of job interviews and from what I was hearing from friends in the industry, sales jobs were scarce. I liked selling to librarians regardless of their lamentable budgets; it was my career. I planned on sticking around, if not at WAS, then with another publisher in the library market.

My 57th birthday spurred reflections on life, namely dualism. Dualism is inescapable; it's the nature of thought. Future and past, conscious and unconscious, sad and happy...you can't have one with the other. Without sunlight, there would be no shadows. Shadows are frequently problematical; aspects of the ego or small self or little one (whatever term you prefer) that aren't acknowledged. They can manifest as addictions and afflictions. Celebrities', politicians', and religious leaders' stories of their struggles with any number of shadows are media favorites.

> The dualism of good and evil, beauty and ugliness, black and white, etc. is the inescapable condition of expressing into the world from the place that is free of those dualities. So it's not a case of being free from these things, in the sense that one abolishes them, but of being free from them in the sense that one locates them. They are no longer central. This awareness not only removes one from them – without removing oneself from them - but in the long run and when persisted in, it changes them. (Douglas Harding; 1983 Interview)

For me, astrology offers a good overview of potential problems or shadows via the dark side of planets and signs. The Moon which is known for its dark side is a good place to start. For instance, at the risk of overgeneralization, Gemini Moon's light side is fluent and/or friendly and/or funny; however, its dark side can be snarky and/or snappy and/or sneaky. And, don't forget Pluto. It may have been demoted by astronomers but astrologically is a significant indicator of shadows or wounds. On a cyclical basis, transits and progressions to natal planets can accentuate shadows. That is, shadows come and go and maybe come again depending on the cycle (Saturn's transit cycle is 29 years, Uranus's is 84 years, etc.). I have found it disconcerting to deal with shadows I thought I'd had put to rest, so to speak, only to have an encore performance. By the way, there was no applause for the repeat performance; usually, it was exasperation coupled with resistance (maybe an under my breath "fuck me!" for emphasis). Eventually, surrender would unfold somewhere down the road.

After Chuy's passing, Maya, with Will's assistance, secured Dexter's release from a dog pound in the Hill Country north of San Antonio. Dexter, named after the TV character, had been incarcerated as a serial killer of chickens. He was a sweet, gentle soul. I remember one particular interaction when I spontaneously leaned over and kissed him on his muzzle. Dexter's loving response was an example of what makes dogs so delightful. However, it was obvious when Maya was home, I was second fiddle as far as he was concerned. Rightly so, Maya loved

107

on him big time. I suspect her laid-back approach to discipline appealed to him as well. Maya didn't fault me for my more disciplined approach; she agreed that he should know "sit," "stay," "come," and most importantly, "no." When Maya was flying, I took him on walks around the neighborhood. I taught him to roam periodically with the word "free." That allowed me to walk at a normal stride with him by my side at other times.

Business trips frequently involved flying; occasionally, I worked on my laptop but preferred not to due to cramped conditions, so I read. George Carlin's autobiography, *Last Words*, was my latest pleasure read. My familiarity with George Carlin was his numerous HBO specials I enjoyed over the years. He was a New York City Catholic kid from a dysfunctional family who evolved from being the class clown, something I knew a little bit about as the class wiseass, to one of the greatest standup comedians ever. His "seven dirty words" (shit, piss, fuck, cunt, cocksucker, motherfucker, and tits) was part of a Supreme Court decision central at the time in the government's regulatory power over the broadcasting of "indecent but not obscene" material. I appreciated his deftness with words which didn't fail to entertain, his sharp social critiques which didn't spare the powerful or the popular or golf, and his unapologetic acknowledgment of the pivotal role LSD played in his life.

> Fuck the drug war. Dropping acid was a profound turning point for me, a seminal experience. I make no apologies for it. More people should do acid. It should be sold over the counter. Acid finally moved me from one place to the other; allowed change to take place. (George Carlin)

The children's literacy hardware/software product was selling well despite the challenging economic conditions. I made numerous inroads into large county library systems as well as state libraries. My relationship with various librarians was flourishing. I was invited to library functions not generally extended to sales representatives. Selling a good product was easy; I used onsite demonstrations interspersed with humor to lighten things up. Occasionally, there'd be some contrarian librarian who would raise objections, but the vast majority of librarians recognized the benefit of what I was selling for their children's programs. Typical of the selling process, the vanguards or mavens were the early adopters followed by others in six months to a year or two depending on funding.

The only fly in the ointment was, you guessed it, upper management and their unerring capacity to screw things up from personnel management to mission prioritization. It was an annoyance I was willing to put up with because of the relationships and remuneration. The January '10 sales meeting highlighted their myopia due to a fixation on penetrating the education market and the R&D being devoted to such. As I mentioned before, I was on a quarterly review basis; quitting was tempting, but I didn't cherish the idea of unemployment and securing another job. Some friends and family members were struggling with long-term unemployment; I didn't want to join them. Times were tough; trials and tribulations teemed.

Maya and I visited Layla in February to celebrate her official divorce and gradual healing. Her entertainment and culinary skills were accented with a wine tasting at a local vineyard followed by a homemade sushi dinner. It was rainy the last day of our visit, so we went to the movie, *Up in the Air*, with George Clooney and Vera Farmiga (my ex-girlfriend, Gabriella, look alike). It was an interesting take on corporate downsizing, an entertaining look at frequent flier traveling, and a nuanced examination of romantic mixed signals. I differed with Clooney's character on not checking in baggage. I built in enough time for such because I disliked lugging around luggage along with my briefcase on wheels not to mention finding overhead storage in steerage.

My next pleasure read was Ken Wilber's book, *Integral Spirituality*. Basically, he recommended combining the insights derived from paths of spiritual enlightenment with developmental psychology. He suggested that religions could facilitate human development and evolution by acknowledging the magic, mythic, rational, and pluralistic worldviews thus creating "a global society that honors and includes all the stations of life along the way". Based on what I was reading in the news, I suspected most religions would be resistant to such a suggestion because its sensible and inclusive thus counter to their belief systems.

Speaking of religion, ever since my first course on Buddhism in college, I've appreciated the simplicity of its teaching about life and suffering. Suffering is caused by craving for and clinging to things (possessions, circumstances, etc.) which are inherently insufficient. One can minimize suffering by practicing right view, right intention, right action, right speech, right livelihood, etc. That was pretty logical stuff. However, the Buddhist emphasis on emptiness eluded me; as the Dalai Lama said, "the understanding of emptiness opens the door to true freedom." I didn't "get it" until I "got it" via Douglas Harding's having no head or no face experiments which point out the emptiness; a subtle, silent No-thingness that is overlooked out of habit but always present.

Healthcare on the micro level became an issue; that is, bothersome low-grade headaches and inner ear funkiness. My GP didn't know what to make of it. He suggested I consult with an allergist who conducted a series of allergy skin tests that provided no answers. On a macro level, health care reform or ACA was attracting attention, especially Big Pharma's. Their lobbying effort resulted in a significant increase in earnings per share for their stockholders but resulted in the scaling back of health care provisions in the ACA legislation for you and me, the shareholders.

The Texas library conference was in San Antonio which was one of my favorite cities for such due to the proximity of the River Walk, restaurants, and hotels to the conference center. The bonus was spending some time with Will who was still unemployed but picking up odd jobs. He was struggling with raising his teenage son, not an unusual dynamic, but complicated by his ex who was a few cards short of a deck. During slack moments at the conference booth, I finished reading *Drive: The Surprising Truth About What Motivates Us* by Daniel Pink; an enlightening read that confirmed much of what I have intuitively known and acted on throughout my professional life. The profit motive shouldn't be the prime directive; it is a natural and necessary result of a good product and/or service.

> The best use of money as a motivator is to pay people enough to take the issue of money off the table: Pay people enough so that they're not thinking about money and they're thinking about the work. Once you do that, it turns out there are three factors that the science shows lead to better performance, not to mention personal satisfaction: autonomy, mastery, and purpose. (Daniel Pink; *Drive*)

The WAS sales meeting in June was made tolerable because I had landed the largest library sale in company history. It was the culmination of over two years' worth of persistent, soft sell effort on my part. Sadly, a couple of education sales reps weren't at the meeting. They were fired because of the predictable lack of sales in the education market. Management knew the education sales numbers were unreachable but continued to pretend otherwise; it was the elephant in the room they kept bumping into but tried not to acknowledge. Simply put, they believed their own elephant shit and expected the sales force to believe likewise. My thinking was still on a quarterly basis; if things weren't going well at the end of the quarter, I'd start shopping for another library sales job.

The political Right's fuss about Obama's "shakedown" of BP perplexed me. Anything having to do with government regulation and intervention was a reason to fear the end of civilization as we know it. Even though it was commonly accepted that BP had engaged in reckless behavior that led to the drilling rig explosion and well blowout, the Right roiled against government oversight. Their dislike of Obama led to gross, absurd characterizations verging on, regrettably, hate. Also, their ideological and/or moral issues with abortion (no abortion regardless of circumstances) and gun rights (permission to carry everywhere) defied rationality.

> As far as possible, without surrender, be on good terms with all persons. Speak your truth quietly and clearly; and listen to others, even to the dull and the ignorant, they too have their story. Avoid loud and aggressive persons; they are vexations to the spirit. (Max Ehrmann; *Desiderata*)

Maya and I thoroughly enjoyed the movie *Invictus* with Matt Damon and Morgan Freeman. The theme of forgiveness, despite the brutality of apartheid (think Jim Crow era on steroids), was inspiring. Using a rugby tournament as a symbolic means of healing highlighted how positive political change can happen. South Africa is slowly recovering from apartheid. Another part of the world in dire need of healing was the Middle East. Ever since I can remember there has been war and bloodshed. Hate, especially between Israel and Palestine, Iran and Saudi Arabia, and the Shia and Sunni, had become state-sponsored and contagious. We need a Mandela for the Middle East.

The 2010 4th of July vacation was replete with fireworks in the sky and on the marital front. Maya and I had a nasty argument in the kitchen where our opinions on how to do things sometimes clashed. The explosiveness of these disagreements was fueled by my wine consumption. I knew I had a drinking problem, so I'd not drink for week or two. Then I'd fool myself with imaginations of moderation and end up bingeing again. Cassio in *Othello* captured my predicament, "O God, that men should put an enemy in their mouths to steal away their brains! That we should, with joy, pleasance, revel, and applause, transform ourselves into beasts!"

Chapter 17: Indigestion

All human life is some part failure and some part achievement. (Dalai Lama)

My marriage wasn't the only one in trouble. Bert and Ellie's had been on life support for some time. He was wondering whether Saturn was at play. No surprise, transiting Saturn was opposed both their Moons which was suggestive of problems. Johnny's situation was more humorous. When my mobile phone rang and identified him, I answered. The first thing I heard was "I hate women" which he said with a smirk in his voice. He was at a family gathering in Hawai'i for his mother's funeral and subsequent estate dealings. His sisters and wife were hounding him for his occasional ornery behavior and regular alcohol consumption, not an unusual combination. He mentioned using his inheritance to move to the south of France and didn't include his wife, Phoebe, in the narrative.

WAS sales meetings were potentially contentious; it depended on upper management's mood. The one held in October at HQ was a pleasant surprise. However, for the sales training segment, they hired an overbearing asshole who if questioned would become defensive. That didn't dissuade me from questioning him numerous times, especially about his convoluted sales funnel model. We already had an electronic version via our CRM that was better than his. To top it off, he gave us homework which would require interacting with him on a weekly basis. I deemed the assignments a waste of time and refused (I didn't have to play along because of my sales numbers). Some of my colleagues were cooperating because they felt insecure about their jobs not because they thought it was a valuable exercise. Apart from the group, I explained this to our sales manager. He couldn't have cared less. I started to understand why most folks had an unfavorable opinion of him.

My business trip in early November to Dallas/Metroplex was a success. Several of the Metroplex area libraries had become customers, or better yet, repeat customers. This was accomplished by creating a relationship with the director and/or assistant director and/or children's services librarian. What pleased me most was the occasional business relationship that morphed into genuine friendship. When we met, sometimes over dinner or lunch, in addition to business issues, we shared anecdotes about ourselves. Mutual affection and respect was the result. At times, I would breathe deeply and barely bow my head to the One while saying silently, or under my breath, "Thank you."

Gratitude is the healthiest of all human emotions. The more you express gratitude for what you have, the more likely you will have even more to express gratitude for. (Zig Ziglar)

Maya and I spent Thanksgiving '10 with Layla at her recently purchased fixer-upper bungalow located in a classic little town outside of Durham. Determining the appropriate housewarming gift was part of the evolution. After sweeping up dust mixed with dog and cat hair, a vacuum cleaner became the obvious choice. Of course, a trip to the Durham area wasn't complete without a pilgrimage to Duke Gardens and its bamboo stands. Then we drove to Atlanta for Thanksgiving dinner; a long seven-hour trip due to traffic. We gathered at my brother and sister-in-law's home for the celebration. My two sisters, along with significant others, were present along with various nieces and nephews, all young adults. The turkey and fixings were a feast fit for royalty a la Tudors (Maya and I had just finished watching the TV series). The creamed cauliflower and pumpkin pie took top honors in my opinion. The trip left me with a hangover of sorts. I missed being near my daughter and family.

For my birthday, I purchased an e-reader and, based on my brother's recommendation, downloaded Robert Harris' *Pompeii,* historical fiction about life before and during the eruption of Mount Vesuvius. The main character, an aqueduct engineer or aquarius, was sent to the area to oversee the aqueduct, an engineering accomplishment only matched in recent times. He quickly discovered strange phenomena that proved to be precursors to the volcanic eruption. I found it an engaging read that created a glimpse of life around 79 CE. After finishing *Pompeii*, I downloaded Robert Harris' *Imperium*; part of a historical fiction series about Cicero, the great politician/philosopher. The deceitful and divisive world of Roman politics was not that different from today's arena except that they were more upfront about using violence and murder. Cicero, a consummate politician, had spiritual insight most politicians today lack.

> Be sure that it is not you that is mortal, but only your body. For that man whom your outward form reveals is not yourself; the spirit is the true self, not that physical figure which and be pointed out by your finger. (Cicero; 106-43 BCE)

Over the years I'd often heard about the rise and fall of the Roman Republic and/or Empire and the parallels with today. I realized anybody with an angle had room to opine because the Roman period lasted more than 800 years (roughly 400 BCE to 400 CE). Regardless, the historical/cultural influences are alive and well today. Much of the English in the above paragraph is Latin in origin. The romance languages (Spanish, French, Portuguese, Italian, and Romanian) are spoken by close to two billion folks around the world as either first or second language. Religion, politics, philosophy, science, architecture, astronomy, and astrology reflect strong Roman influence.

Maya and I became enthralled with *Boardwalk Empire* on HBO. It was about life in Atlantic City during the 1920s and 30s when the lead character, Nucky Thompson, the boss, was working his way around Prohibition. Atlantic City was a convention center with plenty of optional vice for the consenting adult customer. The absurdity of various prohibitions was on full display (which is the case in many locales today). Making something people enjoy, an indulgence, against the law doesn't stop people from wanting it. Prosecuting folks for participating in the prohibited pleasure as either supplier or user is counterproductive and expensive (especially if incarceration is included).

> We have whiskey, wine, women, song and slot machines. I won't deny it and I won't apologize for it. If the majority of the people didn't want them they wouldn't be profitable and they wouldn't exist. The fact that they do exist proves to me that the people want them. (Enoch Lewis "Nucky" Johnson)

Towards the end of December, Johnny made it into town after a long drive from Chicago with a pit stop in New Orleans to check out some remodel jobs. I hired him to help with some redesign. The idea was repainting with some sort of brown tone along with nickel metal as a visual anchor on new ceiling fans, door hardware, and plug/light switch plates. Much to my chagrin, the light green paint job I broke my back over didn't work; nor did Johnny's zany humor and, at times, weird behavior. He talked a lot, repeated himself frequently, and engaged in erratic, emotional displays; much of this was due to his daily alcohol consumption. My hands were full trying to get the job done all the while keeping Maya from blowing her top.

However, my attempts to keep a degree of detente fell apart when Johnny exited the bathroom naked in front of Maya's mother. Maya's dislike of Johnny became overt. Within a day or two, I pushed Johnny out the door to my relief as well. I, in turn, out of complete frustration with the whole situation, became angry with Maya over her overreaction. My annoyance prompted me to call a couple of attorneys to inquire about divorce with a prenuptial agreement in a community property state like Texas. I needed to understand the legal and financial ramifications. An unexpected storm had precipitated divorce deliberations and another dark night of the soul.

My relationship with Maya was laced with genuine affection but increasingly beset by growing incompatibility; we argued often. Maya liked the setup in Houston; she was back with her friends, family, and mother (who lived with us). And, her commute to work was much improved. I, on the other hand, was increasingly dissatisfied with my job and had no nearby friends and family. During our frequent absences from each other due to travel, my social outlet was chatting on the phone with various friends and family (Nora wasn't part of the mix due to her new romantic relationship). On my business trips to old hometowns, I'd occasionally visit friends which included a wine-fueled fling with an ex-flame that was a fiasco.

After Christmas dinner, Maya and I had a heated argument about getting another cat. I wasn't in favor of such. With the other guests gone besides her brother, she brought it up knowing her brother would back her up. She had engaged in this political ploy before, and I was tired of her manipulations; I blew up. It wasn't surprising that Uranus was part of the brew being squared by transiting Saturn. Steven Forrest's *Sky Log* interpretation was accurate: "Expect explosive developments and prepare for them in two ways. The first: through dispassionate analysis you can anticipate eventualities and have some tactics for damage-control in place. The second: through imaginative forethought you can recognize some exciting emerging possibilities and be ready to seize them."

The new year began with resigning from my job because of "family issues." Resigning over management issues wasn't the best option from a professional standpoint. And, "family issues" wasn't inaccurate. However, the idea of attending the upcoming sales meeting and being harangued by upper management was less than attractive. I ran some sales numbers for the next year. The company was committed to penetrating the education market; it didn't look promising. The product wasn't ready (I doubted it ever would). I figured it would be best to leave on a high note with an outstanding sales year as number one.

With time on my hands, due to my resignation, I examined my drinking behavior of the last twenty years; I was concerned about the frequency of my binge drinking and my unsuccessful attempts at moderation. Like my smoking addiction years before, I knew cold turkey, the abrupt and complete discontinuance, would work. In a sense, it was easier than moderation; trying to smoke a couple of cigarettes a day never worked for me. Over the years I had abstained upwards of six months and had felt the rewards of such. But I would fall off the wagon, so to speak, and go back to drinking as much as I did before. I was tired of waking up hungover with spotty memories and sharp-toothed shame.

Another deranged mass shooter killed six and wounded numerous others, including Gabby Gifford, Arizona congresswoman. It was the latest example of the ineptitude of our gun control system. The tragic shooting left me disheartened; nothing was being done to avoid a repeat. The NRA/GOP was blocking meaningful legislation and wacko pundits a la Glenn Beck spewed nonsense ("guns don't kill people, people do"). Most gun owners, like me, were responsible and far from crazy. We needed a strict licensing system and a method of identifying folks who shouldn't have access to guns. Another component was eliminating rapid fire guns and assault weapons. Remember, the Second Amendment was written when the guns weren't as sophisticated. Please, keep your muzzleloader if you must.

> I have no f—ing idea about the motives from which the murderous shooter was working. You don't know what a troubled mind will get caught on. (Jon Stewart)

Towards the end of January '11, I took a trip using points for flight, hotel, and rental car. My first stop was Atlanta where I visited my brother and sister-in-law for a couple of nights. We partied hardy one-night dancing up a storm while my brother played DJ. Par for the course, we enjoyed some delicious meals; the shrimp creole was particularly tasty. I also got to hang out with my sister and boyfriend for an evening accented by some succulent steaks. Then I drove to Durham to visit Layla, braving I-85 with its rainy conditions and traffic. She was in a much better place emotionally; not so harried about the home improvement projects (which will never end). While she was at work, I read, wrote, and dillydallied. I also got to take part in selecting a cat, Peppermint, at the local shelter. Spending time with Layla was very special, hard to describe. One of those everything-is-okay-with-the-universe experiences except when she was driving erratically!

After a couple of months of unemployment, I started looking for opportunities in the library market. I contacted friends and acquaintances in the industry as well as recruiters; some folks treated me with disbelief that I had willingly quit my job given the economic climate. Regardless, I had an impressive resume with substantial experience in both public and academic libraries. And, in short order, I had phone interviews for a couple opportunities; unfortunately, they required relocation. I wasn't willing to cross that line.

Arab Spring was in full bloom. Per Wikipedia: "...a revolutionary wave of both violent and non-violent demonstrations, protests, riots, coups, foreign interventions, and civil wars in North Africa and the Middle East." It amazed me how the democratic impulse continued to manifest, even though imperfectly and, in this case, unsuccessfully for the most part. Some of the pictures of the revolution in Egypt were tear jerkers; one that stood out was a father with his daughter in his arms among thousands celebrating the overthrow of the dictator in Cairo's Tahrir Square. Later, I ran across an amusing footnote about pickpockets police had arrested who had taken advantage of the demonstrators. A classic case of "when a pickpocket sees a saint, he sees only his pockets."

> The world is as you see it. (Yoga Vasistha)

Visiting with Will wasn't as easy as was when I lived in Austin. It was a three-hour drive from Houston depending on traffic. Will's economic situation had improved since taking early Social Security; his son's poor academic performance hadn't. He was flunking out of 9th grade due to lack of consistent effort (from A's to F's). Nick was at his wits' end. As I've mentioned before, the commotion was worsened by his ex; her current fixation had to do with extraterrestrial aliens with nefarious plans for humankind. He was getting tired of the struggle and thinking it might be better to "get the hell out of Dodge" by moving from San Antonio.

Taking a break from the brouhaha, Will drove over from San Antonio. We spent eight hours driving along the coastline to the southeast of the Houston metro area checking out the birding opportunities. Our initial objective was High Island which among birders has a great reputation. We checked it out for a while; there were duckbills, irises, and cormorants. Then we drove down to the beach and checked out the gulls and sandpipers. We ended up taking the ferry over to Galveston which we both agreed was the highlight of the trip. We grabbed a bite to eat and drove home on I-45 engaged in pleasant conversation. The following day we played on the same golf course we played before—quality course for the price. There were some decent shots and some real sinkers (i.e., water hazards).

It had been a few months since my first inquiry into the legal ramifications of divorce; my relationship with Maya had deteriorated further, supplemented by emotional distance and dishonesty. We hadn't had sex in months. When Maya expressed interest, I'd claim post-radiation issues; actually, I had lost my appetite. And, to further complicate matters, I wasn't finding any career opportunities based in Houston. I decided to interview for jobs that might require relocation. Something had to give. In other words, transiting Uranus, the planet of impatience with bullshit and the urge to change, was trine my natal Sun (basic self-expression) and sextile my natal Mars (assertion). Oh, due to retrograde motion, Uranus transits can last for months.

115

Some folks think astrology is bunk. If they had an open mind, they'd see an elegant cosmic algebra with various equations populated with variables. Fill in the variables and, presto, the meaning, based on archetypes (universal patterns of thought and behavior) coalesces for you, the final authority. In addition to astrology's personality indicator prowess, astrology provides evolutionary insights and predictive hints that are helpful ("not concretely predictive, but archetypally predictive"). Ascertaining the meaning of planets, signs, aspects, and houses have become standardized and readily available online. Buyer beware; the quality varies substantially. Don't be overwhelmed. Keep it simple. Give astrology some time and effort, and an amazing thing happens…intuition.

During the last couple of weeks of April, I interviewed for two jobs. In both cases, I put my best foot forward. I anticipated offers from both. Within a week, I heard back from the one I was favoring most. The first interviewer, an old business acquaintance, never got back with me which I considered unprofessional and inconsiderate. I accepted the job offer. After almost five months of unemployment, I needed a job. My acceptance meant relocation; I had to live in the territory: Florida, Georgia, South Carolina or North Carolina. They would cover moving expenses. I favored Durham, North Carolina, because I'd be near Layla and a good airport.

Maya wasn't pleased with this development, but not resistant or reactive. With minimal deliberation, we agreed to get divorced. Family and job were foremost for both of us. She was staying in Houston for such, and I was moving for such. Maya promptly started investigating places to live, and I signed a contract with a realtor to sell the home. It was a bittersweet time; moments of sadness, relief, excitement, uncertainty, and thankfulness for how things were evolving.

> Don't be too timid and squeamish about your actions. All life is an experiment.
> (Ralph Waldo Emerson)

By the end of May '11, the divorce paperwork was finalized. The divorce would be official by the end of July. It was uncomplicated because neither one of us was contesting. I agreed to pay off her car loan which would immediately improve her credit score. Maya found an apartment in her brother's complex which would be available in a couple of months. Movers packed my stuff in short order. I drove to Durham, with a pit stop in Atlanta for sales training with my new employer. The trip provided me the opportunity to notice the scenery and commentary pass through Me; the subtle Awareness that is frequently overlooked.

My sales training in Atlanta had a few hiccups. I made calls with a fellow sales representative on three libraries from two medium sized state academic libraries to a small technical college library. In between the calls, the rep spent a substantial amount of time bitching about our supervisor. Then the supervisor called in sick for the week which left me without proper training on various policies and procedures. It was a disappointing introduction to the company (an impromptu meeting with the CEO settled my nerves somewhat). By Friday afternoon I was in my apartment in Durham; the furniture would be delivered the following week. That evening I met Layla and her boyfriend at their favorite sushi restaurant around the corner.

After a couple of months and numerous sales calls in my territory, I was getting a grip on what sold best from an extensive product line. One hurdle was securing necessary information from the inside sales group. A couple of them proved difficult to work with; they considered me either a nuisance or a threat. Then the fellow representative I worked with during my training resigned because of the convoluted office dynamics. The supervisor, who was new to the job and had no sales experience, didn't seem to have an adequate understanding of the dysfunction. An uneasy feeling about the future of my job was dawning.

My divorce was official at the end of July; it took less than five minutes since it was the first case on the docket. Then I stopped by the house to check on things. Dexter, the dog, was confused at first but warmed up; I did miss his company. Maya's mother and I exchanged a heartfelt hug. The house looked great as did the garden. The planters had filled out nicely, especially the bamboo and bottlebrush. Next, I stopped by the realtor's office to inquire about the progress of selling the home. I wanted to sell as soon as possible to get rid of the mortgage expense which combined with rent in Durham was a chunk of change.

Living near Layla allowed me to help her with home improvement projects from painting kitchen cabinets to straightening up the yard while being a sounding board for her tribulations. We looked at her transits; Uranus, the planet of insight, originality, rebelliousness, and recklessness, was in the mix which meant there would be some dynamic changes ("expect the unexpected"). Her difficulties with her immediate supervisor who had OCD got resolved when she was offered a transfer to another department for more pay. And, her unsatisfactory relationship with her boyfriend ended quickly.

Much to my delight, living in Durham allowed me to rekindle my friendship with Terry. We had maintained touch via phone and email over the years on an irregular basis. Her husband, Leo, and she had relocated to the area a couple years before me and settled in a lovely home just east of Raleigh. Terry was going through a rough patch laced with depression along with some inchoate memories of abuse by her father when she was a young child. She was taking anti-depressants and undergoing psychological counseling to examine her difficult emotions. No surprise; transiting Pluto (purging, un/subconscious, etc.) was conjunct her Moon (feelings, emotions, etc.). Pluto aspects with the Moon can be challenging; I speak from experience.

As I had done in previous relocations, I attended the local Unity Church. It was a small congregation composed mostly of folks my age. I appreciated its inclusive approach; the Bible wasn't the only scripture they referenced. I enjoyed the *Tao Te Ching* study group. However, I didn't feel like becoming a member. I attended a handful of times over the next year until the new minister turned me off with her interrogation one Sunday morning before services concerning my spotty attendance.

Become totally empty. Let your heart be at peace. Amidst the rush of worldly comings and goings, observe how endings become beginnings. (Lao-tzu)

As August rolled around, the situation with inside sales had gone from bad to worse. I had a verbal altercation with one of inside managers about an incorrect order form I had used which involved only a minor difference. The inside manager refused to accept the sales which amounted to thousands of dollars in commission. My inexperienced supervisor I mentioned before didn't come to my aid which prompted me to submit my two-week resignation. Things hadn't been flowing, and I was ready to move on. Most importantly, I was in Durham near Layla. All I had to do was get another job and sell the house in Houston.

The 2012 presidential race had begun in earnest. The Republican platform of tax breaks for the rich disguised as trickle down and Trump's questioning Obama's birthplace had grown wearisome. Based on Trump's behavior on the Golf Channel hosting a celebrity golf tournament months before, I figured he was an egotistical asshole. Palin and the other fundamentalist politicians were beyond tiresome. Their supposed monopoly on faith and oh-so-public displays of piety were tedious. Their regressive political platform based on primitive beliefs, prejudices, prohibitions, and failed economic policies was threadbare. Little did I know what lay in store.

Nothing needs to be subtracted from your spiritual path (except, perhaps, any claims for exclusivity); all that is required is adding or supplementing with information generated by Spirit's continuing evolution and unfolding. (Ken Wilber)

The 9/11 tributes were touching and thought-provoking. Ten years after, terrorism had become a regular menu item for folks in the USA. In some countries, it had been routine fare for decades. I remembered years before traveling in the UK and trying to find a trash can at a train station without success. They had been removed for fear of IRA bombs. Here in the US, it had become standard operating procedure to remove shoes and empty pockets at airport security checkpoints before walking through a scanner to dissuade terrorists from using airplanes as guided bombs. Homegrown terrorism was a growing concern.

Economics is a play of impersonal and personal forces combined with macro and micro policies. Unemployed coal miners are the downside, and in-demand internet techies are the upside. Anger is likely when economic realities don't meet expectations. Occupy Wall Street and Tea Party movements were the latest expressions of that anger. Their labels were descriptive of whom they blamed for our economic misfortunes; that is, Wall Street and the government, respectively. The Tea Party types were too angry and too religious for my taste. The Occupy folks were a disparate bunch. To their credit, they brought attention to the Glass-Stegall Act that separated investment and commercial banking activities back in the Great Depression of 1933. Some parts of the Glass-Steagall Act were repealed in 1999 which paved the way for the "too big to fail" banks which devolved into the recent near-fatal financial meltdown perpetrated by Wall Street, greased by Congressional legislation, and underwritten by the American taxpayer. Phew, say that quickly!

The world's most powerful and most highly paid had been entirely discredited; without government intervention every single one of them would have lost his job; and yet those same financiers were using the government to enrich themselves. (Michael Lewis; *The Big Short*)

Another political issue that had become a flashpoint was the reactionary anti-immigrant law passed in Arizona. I figured every country had the right to know who comes and goes across its borders, especially in light of terrorism. However, the law promoted racism. Pulling folks over because they look Mexican was barking up the wrong tree. Mexican American citizens have lived in the what is now the US for generations. As Eva Longoria said, "We didn't cross the border. The border crossed us." My concern was ICE's arbitrary roundups that violate basic human rights and the private prison industry that profits; remember, one day it might be your group, race, and/or religion that is targeted.

I had a couple of job interviews but didn't feel enthusiastic about either. Various friends and contacts in the industry were telling me that companies weren't hiring because business was slow. My house in Houston had not sold yet. Given rent, mortgage, and being unemployed, finances became paramount. If I didn't secure a job in the following few weeks, my contingency plan was to move back to Houston to eliminate the rent portion of my expenses. With time on my hands, I read; I thoroughly enjoyed *1491*, *1493*, and John Lithgow's memoir, *Drama*. I appreciated his account of how he met his current wife of thirty plus years. He was given a choice of two acting roles in NYC where he lived and ended up choosing the one that flopped. Because he had no job prospects in NYC, he went to LA to check out an acting opportunity there. While in LA a friend introduced him to his future wife. He noted, "None of these things would have ever happened if I hadn't made the biggest mistake of my career." Sometimes it is good to fail.

So far my job search had failed. In November with no immediate job prospects, my contingency plan was set in motion. I moved back to Houston to free myself from rent expenditure. A few weeks later, Will and I got together and played golf and, because we were willing to wake up early, we had the course to ourselves. Then we tied one on with that immigrant from France and watched football. The next day we relieved our hangovers at a local spa I had discovered that provided massages with happy endings. Throughout the weekend, Will's breathing was labored; he got winded readily. I tipped my hat to folks like Will dealing with debilitating diseases. Ken Wilber had this to say about his REDD disease: "My I is free and radiant, but my me is fucked, and it's just a matter of which side of the identity street you want to play on."

A few weeks later I accepted a sales representative position at WAS, my employer before last. I was replacing the previous representative who had quit. It happened in a matter of days. Because I hadn't burnt any bridges when I left a year before, I was welcomed back. It meant I could move back to Durham. I wasn't under the illusion that management had changed their tune, but I needed a job and income; I figured I could handle their mis-fucking-management. They had rearranged the sales force; there were two sales divisions, one for libraries and one for education sales. I wouldn't be responsible for the education sales numbers; that is, the likely lack of sales. The agreement was I'd commute to the territory (Florida, Georgia, South Carolina, and North Carolina) until my house sold. There would be a learning curve concerning North Carolina and South Carolina which I had never covered on the public library side. However, I knew the other part of my territory quite well, Florida and Georgia, and their long-standing budget woes.

> Nearly all the best things that came to me in life have been unexpected, unplanned by me. (Carl Sandburg)

Just before Christmas, Will inherited a sedan in great shape and a two-bedroom condo from a recently deceased friend. Will had assisted him over the years with doctor appointments and hospital visits as he struggled with terminal cancer. To lend a helping hand, I drove over Christmas day. I don't think a half hour passed before we were cleaning and rearranging things. I was super pleased that he had his own space again and transportation (his previous car had been recently totaled which insurance had inadequately compensated). Golf took a back seat. A couple days later I drove back to Houston.

Chapter 18: Relocation

> What saves a man is to take a step. Then another step. (C.S. Lewis)

2012 started off with the sale of my home in Houston. It was a financial setback; however, I was thrilled to be without the mortgage payment and free to resettle in Durham. I liked living in large university towns; it meant a variety of entertainment venues, young people, liberal politics, and cultural/racial/ethnic diversity. In addition to Black and White folks, the Raleigh-Durham-Chapel Hill area, the Research Triangle, was home to large Asian and Latino communities. Like other moves, this one was an experiment; living in a new town along with an iffy, old job. My simpler lifestyle included being single and, as part of a retirement plan, purchasing a home as soon as possible to eliminate mortgage payments.

Just before my actual move from Houston, I scheduled a medical procedure for the dilation of my urethra due to the recurrence of constrictions from scar tissue caused by radiation treatments five years before (another roto-rooter routine). The resulting drama ranged from stressful to absurd to humorous. The initial stressor was missing my plane Thursday night in Orlando and wondering if I was going to make it back to Houston in time for the procedure which was scheduled for 4 PM Friday (the only time that would work with my planned move to Durham). And, even though my flight was delayed Friday morning due to inclement weather, I managed to make it back to Houston in time for my appointment.

The next stressor was the disconnect between what my new urologist, a far superior practitioner to the previous one, recommended and what the hospital required. The hospital requirement was for someone I knew, friend or family, to pick me up after the procedure (due to possible problems with anesthesia). I could have asked my neighbor but figured it was an imposition. When I mentioned this to my urologist over the phone, he casually suggested I tell the admissions folks what they wanted to hear. From that point on a fabrication was set in motion that would have embarrassed George Costanza of *Seinfeld*. I proceeded to fib repeatedly.

When I arrived at the hospital, the admissions clerk inquired about my pick-up arrangement. I lied about my neighbor picking me up; in actuality, I had arranged for a taxi to pick me up. Then she asked me for my neighbor's name. Oops, I forgot about that! I decided to lie about that as well and invented a name: Bob Estes. Then she asked me for his telephone number. Oops, I forgot about that too! So, I clumsily construed a shaky story about him calling me since he would be out of town and that I didn't have his mobile number.

My faith in my fabrication was floundering, but I wasn't giving up without a fight. I was still committed to the behind the scenes arrangement with the taxi driver. Even though he was South Asian, I thought about asking him to pretend he was Bob Estes! When I arrived at the operating room one of the nurses informed me that she knew about my deal with the taxi driver. Damn, apparently I wasn't the first patient who had tried to bypass hospital regulations. Once again, I lied, claiming I forgot to cancel and that Bob Estes would be picking me up. The operating room nurses insisted they wouldn't release me until they met Bob Estes. I felt relieved; at least they were going ahead with the dilation.

> Just remember. It's not a lie ... if you believe it. (George Costanza; *Seinfeld*)

After I woke up from anesthesia, I introduced some playfulness by dancing with one of the nurses. However, the absurdity of my duplicity had become too embarrassing. I fessed up about Bob Estes being a lie. I was tired and just wanted to go home. Due to the regulation, the idea was floated that I might have to stay overnight in the hospital. Thankfully, one of the nurses volunteered to take me home. The result of the procedure was boon; I was able to urinate and void my bladder effectively (efficiently, if you prefer) and have been able to do so since.

My new old job was like putting on a seasoned pair of shoes; easy, comfortable, and habitual. My two new states, NC and SC, would require acquainting myself with the significant libraries, players, and fiscal peculiarities. The dark side of the company was the same. Apparently, management MO had been very heavy handed the year I was gone. Upper management motto was: "beat 'em up until the morale improves." The sales meeting was a big disappointment accented by the president's ornery behavior. I reinstituted my quarter by quarter review tenure-wise at WAS.

Since my SMP days, Ben and I had managed to stay in touch. A more pleasant man was hard to find. Our communication was primarily phone conversations with a few emails in between.

Ben's wife had Chronic Obstructive Pulmonary Disease (COPD) due to years of smoking complicated by intermittent bouts of pneumonia. Ben had struggled irregularly with arrhythmia for years and in the last year had cataract issues, one of the most common age-related diseases. Then he was diagnosed with prostate cancer. We discussed at length the pros and cons of the various prostate treatment options. His preferential attitude, some folks call it detachment, was commendable.

The advent of texting was an adjustment for me. My daughter, like the rest of her generation, preferred such. I found it a convenient form of communication if limited feedback was suitable. However, if more substantive communication was desirable or necessary, I preferred telephonic communication. In the spirit of experimentation, I sent Layla a text about her mother's upcoming birthday. Her reply struck me as dismissive which pissed me off. Later when I brought it up, she said it wasn't her intention at all. We both laughed and agreed that one of the dangers of texting is the lack of emotional nuance and misinterpretation.

Business wise things were perking up with a handful of significant sales. In addition to being left alone, all I needed from management was to continue producing a good product. I was traveling extensively throughout my territory calling on public libraries in small towns, suburbs, and major metro areas. On one trip to north Florida, I cashed in on some hotel points and extended my stay over the weekend in Jacksonville. I visited old friends including Bert, Donna, and Sarah. Despite our brief affair, Sarah and I had managed to stay friends. We shared our concerns about getting older; that is, problems with health, wealth, family, and political dysfunction. It seemed to me that growing old with minimal anxiety had to do with seeing Who I really am and recognizing where problems belong..."out there." That didn't mean denying the problems. Actually, the essential seeing is the source of clearer thinking for fixing problems if deemed possible or preferable. The unpredictable moments of grace were gravy.

> These brief occasions of Grace are unpredictable and beyond one's control, coming and going as they please. What comes will go. The essential seeing, on the other hand, neither comes nor goes. (Douglas Harding)

Later that spring Will flew in from San Antonio to get away from the drama with ex and son. The ex's obsession with the extraterrestrials had been replaced by some demented diet trip. His son needed to start making good decisions and developing good habits; the school of hard knocks was tuition free and always recruiting. Eventually, we made it to the golf course but had to skip numerous holes because of the heavy rains the day before which also made for slow play. Finally, we hit a couple of drives; Will's went right, and mine went left landing in a large puddle of water. I didn't realize the depth of the puddle and got the golf cart stuck. Will got behind the cart to give it a push as I depressed the accelerator. The back tires dug into the fairway and sprayed him with mud from head to toe. His face dripping with mud was the epitome of forlorn resignation. Even though I felt guilty, I couldn't help laughing till my sides ached. Will deserved credit for being a good sport. That was the last time I swung a club.

As expected, the amendment to ban gay marriage passed in North Carolina. The religious Right's gospel of fear and prejudice carried the day. A couple days later, on my stroll back from the local market with some wine, I ran across two women walking and holding hands. They were a good five meters ahead of me when I yelled, "Y'all should be careful. That's against the law." Both turned around simultaneously, knowing I was goofing, and greeted me with glee and thanked me for my "magic." A few months later Obama came out in favor of gay marriage which provided the necessary catalyst for changing the prohibition.

On my business trip to the Tampa Bay area, I extended my stay, once again, using hotel points so I could visit Johnny; he was staying with some friends in the St. Pete area. We met at a funky restaurant on Clearwater Beach where we shot the shit and sipped on a couple of sangrias. He was still trying to be the nice guy with his estranged wife, Phoebe. It was a pattern I had witnessed before when he broke up with other women and only added to his emotional turmoil. When was Johnny going fish or cut bait? That is, stop vacillating and act. After our meeting, I headed back to the hotel where I overindulged in wine at the bar. I woke up the next morning hungover with a nagging question. When was I going fish or cut bait concerning my drinking problem?

In June '12 I attended a Headless Way workshop at Unity in Raleigh conducted by Richard Lang who met Douglas Harding back when he was a teenager in the early '70s. About 25 folks attended. Most of the folks in attendance were seasoned seekers but new to the efficacy of having no head or no-face. Richard expertly conducted the experiments like the no-face to face which points out the fact that the only face you can't see is yours; in place of an imagined face is Aware Space for others' faces. That may sound silly or absurd but is profoundly freeing if practiced regularly. Another experiment consisted of the placement of colored dots on everyone's forehead without them knowing the color. Then, without talking, folks meander about attempting to segregate according to the unknown colored dot based on non-verbal cues from other participants. It brought up feelings of confusion, separation and/or belonging highlighting the problematic adult stage. Problems that prompt us to seek a solution; that is, we stop ignoring our headless view, Aware Capacity. We acknowledge our birthright as Seers.

> The adult is fully committed to the external view - 'I am what I look like' - and dismisses the validity of the original headless view. The fourth stage of the seer is where you re-instate the original headless viewpoint, accepting its validity - and then, with fresh eyes, discovering how important and meaningful it is. This fourth stage develops naturally from the adult stage, and really is everyone's birthright. If you don't go on to the fourth stage you are missing something important. (Richard Lang)

Life invites experimentation; being decisive was my favored routine. In that light, I started shopping for a home regardless of the tenuous situation at work. If circumstances changed, I'd adjust. I favored something along the lines of a bungalow with a nice view and some land to play with. The adjacent neighborhood to my apartment was high on my list with its walking trails. It was centrally located and not too far from the airport, near a shopping mall, and equidistant from the UNC and Duke campuses. That meant I was near Duke Gardens;

approximately 55 acres of landscaped and wooded areas within the campus laced with trails affording many photographic miracles along the way. Albert Einstein captured the essence of this reality eloquently when he said, "There are only two ways to live your life. One is as though nothing is a miracle. The other is as though everything is a miracle."

The Second Amendment reads, "A well-regulated militia, being necessary for the security of a free state, the right of the people to keep and bear arms, shall not be infringed." The NRA's campaign of fear, paranoia, and disinformation had bastardized an amendment written in the time of muzzleloaders and volunteer militias. Somehow yesteryear's militia, today's National Guard, had been reinterpreted as a right for everyone to carry a gun; that is, rapid-fire guns, military-style weapons. I find it difficult to believe the Founding Fathers would condone the insanity we suffer from today with more and more guns resulting in more and more mass shootings and gun-related deaths.

> Things started to change in the 1970s as various right-wing groups coalesced to challenge gun control, overturning laws in state legislatures, Congress and the courts. But Chief Justice Warren Burger, a conservative appointed by Richard Nixon, described the new interpretation of the Second Amendment in an interview after his tenure as "one of the greatest pieces of fraud--I repeat the word fraud--on the American public by special-interest groups that I have ever seen in my lifetime." (Fareed Zakaria)

The debate over gun control was one of many disagreements contributing to political polarization between conservatives and liberals. In *The Righteous Mind: Why Good People Are Divided by Politics and Religion* Jonathan Haidt contends that our values are "expressions of our tribal, groupish, righteous nature." Conservatives are motivated by loyalty, authority, and sanctity while liberals are motivated by pluralism, caring, and fairness. Each tribe or side emotionally backs their claims of superiority along with various justifications or rationalizations all the while not recognizing the worth of the other side's values resulting in "my values are the only correct values" pissing contest; a political face game with confrontation the result. How do we work it out? Integral Theory recommended accommodating "the gifts of all previous worldviews, including those which have been historically at odds: science and religion, Eastern and Western schools of thought, and pre-modern, modern and post-modern worldviews." (Jeff Salzman; *The Daily Evolver*)

Given the political disagreement, the cultural discord, the economic roller coaster, the pervasive environmental degradation, and the dozen or so armed conflicts, humor was appreciated. When I was younger, I enjoyed numerous sitcoms such as *I Love Lucy, Dick van Dyke,* and *Gilligan's Island*. Those had been replaced by *Three's Company, All in the Family, MASH,* and *The Cosby Show* which had been replaced by *Seinfeld, Cheers, Frasier,* and *Friends.* Thankfully, new sitcoms were providing a good laugh as well such as *The Big Bang Theory* and *Mom*. I'm a pushover for such entertainment; I laugh on cue every time.

> As soap is to the body, so laughter is to the soul. (A Jewish Proverb)

I was a pushover when it came to Nora as well. When she hit a rough patch with her boyfriend, our communication via phone and email increased. Our conversations quickly escalated into planning a romantic rendezvous at Nora's place in California along with a couple days in nearby Napa Valley. Both of us were excited about the prospect of consummating our relationship. It wasn't to be. A home in the neighborhood I had been eyeing became available. I couldn't afford both the trip to California and the purchase of the house along with renovations.

The house was a bit over 1550 square feet (almost bungalow size), two stories, three bedrooms, and two baths. Before moving in, I arranged for the replacement of window treatments and carpeting on the stairwell, hall, and second-floor bedrooms along with repainting the entire interior (the raspberry colored kitchen and lavender colored bedrooms weren't my cup of tea). After moving in, I upgraded the kitchen and bathrooms with new tile floors, granite countertops, sinks, and toilets. Landscaping with ground cover, bamboo, and other ornamentals would have to wait until spring. While relaxing in the living room in the midst of this creative flow, I had a remarkably clear déjà vu about the entire scene. *And*, I remembered when I saw the scene. It was five years before back in my home office in Houston when I was unpacking. Call it a wrinkle in time.

Chapter 19: Intimation

Only at Centre are you All Right! (Douglas Harding)

In the preface to this memoir, I refer to myself as a pessimistic optimist. I drive a car, but I wear a seatbelt. I have learned the value of considering worst-case scenarios. However, in romantic endeavors, career choices, and political considerations, blind optimism has proven to be an inclination with a long half-life. For instance, the reelection of Obama to a second term. I thought there would be some progressive changes; that proved wildly optimistic. I didn't realize the extent and effectiveness of the political propaganda and social conditioning being orchestrated by the GOP, Fox News, and other right-wing organizations at the expense of the country's welfare.

Another example of indoctrination or brainwashing was Big Pharma marketing. The "talk to your doctor" mantra on TV advertisements flirted with selling diseases, rare or recently concocted. The long-winded list of possible adverse effects including death was almost funny. However, the most outrageous practice was the marketing of opioids which resulted in the over-prescription *and* knowingly producing and distributing more product than necessary given standard treatment protocol. Eventually, this would lead to an opioid addiction crisis. Health care combined with the profit motive is a slippery slope.

Peter Anton by Salman Rushdie was an eye-opener. It was a third person account of Rushdie's years in hiding under the name Peter Anton due to the fatwa issued by the Ayatollah calling for his assassination because of a book he wrote considered anti-Islamic, *The Satanic Verses.* It was a frightening example of a state, Iran in this case, using "religion as political repression and as international terrorism." There are religious folks in this country with similar proclivities engaged in undermining constitutionally mandated separation of church and state. The 1st Amendment was put in place to protect us against the very horror Rushdie suffered. Inquisition, repression, and terrorism are propensities religious fundamentalists through the ages, regardless of the particular religion, have repeatedly succumbed to at humankind's expense.

Rushdie's travails prompted me to do some research on The Universal Declaration of Human Rights (UDHR). It was drafted by the United Nations General Assembly in Paris on December 10, 1948, as the universal standard of rights for all peoples and all nations. Article 18 and 19 apply to the above paragraph. The complete declaration is available at www.un.org/en/documents/udher/indes.shtml.

> Article 18. Everyone has the right to freedom of thought, conscience, and religion; this right includes freedom to change his religion or belief, and freedom, either alone or in community with others and in public or private, to manifest his religion or belief in teaching, practice, worship, and observance.

> Article 19. Everyone has the right to freedom of opinion and expression; this right includes freedom to hold opinions without interference and to seek, receive and impart information and ideas through any media and regardless of frontiers.

Layla and I decided to celebrate my 60th birthday a week earlier than my birth date due to the potential conflict with folks' Thanksgiving plans. Layla and boyfriend chose a Mexican theme with burritos, guacamole, sombrero, and piñata along with an entertaining mix of folks. There was flagrantly flirtatious Terry and her husband, Leo; my loquacious neighbor Pat minus her husband, Peter, who was sick; my brother and sister-in-law who had driven up from Atlanta with some much-needed mattresses for my guest bedroom; and two other couples, friends of Layla's she'd known since college. En otras palabras, fue una gran fiesta!

For our Thanksgiving dinner, Layla and I went to Cafe Parizade to participate in their annual vegetarian feast. There were numerous delicious dishes to pick from; the pumpkin bread and mashed sweet potatoes were exceptional. The restaurant was packed, but we slipped in and out quickly because we preordered tickets and opted for outside seating. Layla and I complemented each other on our preference for such efficiency. The next day was my official body/mind 60th birthday, by most definitions a senior citizen! I woke up to a text from Nora wishing me a happy birthday and that she missed me. After seeking romance for most of my adult life, I was pleasantly surprised that I was enjoying being single. And, yes, there was an astrological correlation: transiting Pluto (transformation, power) conjunct Venus (romance, creativity) in the 5th house (self-expression, creativity). Call it a hint from the Universe about romantic and creative transformation.

After an intentionally long break in communication, I spoke with Johnny. His marriage was topsy-turvy as usual; however, due to his recent stay at an alcohol detox unit, he felt like he had turned the corner. It's curious; alcohol for most folks isn't an issue. However, for some of us, it's a problem. One man's pleasure is another's pain. Bert's main pain, his marriage, had finally dissolved; he had been unhappy for a long time. He was relieved but suffering from PDS (Post Divorce Syndrome) along with an alcohol issue. I emailed him a *SkyLog* report (transiting Pluto squared Mars, progressed Moon squared Mars, etc.). Bert's response was, "that's some heavy shit." Indeed. I sent him an email with one of my favorite poems by William Blake.

> Man was made for joy and woe;
> And when this we rightly know,
> Thro' the world we safely go.
> Joy and woe are woven fine,
> A clothing for the soul divine.
> Under every grief and pine
> Runs a joy with silken twine.
> (William Blake; *Auguries of Innocence*)

The Sandy Hook Elementary School massacre in Connecticut was horrific; 20 children and 6 adult staff members killed. Innocent souls murdered by an unhinged young man armed to the teeth. I found it hard to fathom how families and friends of the victims were grappling with their grief. There was an outcry for more effective gun control, assault weapons ban, and stringent background checks. It was time to counter the idiocy and disinguousness of the NRA/GOP. Their resistance to gun control had resulted in a glut of guns in the wrong hands which had encouraged more killing, drive-bys, and mass shootings. The idea of everybody going about their business carrying a gun was insanity.

The situation between Will's son and his ex was getting no better, maybe even worse. The details of various battles between them varied, but results remained the same; his ex would tell one tale and his son another. Will would go back forth trying to get the straight scoop, if at all. For a while, things would improve, and he'd think the basic dysfunction had changed. A month later another triangulation would occur, and he'd get caught in the crossfire. "Getting out of Dodge" gained urgency; that is, moving to Utah as soon as his son graduated from high school. One roadblock was getting the final legal ownership of his condo. A wicked witch, an aunt of his deceased friend that gave him the condo, was the glitch.

To get away from the maddening drama, Will flew into town in time for the holidays. Peter and Pat's Christmas party was a big hit; her shrimp and sausage stir-fry over grits deserved seconds. The rainy conditions put a damper on things, but we managed to visit Duke Gardens which was exquisite as ever. We went to the movies a couple of times, *Lincoln* and *Django Unchained*. Both dealt with slavery powerfully and poignantly. *Lincoln* was outstanding. *Django Unchained* was tough to stomach at times with lots of graphic violence. Naturally, we discussed what was happening with friends, family, and exes. He was concerned that his ex, the mother of his son, had some sort of personality disorder. Given her behavior, that wasn't a surprising conclusion; experts think roughly 10% of the population suffer from such.

I continued making significant inroads in my sales territory. Basically, it was a matter of creating relationships with librarians and being sensitive to their needs. Most of them were overwhelmed with their duties, often doing the job of two or three librarians due to budget and staff cuts over the years. Thus, due to no fault of their own, they weren't responsive to voice messages or emails. And, yes, some were resistant, even reactive, to sales folks like me. I didn't take it personally; well, I may have bitched a bit to myself. One of the benefits of calling on libraries in person was the valuable insight I garnered about possible purchasing decisions and management dynamics that were difficult, if not impossible, to discern via email or phone because of the reasons stated above.

The sales meeting in Orlando was better than expected. The president was busy with the education sales reps which meant we, the library reps, were off the hook. As usual, their camaraderie was enlivening. The sales trainer's message was "know yourself" which was a welcome relief from the usual corporate sales training bullshit. In this case, "know yourself" was self-assessment, meditation, and curiously, journaling. The major negative of the meeting was the sales goal inflation of 30% and the lack of new product tapping into needs librarians had repeatedly expressed such as adult literacy. The president was devoting most of the R&D to penetrating the education market.

Because of my home's proximity to her office, Layla stopped by frequently. Her fortunes in romance, car repair, and dentistry had taken a turn for the worse. She decided to break up with her boyfriend due to his lack of direction. As for her car, the mechanics couldn't locate the sound Layla was concerned about. And, her dentist was advising gum surgery. She was feeling discouraged. However, her mood changed rather quickly, though more than likely temporarily, when we played a game of Zilch. I went ahead early but suffered through a handful of mediocre dice rolls. Gradually, my fortunes improved until the score was even. However, on her last roll, Layla got a straight flush and won outright. She was thrilled with the victory. I was glad for her. She was no longer down on her luck.

> The self is best thought of as some kind of a fiction, albeit an extremely useful one – and that realising this, instead of doing everything we can to deny it, might be the route to fulfilment. (Oliver Burkeman; *The Antidote: Happiness for People Who Can't Stand Positive Thinking*)

The Robin Williams and David Steinberg show at the impressive DPAC venue in downtown Durham was a lot of laughs. Karla, a friend I met through work, organized the evening. The production consisted of Robin and David talking about their films, sitcoms, TV appearances, stand up comedy, and various biographical incidents with Robin having most of the time and laughs. Robin's reenactment of his falling off the wagon (drinking again) at a movie shoot in Alaska was hilarious. The local convenience store had only little bottles of booze, so he stocked up on a handful and headed back to his hotel with them clinking in his pocket. In a way, it reminded me of the biweekly collection of my recycle bin filled with wine bottles. As the garbage truck's robotic arm hoisted the bin and dumped it, rather than a clinking sound, there was a loud clanking sound along with noise of breaking bottles.

Every few weeks, Terry and I talked on the phone after her husband went to bed. Sometimes fueled by wine and our sexual history, we'd flirt with each other. We also spoke in depth about family issues, especially our children's situations, spirituality, and gardening with her taking the lead; she was a master gardener. Her combination of humor and honesty was refreshing. She once suggested it would be better, and more efficient if we went around smelling each other's asses like dogs. Maybe you had to be there to appreciate it; it was hilarious.

Over the years communication with my siblings had increased in frequency via phone or email. My brother and I chatted every other day or so. Often, it was merely checking in; however, occasionally our conversations took on a more serious tone regarding family dramas or political events. Our political opinions had become more similar over the years; we agreed more often than not. Even though our children were adults, parenting wasn't an unusual topic. Dealing with their trials and tribulations wasn't easy at times; a healthy dose of minding one's own business and letting go was required.

Right up my reading alley was *Cosmos & Psyche* by Richard Tarnas. It's a thorough historical analysis of astrological world transits through the ages, but mostly concentrating on the last handful of centuries. The central premise: The Universe is alive and pulsating with meaning freely provided by Being wrapped in archetypes. Astrology offers a way to dislodge "the modern mind from its disenchanted cosmological condition." Tarnas' *Cosmos & Psyche* is unequivocally in a class by itself. His book is a must read if you're an astrology aficionado and a recommended read if you appreciate history, philosophy, psychology and/or spirituality. Below is an excerpt.

> The objectifying ascetic rationalism and empiricism that emerged during the Enlightenment served as liberating disciplines for the nascent modern reason, but they still dominate mainstream science and modern thought today in a rigidly undeveloped form. In their simplistic myopia and one-sidedness, they seriously constrain our full range of perception and understanding. (Richard Tarnas; *Cosmos and Psyche: Intimations of a New World View*).

Tarnas' analysis is predominantly a macro-historical perspective using astrological transits. However, occasionally he'd comment on some personal or micro aspect in the birth chart. One planetary combination I never had a good grasp of was my Saturn-Neptune conjunction (present in charts of millions of folks born late '52 to late '53). It's a curious one; sober-minded Saturn joined at the hip with spiritually inclined Neptune. Tarnas' interpretation is spot on: "...sensitivity to the suffering and sorrow of life, whether experienced by oneself or others...more than the usual concern with death and its spiritual implications; also associated with individuals whose philosophical outlook showed an emphatic tendency towards skeptical realism, which ranged in character from, on the one hand, agnosticism or atheism to, on the other, a critical attitude towards conventional religious belief combined with a serious, sometimes somber spiritual vision of life of a highly pragmatic, this-worldly nature."

The Boston Marathon bombing was executed by two young brothers, ages 27 and 19, on April 15, 2013. Their objective was to murder and mutilate innocent bystanders gathered to enjoy the spectacle of the race. The brothers emigrated to the US from the Caucus region of Russia in 2002. It is thought the older brother became a radicalized Islamist during a trip back to Dagestan to visit family in 2009. They learned how to build the two homemade pressure-cooker bombs from an al-Qaida website. They killed 3 and maimed 264.

Another graphic horror story broadcasted daily on TV and online was the Syrian civil war. Pictures and videos of Syrian parents grieving over their dead children were heartbreaking. The Syrian regime with the support of Russia and Iran has slaughtered tens of thousands of innocent civilians via poisonous gas, massive bombardment (including hospitals), hanging, and torture. Accurate estimates varied on the number of deaths in the civil war; it was probably somewhere around 220,000 with roughly 3 million refugees mostly living in camps in Lebanon, Jordan, and Turkey. There was no end in sight.

> Keep me away from the wisdom which does not cry, the philosophy which does not laugh and the greatness which does not bow before children. (Khalil Gibran)

Will's next visit provided a stark reminder of his health issues. After picking up his luggage at the carousel, we proceeded to walk back to my car in short-term parking. We hadn't gone a hundred yards before Will asked to take a break to catch his breath. That didn't stop us from having fun; we partied with my neighbors, Peter and Pat. Then we drove down to Carolina Beach where we spent the day. On our way back, we visited the USS North Carolina battleship moored in Wilmington which included a serendipitous tour provided by one of the maintenance engineers. And, of course, we performed our pilgrimage to Duke Gardens.

His visit prompted a meditation on our eventual bodily demise; a contemplation about each of us having to "shuffle off this mortal coil." His passing more than likely would be via congestive heart failure. I figured mine would be cancer, foreshadowed by my prostate cancer episode a few years ago. Alzheimer's was another option being that my mother died of such. Death might be unpleasant, even painful. So, at the risk of sounding melodramatic, I planned to work a few more years, retire, read, write, and, get ready for death by continuing to remember Who I really am, Awareness.

While driving from one library to another, I caught an NPR interview with Amy Grant. I was intrigued; I had always liked her voice and knew she had gone through a divorce and remarriage to Vince Gill, a great guitar player. I caught the part when she was talking about her parents' struggle with dementia and death. Her account brought a tear to my eye. I thought of my mother slowly disintegrating from Alzheimer's; it was emotionally excruciating at times. Her comment about the politicization of religion struck a chord as well. It's a sticky situation. There are good religious folks who are helpful, harmonious, and holistic; and there are bad religious folks who are disagreeable, disruptive, and destructive.

Western North Carolina and South Carolina are graced by the Blue Ridge Mountains which provided the backdrop to a visual cornucopia of spring green; a mixed leaf salad crossed my mind. However, my culinary reverie was conditioned by concerns about Layla's health. She was suffering occasional stomach aches along with episodes of nausea. We figured it was a problem with her gallbladder; her grandmother and mother had their gallbladders removed years before. According to her doctor, the tests were inconclusive of such; she opted for the desperation diagnosis: stress.

My next business trip was to the panhandle of Florida, my least lucrative market, to stir up some business which inadvertently stimulated some memories and commentaries. Due to my father's job transfer, we moved from Venezuela to Florida in 1963. I was in fifth grade; the state population was roughly 5 million. By 2013 it was approaching 20 million. As I drove through Destin Beach along US 90, I was amazed by the amount development and the traffic to match. I remembered when there were just a few motels scattered along the crystalline white beaches. This was true wherever I went in Florida; especially along the coastlines and the central section around Orlando (think Disney World). Regardless, driving was a meditation of sorts noticing the scenery, thoughts, and feelings pass through me, Conscious Capacity. Later, I made a pit stop at a truck stop for a biological break. On the bathroom stall someone had etched, "Let go, let God." Ahhh...synchronicity, ya gotta love it.

Then tropical storm Andrea made her presence known. There is something about a tropical storm in Florida with the spacious skies and towering cumulus nimbus clouds that is like no other. I got caught in her deluge while making calls on public libraries in Sarasota where I was assisting with implementation and conducting training. At one point, I had to take my shoes and socks off to make it to my car; the water was up to my ankles. Then Andrea followed me on my trip back to Durham where there was localized flooding. The next morning, I strolled through Duke Gardens photographing some post-rain magic.

Layla and I met for Father's Day brunch at Antonia's and feasted on huevos ranchero. Unlike my mother's tomato-based concoction, this one was black bean based with a couple of corn tortillas topped with two fried eggs, mango salsa, and sliced avocado. ¡Igualmente delicioso! With our afternoon wide open, we decided it would be a good time to paint her front porch with some leftover paint from my home improvement projects. The color left a lot to be desired but it certainly looked cleaner, and it provided a pleasant diversion for Layla. She was chewing on some difficulties, namely her job and romance; a predicament I knew all too well. Letting the dusty ego bitch and moan a bit wasn't so bad. After all, you can't throw mud at the Sun.

Later that summer Johnny stopped by on his way down to Florida to visit family. He was aggravating from the get-go with his almost constant moaning about his dysfunctional marriage and divorce deliberations, which had been going on for years. It was difficult to get him on task

131

constructing a blind with 4'x 6' lattices even though he was short on money and I was paying him handsomely. And, there was his around-the-clock drinking. Once the blind was completed, I nudged him out the door. I had no room to be judgmental about Johnny's drinking problem; mine meant too many mornings waking up with multi-star hangovers. The culprit was me, and the crime was wine; as *UB 40* sang, "red, red wine, you make me feel so fine." By hook or crook, cunning subconscious rationalizations held sway convincing me one more buzz was okay.

> There is clarity: luminous, still and silent clarity. It is with you and in you. It is you. It always exists. No it never takes a break; no it never goes out for just one cigarette. It is the wholeness you can never fall out of. Not in your drunkest, sorriest, most hysterical moments, not even then can you fall out of this clear and sacred perfection. You know that. (J. Jennifer Mathews; *Radically Condensed Instructions for Being Just as You Are*)

The beginning of fall brought increased pressure from upper management for more sales due to the approaching end of the fiscal year on December 31. My metrics were at a historic low for that period of the year. My explanation was simple; due to an upcoming special discount, customers had delayed their purchases. My immediate manager knew this but was getting hounded by the president. I also explained that three out of my four state libraries were planning to purchase using either federal or state funding that wouldn't be available until later in the fall.

WAS wasn't much different from other dysfunctional companies I had worked for; that is, upper management that was slow on the uptake in acknowledging and taking responsibility for their poor personnel policies and short-sighted philosophy. However, to their credit, they had produced an exceptional product that promoted children's literacy via local public libraries. I thoroughly enjoyed selling it. By the end of November, much to the surprise of upper management I had surpassed my sales quota, and I could go ahead with my bathroom remodel plans.

> I'm not convinced salespeople are somehow radically different from the rest of us. We all want to be paid fairly for our efforts, of course. But that's just a starting point. We also want to do good work, challenge ourselves, get better at something that matters, and make a contribution. That's true for everyone. (Daniel Pink; *To Sell Is Human*)

Most Americans and the Obama administration were against intervention in Syria. Our failed effort next door in Iraq was a stark reminder of the quagmire we wanted to avoid. The estimated cost of our Iraq debacle was $3 trillion (that's the letter T). That would have paid for a very robust healthcare system, updated infrastructure, free college tuition, and much, much more. Roughly, 500,000 Iraqis, civilian and military, died. 4,491 U.S. service members along with 1,487 contractors were killed; 10's of thousands were wounded. One in four U.S. troops came home with a medical or mental health problem that required treatment that, in some cases, is still ongoing.

Regardless of the repercussions of the Iraqi debacle, some Congressional members wanted to intervene militarily with "boots on the ground" in Syria. I registered my objection to such via the websites for my two senators and one representative. The Syrian civil war was a religious/sectarian/tribal conflict, a clusterfuck, reflective of similar problems in other Muslim countries (Pakistan, Egypt, Lebanon, Yemen, Libya, etc.). Somehow, the Islamic world needed to take the lead and figure out how to live and let live with each other and others...soon. Unlike other religious/sectarian/tribal conflicts of the past, weapons of mass destruction were readily available.

> Spare me the political events and power struggles, as the whole earth is my homeland and all men are my fellow countrymen. (Kahlil Gibran)

While I was on my soapbox, I had a few things to say about Cuba. The Castro regime was no doubt fucked up; their economy was hanging on by a thread and their political ideology in tatters. Maybe because I lived in Miami for years, I had grown tired of the anti-Castro folks getting their calzones in a bunch. The latest tumulto was Jay-Z and Beyonce's trip to Cuba. Maybe it was time for some civil disobedience by encouraging as many Americans as possible to violate the embargo. Or, hold a lottery and use the proceeds to fund trips, via Mexico if necessary. Heck, there could be consolation prizes such as trips to Vietnam or China; other Communist authoritarian regimes with whom we've waged war against where travel *is* allowed.

Chapter 20: Liquidation

> In any moment – in this moment – you can notice you are looking into time from the timeless. (Richard Lang)

As mentioned before, time isn't a constant. Have no fear, an hour is still sixty minutes. However, there was no doubt that as I got older time passed more quickly. Better yet, "life is like a roll of toilet paper; the closer I get to the end, the faster it goes!" That included the holidays which flew by. Thanksgiving at Layla's included some of her old college chums, her mother and boyfriend, Will, and a savory veggie casserole; the dessert was delicious pumpkin pie and cordial conversation. I spent New Year's Eve with Terry and Leo at their home outside Raleigh. We ate, drank, and chatted about everything from pets to politics. Both being well read meant good conversation and ample opinions; right up my alley. Terry and Leo had gone through a rough patch earlier in the year but seemed to be meshing well.

Occasionally, I read about various spiritual paths to familiarize myself with the marketplace, so to speak. Each path had a style or orientation depending on the scripture's or teacher's prescriptions and proscriptions; frequently, suggesting their primacy or superiority. Many of the recommendations seemed antiquated, complicated, and/or superfluous to me. Some paths, namely non-dual, were unduly concerned with denial of the ego and the use of the words "I," "me," and "mine" as if Awareness is the result of syntax. Essential seeing is not dependent on a specific vocabulary, belief system and/or spiritual qualities. Joyful simplicity is recommended.

> There are no preliminary or private views or privileged showings, no more enlightened or less enlightened versions of This, no heights to mount to or fall away from, and certainly no religious or spiritual or aesthetic qualities to cultivate. (Douglas Harding)

As you probably have discerned, I wasn't a big fan of Big Pharma because of the political clout they wielded as evidenced by their influence over ACA's lack of price controls. Their product, drugs, wasn't the problem per se; Alka Seltzer is great for a hangover. I objected to the legislative favors they purchased through Congress, the two chambers of commerce. The Agrifood complex (ADM, ConAgra, Nestle, etc.) was no better. Our health was secondary to the profit motive. The FDA and USDA had been compromised by Congress which had been bought off by the various industries via their lobbying efforts. The congressional initiative to improve food labeling was an example. Sugar producers were against it; they had the balls, the unmitigated gall, to argue that there was no scientific link, a tactic used by Big Oil and Big Tobacco for decades, between excessive sugar consumption and disease. And, don't get me started about the telecoms (Verizon, ATT, TWC, etc.) and their push to further corrupt the internet by eliminating net neutrality and raise prices.

Pretty much where ever I traveled in the USA the Latino cultural influence was apparent. Ray Suarez's *Latino Americans* was an engaging read. It offered an impressive historical overview of the last 500 years of Latino presence in North America. Our Latino minority has been a win-win for all of us with a more vibrant economy, varied culture, and expanded cuisine. Oh, and better baseball teams. Due to growing up in Venezuela, Puerto Rico, and South Florida, I had an affection and appreciation for Latino culture. Living in Texas for ten years and getting married to a Mexican American sealed the deal, selló el trato. And, growing up as a kid in Latin America engendered an empathetic bond. I knew what it's like to be treated in an unfriendly manner as a minority, as a gringo.

> In 2008 and 2009, more than one of every two newborn Americans was a Latino, and the youth of the population means that number ought to rise even higher as more Latino teens enter adulthood. Sixteen states counted more than half a million Latino residents, and in twenty-one states Latinos were the largest minority group. (Ray Suarez; *Latino Americans: The 500-Year Legacy That Shaped a Nation*)

Growing up in a Spanish speaking country meant the benefit of two languages. English was spoken at home with Spanish thrown in when convenient; call it Spanglish with emphasis on the lish part. Spanish fluency varied among family members with Dad speaking fluently. Possibly because Spanish was much easier to spell, I struggled with English spelling as a child. Out of curiosity, I downloaded *Spell It Out: The Curious, Enthralling and Extraordinary Story of English Spelling* by David Crystal. The basic problem with English spelling is the number of letters; 26 letters doesn't cover the 40 plus sounds, depending on dialect. Can you imagine being a scribe in a monastery in 7th century England trying to figure out how to capture Anglo-

Saxon sounds that varied regionally with mostly Roman letters? A few centuries later the Norman invasion introduced French and Latin. Mon Dieu, no wonder English is so difficult to spell!

Another January sales meeting came and went, this time in Scottsdale, Arizona. The rapport with my fellow salespeople was enjoyable and uplifting. We, the sales force, conducted ourselves with grace; it took a lot of grit to put up with management shit; namely, their poor attitude and tunnel vision. They were still gung-ho about breaking into the education market and were dismissive of anyone who thought otherwise. I think some of them, namely the president, were in over their heads and not sure how to extricate themselves. They had committed valuable resources and had very little to show for it. Cash flow problems were cropping up.

After the dispiriting sales meeting, to recharge my depleted batteries, I got back on the road calling on libraries. The Orlando/Orange County system was one of my best customers; credit my primary contact, she was a professional librarian through and through. However, my scheduled return flight was delayed due to a snow storm closing RDU. I lost little time bemoaning my fate; I took it as a chance to call on other libraries. The area was peppered with small-town libraries such as Mount Dora, Winter Park, and Leesburg; excellent facilities that offered terrific programs for children, teens, adults, and seers; I mean seniors.

The efficacy of having no-face to customers' faces was beneficial; my imaginary face, based on present evidence, wasn't getting in the way. This openness or spaciousness was receptivity to my customers' needs which they appreciated. That didn't mean everything was orange blossoms. There were circumstances I wanted to change and worked to improve. A Friends of Library group had been holding up a sale for nearly six months, so I called the Friends president asked if there was anything I could do; there wasn't. Life is a parade of preferences.

> Non-attachment is not the elimination of desire. It is the spaciousness to allow any quality of mind, any thought or feeling, to arise without closing around it, without eliminating the pure witness of being. It is an active receptivity to life. (Stephen Levine)

Mercury retrograde is possibly the most popularly understood astrological transit. Mercury rules communication. When in retrograde, communication is adversely affected; nothing catastrophic, simply not as clear or crisp. Things that require clear communication should be double checked: contracts, buying, selling, negotiating, email, etc. During Mercury retrogrades, I found it entertaining to see what kind of glitches appeared. In my case, I dropped and damaged my cell phone which impeded communication. I also had to deal with my ISP on an unsatisfactory internet download/upload issue.

After calling on libraries, I would check into a Hilton property (for points) near where my calls would be the next day. Once settled in my room, I would sign-in on my laptop to check for email. The information age had its advantages but not without its challenges. Through trial and error, I learned how to use digital productivity tools. Professionally, I couldn't imagine selling without CRM (customer relationship management software), Word, Excel, and email. When those didn't work because of a power outage or some ISP glitch, it was difficult to get things done. My contacts and notes were in the cloud; I had no hard copy.

When orders were received, WAS HQ sent an email to everyone announcing the deal. Usually, there were a half-dozen or so congratulatory emails in reply; sort of a high five. One morning while calling on a library, I used one of their public access computers to check email using the web-based version of Outlook, not the VPN version. Among the emails was one from the president about a recent Orange County order of mine. It read: "I am assuming there is more to come from down there." I became indignant. The fusty, dusty little one, my ego, got riled up and went into overdrive. I was tempted to send a reply telling him to fuck off. That evening in my hotel room I signed on the VPN version as usual and reread the email. Plain as day was: "Great order" and the rest of the email. I didn't notice it on the web-based version before because it blended in with some gibberish at the top of the email. Moral of the story: be careful before you tell someone to fuck off and click SEND and be extra careful during Mercury retrogrades.

Layla decided to buy a larger home in the same neighborhood. She realized during the recent Thanksgiving's celebrations that her bungalow was too small. With impressive decisiveness, she put her house up for sale and, before it sold, bought the other. In addition to more square footage, it had a much larger yard. "The boys" (the goats) were going to love it; more to chew and tear apart. When it came time to move, we walked Caspar and Domino through the neighborhood to their new home. Folks along the way were charmed.

Layla wasted no time launching various home improvement projects. Along with painting her bedroom and kitchen cabinets, we put together a day bed frame which proved much more difficult than we anticipated. The directions left a lot to be desired, written by engineers in English, their second or third language. Between the two of us, along with plenty of cussing, we figured it out. The next day I woke up with searing pain in both elbows. Tendonitis was my diagnosis, a painful reminder of my physical limitations. Yep, I overdid it, a propensity I was familiar with in other areas of my life.

My next business trip to Florida went according to plan without a hitch. I closed two new accounts after a long sales cycle which always felt good. I especially enjoyed the training sessions. It was my stand-up routine, if you will, with a few jokes that were guaranteed laughs; at times it felt magical. One of the challenges was overcoming some librarians' fear of feeling stupid because they didn't know all the answers. A few of the apps included difficult content or material easily forgotten such as state capitals and the like. So, I did my best to calm their fears by highlighting questions I didn't know the answers to in a lighthearted fashion. No two software training sessions were alike, in part because of time. As with sales presentations; I had a 15-minute version on up to a 1-hour version. I was the Source, "the unthinkable Origin," of my show, and, forgive my Leo rising, I was the star of it!

Libraries are a prime example of a public service funded by the local, state, and federal governments. In April '14 Congressman Ryan recommended the defunding of the Institute of Museum and Library Services (IMLS). It would have had a devastating impact on public libraries. It was part of the constant Republican/libertarian drumbeat about the government and public services being the problem. Their answer to all that ails our society was eliminating regulations, lowering taxes, and privatizing. The private sector, on the other hand, was sacrosanct and prescient. Tell that to the folks downriver from the secret dumping of pollutants for years into the Cape Fear River by a DuPont spin-off. Tell that to the millions of Wells Fargo customers who without their consent had fraudulent savings and checking accounts opened in their name. One of the many blatant examples of private enterprises engaged in unconscionable (i.e., immoral and unethical) behavior.

Together with that drumbeat was the religious Right's incessant chant about the "war on religion," especially around Christmas. The promoters of this delusion were self-righteous types. Religions, stripped of their divergent beliefs and baloney, essentially promote trust in spiritual Being which I subscribe to. However, these religious partisans didn't strike me as spiritually inspired but politically motivated. They disguise their desire for power with a veneer of religious beliefs, a dangerous potion of specious prophecy and spurious persecution which induces resentment (or worse) of nonbelievers or nonmembers. Some advocate Dominion Theology; the belief that the USA should be governed by Christians and biblical law which was disturbingly similar to Muslim fundamentalists' caliphate and sharia law.

Fundamentalists, regardless of the brand, believe their religion is an exclusive country club, yet with mandatory membership. If you belong, you get all the benefits. If not, tough luck, you are fucked; you deserve to be discriminated against at best and killed at worst. Fundamentalists forget that the Indivisible is nonsectarian; a non-verbal Awareness that is always available.

Religion makes good people better and bad people worse. (H. Richard Niebuhr)

Wikipedia defines oligarchy as "a form of power structure in which power rests with a small number of people. These people may be distinguished by nobility, wealth, family ties, education or corporate, religious or political, military control." That definition would suggest that the USA is an oligarchy with a veneer of quasi-representative democracy. Corporations and special interests with vast amounts of wealth control the country through the acquiescence of Congress; a process lubricated by campaign contributions and gerrymandering. Researchers at Princeton conducted an analysis of policy decisions over the last handful of decades and determined that "big corporations, the ultra-wealthy and special interests with a lot of money and power essentially make all of the decisions. *Citizens wield little to no political power*." (Tom McKay, *PolicyMic*) A complete overhaul our tax code was needed which I didn't see happening. The chicken coop, I mean Congress, who wrote the tax code, was bought and controlled by the fox and friends; oligarchs and corporations that profited from the system. The Republican tax reform was for their benefit and brazenly sold as trickle-down fertilizer but actually was poop based on foul-smelling economic theory.

Connected and equally disturbing, was the deceit and misdirection employed by Wall Street. *Flash Boys* by Michael Lewis was an enlightening read about the fleecing of average investors via high-frequency trading. The trustworthiness of Wall Street had sunk to a new low. Thankfully, Brad Katayama and associates (IEX) exposed the fraud and set about creating a fair exchange. At best the Securities and Exchange Commission was asleep at the wheel, at worst colluding; financial pilferers always seemed one step ahead waiting to rip off the unsuspecting. Fed up with being taken advantage of, I considered liquidating my very modest stock market investments.

Sages through the ages have warned about "wine, women, and wealth" being problematical. Stripping away the oversimplification, generalization, and sexism, the essence of the warning was to be careful in these areas or endeavors. Wine covered intoxicants. Women referred to romantic relationships and sex. Wealth involved accumulation of money and valuable possessions. That was spot on advice; I have found to some degree or another all three to be problematic at one time or another. You might say, life is a "country of problems."

> The one here is the solution of all the problems that proliferate out there, in the country of problems. They are wholly resolved by discriminating between this central region which is visibly clear of problems (and everything else) and the surrounding country where no problem is ever cleared up. (Douglas Harding; *The Face Game: Liberation without Dogmas, Drugs or Delay*)

I was ready for spring after a long winter; as a warm climate native, I was still acclimating. Gardening opportunities were ripe for the picking; namely, sprucing up the front and side planters with a few strategically placed hostas and variegated liriope. I have enjoyed ornamental gardening since I was a kid. Once, I spent an hour waiting for a spider lily flower to bloom, a sight to behold. My parents were convinced I'd major in botany; I entertained that fantasy until high school chemistry. And, of course, there were lessons to learn. I remember feeling forlorn when a large water oak died in my backyard due to drought. However, minus its substantial canopy, various plants flourished because of increased sunlight. The puny split leaf philodendrons shot up to over 6 feet in height with leaves the size of golf umbrellas.

Cancer was the diagnosis del día. My oldest sister was diagnosed with colon cancer and my youngest sister with breast cancer. In both cases, surgery was the recommended course of treatment with positive prospects. In my family, there seemed to be a genetic predisposition in regards to cancer. Basically, cancer occurs when the genes' control mechanism goes topsy-turvy and rampant cell production occurs. Whether from cancer or whatever, being human eventually entails the death of "human me" thus the designation "mortal me" in some circles. I sense it will be akin to having just played in the garden and letting the soggy, soiled clothes of "human me" drop to the bathroom floor and stepping into the refreshing shower of Immortality. No more need for soap until the next body/mind!

Another cancer was societal in nature; that is, mass shootings, a preventable disease ravaging our country caused by the unrestrained growth of guns. Per the bbc.com/news/world, "The number of gun murders per capita in the US in 2012 - the most recent year for comparable statistics - was nearly 30 times that in the UK, at 2.9 per 100,000 compared with just 0.1. Of all the murders in the US in 2012, 60% were by firearm compared with 31% in Canada, 18.2% in Australia, and just 10% in the UK." In Santa Barbara, CA, we witnessed another murderer commit another mass shooting. A coldly calculating UCSB student killed seven because of his lackluster romantic prospects and general antipathy towards the world. He planned his attack and purchase three handguns that he admired for their shooting efficiency. The background check indicated nothing amiss. One of the victim's fathers, Richard Martinez, had this to say, "Why did Chris die? Chris died because of craven, irresponsible politicians and the NRA. They talk about gun rights, what about Chris' right to live? When will this insanity stop?"

Needing some enlightening reading, I downloaded Wayne Dyer's memoir *I Can See Clearly Now*. It's an account of his spiritual path from a difficult childhood to a very successful self-help author and spiritual teacher. His spiritual journey began with a psychological orientation and evolved into non-dualism. Over the years I read some of his books, saw some of his PBS specials, and heard him speak publicly twice. He was an engaging speaker who shared openly personal details about his life including family dynamics, divorces, etc. It was a pleasure to hear him sing the praises of Ken Keyes, Nisargadatta, Lao Tzu, and Rumi.

> I now pay much closer attention to what shows up for me, and I'm willing to listen carefully to any inclination I might have and act accordingly, even if it leads me into unknown territory. (Wayne Dyer; *I Can See Clearly Now*)

While wandering around the net I came across a Huffington blog, *The Incomparable Genius of Ken Wilber*, by Arjuna Ardagh, extolling the philosophical ideas of Ken Wilber. Below is Arjuna's synopsis of Ken's philosophy with some parenthetical additions of mine:

- One. While we may experience peak states from time to time, we grow through stages of evolution (peak experiences are nice but not the goal).
- Two. We evolve along multiple lines of development (intellectual, artistic, etc.)
- Three. Tools for development are not one size fits all (meditation, devotion, etc.)
- Four. What is before is not what is after (evolution doesn't go backward).
- Five. We are used to viewing events and relationships through one specific window, without necessarily realizing that we're doing so (ego development stages or memes: traditional, modern, post-modern, etc.)

Along with waking up spiritually and recognizing our multiple lines of development or "gifts differing," we must grow up or "put away childish things." Johnny was finally getting a divorce after years of putting up with a dysfunctional marriage. I figured the dissolution was primarily due to his drinking problem and Phoebe's six planets in Virgo. Johnny had little in the way of a financial cushion. He had invested his inheritance in the condo she owned and wasn't going to see a penny of it. Divorce is like death; the Kübler-Ross stages of grief apply; that is, denial, anger, bargaining, depression, and acceptance. Later Kübler-Ross applied these stages with flexible ordering to any significant personal challenge such as job loss, addiction, incarceration, disease, and natural disaster.

Every 4th of July for the last few years I've watched *John Adams* on HBO. The entire cast is remarkable; Paul Giamatti and Laura Linney are stellar. The photography, costumes, music, you name it, are outstanding. Many scenes are guaranteed to pull a heart string with a tear or two. The dynamic between Adams, Jefferson, and Franklin is exceptional. And, out of tempest, genius, and grit, a flawed but remarkable country was born. And, a Constitution that has stood intact for over 200 years with a few necessary amendments along the way. The amendments are substantial; below are the some of the important ones in my opinion and why.

Amendment 1 - Freedom of Religion, Press, and Expression: obvious.
Amendment 2 - Right to Bear Arms: misinterpreted by SCOTUS a while back: FUBAR.
Amendment 13 - Slavery Abolished: original fuck up by Founding Fathers corrected.
Amendment 15 - Right to Vote: not enforced until the Voting Rights Act of 1965.
Amendment 19 - Women's Suffrage: another fuck up by Founding Fathers; no brainer.
Amendment 21 - Amendment 18 (Prohibition) repealed: cheers. Psychoactive drugs next.

I found calling on customers and prospects in person a more effective way of keeping my finger on the pulse. Late July I traveled extensively throughout southern Georgia and northern Florida calling on libraries and stirring up business. I stayed over Friday night in Jacksonville to enjoy a couple of walks on the beach and visit friends. I met Donna for dinner. We caught up on our respective dramas. She was blown away by the transit and progression report I sent her a couple of weeks before. At one point we talked about some of our favorite movies and why. Both of us loved *Multiplicity* with Michael Keaton and Andie MacDowell. At one point, simultaneously, we both said out loud our favorite line, "I love pizza!" Ain't that a kick?

On August 11, 2014, Robin Williams died from suicide by hanging. He was a gifted comedian and dramatic actor who attended Julliard with Christopher Reeve, Mandy Patinkin, and William Hurt. Once, on Johnny Carson's *The Tonight Show*, I caught his hilarious improvisation on the right to bear muzzleloaders, not the modern weaponry of today. Johnny was in stitches as was I. His personal insights and political commentary were astute. *Moscow on the Hudson, Good Morning Vietnam*, and *Mrs. Doubtfire* were some of my favorite movies of his. His cussing routines were "shit the fuck up" funny.

Friends and family understood I liked to cuss; it was a predilection without termination. Some occasions begged for a cuss word or two; however, at other times it was inappropriate which I offended occasionally. I started cussing as a kid; trying on various curse words for size including a few choice ones in Spanish. Go to hell was a lame version of vete al carajo! By the way, be careful; there are regional differences in Spanish, as in every language. Cojelo suave in Puerto Rico means take it easy; in Mexico, it translates as fuck it easy! I found that out the embarrassing way when I moved to Texas. In English, the various permutations of fuck were, no surprise, my favorite; a bonafide buffet free of charge. One of the finest masters of profanity was Jennifer Carpenter's character, Debra Morgan, on the HBO series *Dexter*. She could put together a string cuss words that left me agog.

Profanity is the chili pepper of language. If used by an idiot or a clod, it can overwhelm the discourse so the meaning is lost, but if used by a linguistic master chef, it can insert a piquant passion to the point where even though your ears may burn and you may want to rinse your mouth out, you cannot say it doesn't sound delicious. (Aasif Mandvi; *No Land's Man*)

My trip to visit my sister and brother-in-law in Louisiana was bittersweet; once again, a play of polarities. My brother-in-law's lung cancer treatment toll was evident with loss of hair and energy. However, I got to see my niece, nephew, and their kids; my, how they had grown, bright-eyed and bushy tailed. My ex-brother-in-law was there as well; it was nice to see the reconciliation with my sister. One night my sister and I stayed up late sipping wine and sharing anecdotes about our family history and dynamics, a subject that to some degree or another is a petri dish of disappointment and resentment for many of us. Thankfully, the Self is a sanctuary.

How can you go wrong reading Stephen King's *On Writing: A Memoir of the Craft*? His advice on omitting useless words made good sense but easier said than done. However, the most significant revelation for me was his take concerning the plot. He doesn't have a predetermined plot when he starts a story. He lets the plot develop as he's writing. I was fortunate with this memoir; the plot was a given. I just followed what I had journaled. Creating a story, especially fiction, from scratch is an incredible feat. There are so many different aspects to consider from theme to character development. Whether I've succeeded in character development in this chronicle is questionable. I suspect several folks mentioned in this memoir, including my ex-wives, would agree.

WAS management hired the recruiter they had used in the past to interview the sales force. With the promise of anonymity, her mission was to identify what was wrong with the sales force resulting in lower sales numbers. It was an example of the old logical argument: a mistake in the premise necessarily leads to an error in the conclusion. The mistaken premise was the notion there was something wrong with the sales force. Actually, the problem was management. We had successfully established our brand in the library market and were failing to take further advantage with additional product. The president didn't want to admit to his miscalculation of the education market and how it had adversely affected the fortunes of the company. The recruiter didn't take a shine to my analysis above and took offense to my characterization of management as "fucked up." She thought my cussing inappropriate, I thought not. No additional feedback on our interviews was ever provided.

Treat employees like they will make a difference and they will. (Jim Goodnight, CEO SAS)

I attended the state library conference in late October. As usual, the conference provided me with the opportunity to meet and greet and catch up with librarians and friends. The conversations varied from library shoptalk to industry gossip. Librarians, especially public librarians, are not easily pigeonholed; primarily because of what type of library they hail from (i.e., urban, suburban or small town). Almost to a tee, they are conscientious and compassionate. I loved selling to libraries. It was a skill and a thrill, no denying. The buzz kill was the cash flow crunch. Management had miscalculated revenue and was in panic mode. Commissions were withheld, expense reimbursements delayed, and the president fired my immediate manager and VP of sales. For the first time in my WAS career, the idea that the company might not survive crossed my mind.

The following week I conducted training sessions in Fort Myers and Sarasota which were designed to show the library staff how to use the software and further highlight the educational benefits for the kids. Training was fun. During one of my sessions, I was hitting all the notes and was asked if I was a stand-up comedian on the side. To avoid traveling on Friday nights, I cashed in some hotel points and stayed at the downtown St. Pete Hilton with a lovely view of Tampa Bay. I planned on meeting Johnny but didn't feel up to his plan. I ended up at the hotel bar where I carried on with a cute lady resulting in the exchange of telephone numbers; however, the next morning's hangover had no redeemable value.

October '14 ended with a bang. The state librarian informed me of the plan to purchase numerous learning centers for public libraries across the state in December. It meant my sales quota was given to me gift-wrapped in time for the holidays. However, the thrill of the sale was dimmed by the prospect of the company declaring bankruptcy and/or being purchased. Morale was plummeting. I was asked for sales forecasts twice a week (forecasts don't change that quickly). Fellow sales reps and I reviewed the worst-case scenarios. Misery shared, misery halved.

Congress with a religious, radical Republican majority was worse than I feared. Their belief in the good old days was based on fantasy and fiction; a dark dystopia set in the well-armed Wild West town of Bethlehem. What they were trying to implement concerned me; that is, further erode the separation between church and state (i.e., achieve a theocracy). They also wanted to add more uninsured with the repeal the Obamacare as well as split up families by deporting as many undocumented immigrants as possible. And, last but not least, they wanted to conduct another expensive ground war and ineffective occupation in the Middle East.

> That mismatch between parties and governing institutions is exacerbated by the fact that the polarization is asymmetric. Republicans have become a radical insurgency— ideologically extreme, contemptuous of the inherited policy regime, scornful of compromise, unpersuaded by conventional understanding of facts, evidence, and science; and dismissive of the legitimacy of their political opposition. The evidence of this asymmetry is overwhelming. (Thomas Mann; *The Atlantic*)

Layla and I scheduled my birthday party the weekend before Thanksgiving. Layla and boyfriend, Terry and Leo, Peter and Pat, Cindy, Tim, and Karla were of good cheer. The weather was cold but clear. The food was delectable; once again, a Mexican mix: tostadas, queso, guacamole, salsa/chips, refried beans, corn on the cob, and flan. Beer, weed, and wine were plentiful as well. Good-natured conversations flowed freely, each of us wearing some sort of hat which added to the frivolity. The only hiccup occurred when Karla made a romantic overture which I turned down. She got angry and left in a huff. She apologized the next morning and acknowledged that I had been upfront about having no romantic interest since the get-go years ago when we met. Karla, much to her credit, didn't hang on to the hurt feelings and let it pass.

A new Thanksgiving tradition had been established. Celebrating Thanksgiving in Atlanta with my brother, sister-in-law, and family had seen its day. Like last year, Layla's mother and boyfriend drove up from Jacksonville to celebrate the holiday. Layla's recently divorced friend and her family joined in the celebration. Everyone had a good time sharing entertaining anecdotes. We feasted on a variety of dishes with the quiche getting top ranking in my opinion. Layla's new home easily accommodated the numbers. I was pleased to see her happy with her new place; pleasure shared pleasure doubled.

I finalized the large sale with the state library in mid-December. The director and her staff exuded personable professionalism. I walked out of the meeting feeling fine with a contract in hand. An hour later, the WAS CFO informed me that a down payment of 50% would be necessary because of limited credit due to bankruptcy. I got angry at the CFO for dropping it in my lap at the last moment. Had I known beforehand, I could have made it part of the final negotiation. I hoped the customer wouldn't get unnerved. Thankfully, the state librarian handled it with aplomb. I was having an award-winning year. However, the commission would not be paid until the end of the next year's 1st quarter. Whether the company would still be in business and able to honor such was debatable.

For the most part, I was handling the tenuous business situation with equanimity. However, I started feeling an occasional low-grade headache and dizziness not unlike what I experienced years before when I lived in Austin. I figured it was HBP. I went to the doctor to adjust my medication. However, my HBP was better than before; even took, an EKG—numbers were good. Blood work numbers were decent as well. The doctor opted for the fallback diagnosis, stress, and recommended mindfulness, another term for seeing, which I practiced regularly. So, I racked it up to the inevitable discomforts of an older body.

To celebrate Christmas, Layla and I ate dinner at one of our favorite Indian restaurants. She was feeling blue due to boyfriend problems; issues that had been swept under the rug or not acknowledged at all. Transiting Pluto (subconscious, purging) conjunct her Uranus (unexpected change) and squared her Sun (basic identity and expression); not to be outdone, transiting Neptune (inspiration, confusion) was squaring her Moon (needs, reactions. Her relationship drama and my romantic failures reminded me of why I had remained single for the previous three years. Solitude was a restorative and a prerogative.

Chapter 21: Resignation

> You are not a person, but the awareness in which the person arises. (Greg Goode; *Standing As Awareness*)

Another company sales meeting was scheduled for January '15 in **picturesque** Scottsdale, AZ. I considered feigning sickness by using HBP as an excuse. However, I was the top salesperson, and I didn't want anything getting in the way of my commission payment. I asked Self for forbearance. It was curious how the word forbearance popped up, came to mind. I couldn't remember ever using the word before. I looked up the definition: restraint and tolerance. Not exactly my strong suit. Based on some of my mental chatter about the meeting, I was going to need such in spades.

After my flight to Phoenix, I started feeling inner ear congestion, ringing, and occasional dizziness. On the second day, the wooziness got worse, so I went back to my room to lie down. The good news, I missed substantial portions of the sales meeting which consisted of some new sales reporting technique that was supposedly going to change WAS's fortunes. It was some rah-rah cheerleader crap some of which I already did without the pom-poms and acrobatic stunts. The purveyor of this nostrum was the new sales manager.

The president behaved with disdain. His declarations and digressions sucked the air out of the room. It was difficult to witness; his wounded ego, the result of mismanaging the company into bankruptcy, was disguising his basic decency. The most likely buyer was a company that specialized in turnarounds. I planned to stick around until I got my commission payment; unfortunately, not a done deal due to the uncertain financial footing of the company.

On the flight back home, I had the chance to read *The Sense of Style: The Thinking Person's Guide to Writing in the 21st Century* by Steven Pinker. He's a professor of psycholinguistics at Harvard. Along with my misgivings about spelling in English was my apprehension about grammar. I found his analysis and recommendations about writing refreshing, especially his advice about having a clear conception of what I wanted to communicate. However, in my darker moments, I doubted I'd know a clear conception if it bit me in the ass. By the way, hail the serial comma!

> The graybeard sensibilities of the style mavens come not just from an underappreciation of the fact of language change but from a lack of reflection on their own psychology. As people age, they confuse changes in themselves with changes in the world, and changes in the world with moral decline—the illusion of the good old days. And so every generation believes that the kids today are degrading the language and taking civilization down with it. (Steven Pinker; *The Sense of Style: The Thinking Person's Guide to Writing in the 21st Century*)

Back home, the discussion with my GP about the wooziness was inconclusive; however, we did conclusively determine that my BP monitor was malfunctioning. My BP was above average but not enough to account for the symptoms I was suffering. Once again, stress was the fallback diagnosis. To be on the safe side, he recommended I see a cardiologist. I didn't bother to mention my inner ear congestion and ringing, figuring it had to do with flying.

Terry called a couple of days later needing to chat. She was struggling with an emotional funk. Leo was working from his home office instead of the HQ office. Her alone time had been substantially curtailed. I recounted my recent brush with Obama and his large entourage at the hotel in Scottsdale where both of us had stayed. I never actually saw Obama; though I did converse with a couple of his security team members at the restaurant. After my description, Terry went off on a political tangent that smacked of racism. I was taken aback and hung up. She called the next day and apologized citing too much wine. I had no room to judge; I was hungover from drinking too much wine. Let opinions come and go like clouds in the sky. Here we are Aware Space where there is no divide.

Given my uncertain future with WAS, I warmed up my ideas of retiring to Central or South America. I was 62 which meant I could claim Social Security. Via the internet, I researched retirement options in various countries; Panama and Costa Rica stood out. They offered a significantly cheaper cost of living and inexpensive health care due to some form of universal health care. I wouldn't qualify for the American single payer system (Medicare) until age 65. Private health insurance premiums were prohibitive having risen close to 40% since 2008. The biggest drawback would be the long distance between my daughter and me.

The national annual library conference was in Chicago. As I've mentioned, I enjoyed conferences due to the ease of meeting, greeting, and hanging out with librarians and friends. However, the idea of spending time with upper management and their desperation was less than attractive. I decided not to attend claiming health issues which wasn't inaccurate; I was still bothered by inner ear funkiness and afraid flying would be aggravating. Two field sales reps and two key HQ folks had jumped ship for more promising jobs which spoke volumes. There was a lot of bitching going on, and morale was scraping the bottom.

On my first sick day I treated myself to a weekday movie matinee; it's a great time of day because there are no crowds to contend with. I saw *Fury*. It took place in 1945 towards the end of WWII. Brad Pitt led a group of tanks in a battle against superior German tanks. It was a vivid depiction of "war is hell" (attributed to Civil War General Sherman which is the type of American tank highlighted in the film). I gave it thumbs up. Typical of my routine, after the movie I had a club sandwich at Cheesecake Factory. Then I strolled through the mall; everything was lit up.

> Heaven is more Earth than Earth is Earth. The scenery of Heaven is Earth's scenery viewed as it really is. Which is to say, lit up and profoundly transformed in the Clear Light of Heaven. (Douglas Harding; *Look For Yourself*)

At the beginning of February, the bankruptcy process was delayed by management; they wanted to consider other bids, hoping to get a better offer. It smelled of more desperation. I maintained a wait and see mode (better yet, a see and wait mode). That is, stay on board, so to speak, until receipt of my commission which was scheduled for the end of March; however, given the impending bankruptcy, an uncertainty. The quarter before management had delayed commission payments for a couple of months.

I was about to drift off to sleep when Johnny called. He needed to talk, to tango, to tell a story or two. His divorce was starting to take shape; within a month or two he would be on his own. I was happy for him. My two divorces were difficult yet very different experiences due to having a child (or no child), finances, stage in life, personal goals, professional status, etc. However, both marriages were stews lacking an essential ingredient or two. Regardless of what I did or didn't do, the mishmash proved unsuitable. Finally, I gave up, threw in the kitchen towel, so to speak. The relief of letting go was the relish!

> Some people think that it's holding on that makes one strong; sometimes it's letting go. (Unknown)

It took weeks to arrange an appointment with a cardiologist. The consultation was inconclusive. My numbers showed no abnormalities or areas of concern. In fact, he lowered the dosage on my HBP medication to the minimum. And, because he had no definitive answers, he recommended a test for a rare adrenal gland condition which I refused. I got the impression the profit motive was at play which reinforced my opinion about the need for a universal healthcare system that covered the costs of essential healthcare. Contrary to public perception, the federal government funds most health care via billions of dollars in tax subsidies. It also funds healthcare for the elderly (Medicare), veterans (VA), etc.; however, taxpayers are paying more and getting less because of the profit motivated pharma/medical/insurance complex.

Along with bitching about Obamacare and/or universal health care, the radical and religious Right was trying to repeal Common Core educational standards and expand school voucher programs. First, *not* having a "clear set of shared goals and expectations for what knowledge and skills will help our students succeed" is fucking stupid. Standards provide parents with the necessary metrics to make informed decisions about their children's education options. Second, parents deserve good schools for their kids; if the local public school is deficient, there should be other options, Third, based on having attended *and* taught in public, private, and parochial schools, there is no single answer. Each child's needs are different including learning style, motivation, prior knowledge, family circumstances, and health. Fourth, school voucher programs aren't a panacea; there has been financial wrongdoing and grave education lapses due to lack of regulatory supervision. The idea of my tax dollars funding a religious fundamentalist school teaching anti-science, superstition, and sectarianism isn't appealing to me. Last, the cohesiveness or team spirit engendered by kids attending the same neighborhood school shouldn't be underestimated.

The religious Right was also furrowing their brow about the decline in religious observance; they still hadn't figured out that religious participation and righteousness aren't synonymous. According to a Pew Research analysis conducted in October 2012, religious service attendance was falling. 20% of Americans don't have a religious affiliation, and a growing number are less observant. Even though Christianity is the dominant religion in the USA, the religious Right was claiming persecution all the while discounting and disparaging fellow Christians, Jews, Muslims, Buddhists, atheists, agnostics, and spiritual-but-not-religious. This judgmental attitude was promoted by a few prominent politicians and preachers with questionable agendas. Spirit is open; we are built for loving.

Sam Harris' book, *Waking Up: A Guide to Spirituality Without Religion,* caught my attention with its catchy title. From what I gathered he was a neuroscientist into spirituality which struck me as an unusual combination. I checked out the eBook contents on Amazon; one of the chapters was titled "Having No Head." It was a recommendation of Douglas Harding's headless experiment that directs attention to What or Who we really are. I downloaded Harris' book.

> Harding's assertion that he has no head must be read in the first-person sense; the man was not claiming to have been literally decapitated. From a first-person point of view, his emphasis on headlessness is a stroke of genius that offers an unusually clear description of what it's like to glimpse the nonduality of consciousness. (Sam Harris; *Waking Up: A Guide to Spirituality Without Religion*)

Then, via a Google search on Sam Harris, I discovered he's a famous atheist who considers religion the reason for many problems in modern life. If I have characterized his opinion correctly, I have no problem with such. There's no doubt that most religions have condoned irrational, irresponsible, and reprehensible behavior through the ages. However, I believe and/or hope religions will evolve and shed their divisiveness through an emphasis on inclusive and transcendental beliefs based on the recognition of the nonduality of Spirit that is often ignored or not emphasized.

In addition to not having to rely on antiquated belief systems, having no head brings about self-acceptance. I don't have to change my personality; a quixotic quest at best. In fact, trying to do so, gets in the way. Awareness always is regardless of culture, karma, class or other considerations (genetics, planetary aspects, family dynamics, etc.). All I do is turn my attention around 180 degrees and be at Home. In place of an imagined face, I find Aware Space for everything sparkling. What a deal, I lost my head and discovered Love.

> How wonderful is the path of love, where the headless one is exalted! (Hafiz; 1315-1390)

My business trip to southern Georgia and northern Florida was successful. I accomplished my business objectives; namely, I met with the state librarian and firmed up a couple of future sales. The trip offered some lovely vistas; that is, live oaks draped in Spanish moss along with spacious skies dotted with cumulus clouds. However, there were clouds of a different sort as well: concerns about career and retirement. To avoid Friday evening travel, I took advantage of some points and checked into a hotel on Jax Beach. Then I settled in at the bar and wallowed in self-pity; loneliness's favorite indulgence. The next morning, I met Bert at one of my favorite breakfast spots on A1A. His romantic complications with a lady he was dating provided comic relief and reminded me of why I was single. My drive to the airport reminded me of Who I am as the world, clouds and all, passed through me, Awareness. No longer lonely, I relished my Aloneness.

Just after I got back from my trip, Johnny called. I knew I was in for a doozy when he started out by saying I wouldn't believe his tale. He was staying with friends he'd known for years in St. Pete. His recently divorced wife, Phoebe, who lives in Chicago, convinced the St. Pete police that Tommy might be suicidal. The cops followed up and readily determined he was no threat to himself. Johnny, with his Venus conjunct Neptune, was a romantic who drank too much, but he wasn't suicidal. Later that same evening Will called. The sale of his condo was proceeding as were his plans of moving to Utah along with his son. I shared Johnny's story. We laughed and commiserated. Both of us have been bamboozled by romance, a drug like no other.

In Chapel Hill, the town over from where I live, a maniacal man murdered three UNC students in cold blood. Initially, it was portrayed as some quarrel about parking lot spaces at the apartment complex where all of them lived. However, from his Facebook postings, it became apparent it was a hate crime. The victims were Muslim, and he shot them in head execution style. They were UNC students and outstanding citizens that deserved the chance to live and pursue their dreams. Dreams cut short by an angry man with a large arsenal and a license to carry a concealed firearm.

The increasing number of mass shootings and gun-related deaths in the USA was a classic case of the elephant in the room nobody was doing anything substantive about out denial and/or fear. Around 1.4 million Americans have been killed, excluding suicide, by guns between 1968 and 2011. The NRA/GOP answer was more people with more guns shooting more people while repeating the mantra "guns don't kill people; people kill people."

> Bazookas don't kill people; people kill people. Although it is obviously true that bazookas are only proximate causes, it clearly does not follow that bazookas should be legal. Yes, bazookas don't kill people, people do—but bazookas make it a lot easier for people to kill people, and in great numbers. Further, a bazooka would not be useful for much else besides mass murders. Bazookas clearly should be illegal and the fact that they would only be proximate causes to mass murders does not change this. (Professor David Kyle Johnson; *Psychology Today* 2/12/13)

A winter storm came through town with 20 centimeters of snow; fortunately without freezing rain experienced by neighbors in the southern part of the state. I still got a thrill when it snowed; it created different visual elements that invited a photograph or two. There were scattered power outages coupled with impassable roads. Without the din of traffic, there was a pleasant silence. I spent the morning clearing pathways and steps; my sore lower back told me stories the rest of the day. Two days later the paths and stairs I cleared were covered again by another snow this time topped by ice. I figured another sore back wasn't worth it.

At the beginning of March '15, my commission was paid which provided me financial maneuverability. The sale of the company was completed at the end of March. Things started unraveling quickly with the new management team. The new sales manager proved to be a snake. He fired two library reps and replaced them with friends of his, reps from a previous job who didn't know libraries and had no relationships. It didn't make good business sense. My enthusiasm, my strong suit, dimmed to a flicker. I figured it best to cover some dental expenses with company provided insurance as soon as possible. It looked like my WAS career, spanning eight years in all, was ending.

Layla came by one afternoon after work; both of us questioning our particular career trajectories. My struggle has been documented in this account. Layla's situation had many moving parts contributing to her angst; basically, she was getting burned out. As we chatted and visited vino, she trimmed my hair; I feigned she was cutting too much while she dramatized her Virgo fastidiousness. We had a good laugh. After she left, I found some cleaning inspiration; a bit here and there was my preference instead of letting it build up into a larger task.

It seemed for every step forward on issues such as gay rights, we seemed to take two steps back in this country. The radical and religious Right's political prowess was impressive. Even though they were a minority of the electorate, they had majorities in many state legislatures due to gerrymandering and ALEC, a nonprofit organization devoted to weakening environmental regulations, disenfranchising voters, undermining labor unions, and opposing gun control. Their latest salvo of fear and fantasy was the Religious Freedom Restoration Act. It was a legislative brew by a self-righteous crew with a frothy top of fictional persecution. It's a pale substitute for what really ails us.

Equally flustering to me, as I've mentioned before, is how business is idealized in this country. Don't get me wrong, I'm pro private enterprise. I've made a nice living via such; however, I didn't put it on a pedestal. Forgetting the Wall Street collapse of 2008, a Ponzi scheme that almost sank the world economy, politicians love to extol the supposed virtues of running government like a business (I have witnessed ethically challenged and poorly run companies). I hope compassionate or shareholder capitalism will become the norm, rather than the exception, in our society; that is, where the profit motive *and* heart become the de facto business model.

> We are a country based on capitalism, but we should just have a more compassionate capitalism. It shouldn't be just about shareholders but, more broadly, stakeholders, from your customers to the environment. (Marc Benioff, Salesforce CEO)

The new WAS president's teleconference was one of the worst I had experienced. Giving him the benefit of the doubt, I'd say he was a jerk (based on a taxonomy of bad managers I had recently developed: psychopath, asshole, or jerk). His new travel and entertainment rules were unrealistic, onerous, and not business friendly. I resigned via email which prompted him to call me. I enjoyed the luxury of speaking my mind about the new T&E, the keyword being bullshit.

He assured me they were guidelines, not written in stone, and offered me a 15% salary bump to come back. I accepted the offer despite my doubts about his management style.

Angles between planets are called aspects whether in the birth chart or via transits and progressions. The most noticeable aspects are 0° (conjunction), 90° (square), and 180° (opposition) followed by trines (120°) and sextiles (60°). Angles are operative within 2 to 8 degrees exactness depending on the planets involved. At the risk of too much more astrologese, transiting Saturn was conjunct my Sun. I experienced a downshift in physical energy coupled with enhanced self-reliance and solitude. Another obvious one was transiting Uranus square my natal Uranus and trine my ascendant; ridiculous rules and regulations were not my cup of tea evidenced by my recent resignation.

On the developmental or predictive side, I was looking forward to the promising transits of Jupiter (expansion) and Pluto (transformation); that is, transiting Jupiter conjunct my natal Pluto (in 1st house of self-expression) and transiting Pluto trine my natal Jupiter (in 10th house or career). Think of it as a double dose of Jupiter and Pluto that boded well for personal freedom and career change.

> Astrology in its most general definition rests on a conception of the cosmos as a coherent embodiment of creative intelligence, purpose, and meaning expressed through a constant complex correspondence between astronomical patterns and human experience. (Richard Tarnas; *Cosmos and Psyche: Intimations of a New World View*)

A few weeks after the T&E regulations drama, the WAS president issued a non-compete agreement requiring my signature. My sister's significant other, a corporate lawyer, tore it apart as vague and indefensible. He recommended I not sign it unless substantial changes were made. Then the president issued the revised Personal Time Off numbers. They took last December's numbers as part of the current year's PTO total. I took a whole week at the end of December based on the previous year's numbers. It was a shitty thing to do and another reason to resign, another nail in the WAS coffin, so to speak. The upcoming Florida state conference would be my last WAS commitment.

The library conference in mid-May was bittersweet. It was fun interacting with librarians and various industry friends. However, it was sad knowing it was my last foreseeable function as a sales representative calling on public libraries. And, I was passing on some good business deals I'd been working on for weeks if not months. The conference was held at a resort near Disney World; the grounds garnished with colorful tropical landscaping and a big cage with a macaw parrot. He dropped a large tail feather which I accepted as a parting gift and is now part of my home decor. When I got back to my home office, I submitted my two-week resignation notice...again. It was a relief knowing I would no longer have to put up with management manure. With a resume reflecting success, I was leaving on my own terms with a comfortable financial cushion. I could relax (my new favorite mantra) before embarking on another job quest. Using airline points, I planned on visiting Will in Utah.

Chapter 22: Solution

Why should one who knows his Self to be That in which universes rise and fall like waves in the sea, run hither and thither like a suffering creature? (Ashtavakra Gita)

My plumbing problem with an outside faucet proved challenging. I felt a bit out of my league. However, with mobile phone pictures, I was able to explain to the Home Depot associate what I needed. His advice was a boon; a crimping tool which I rented. A few strategic crimps later the leak was no longer. Since I had cleared out the storage closet to get to the plumbing, I figured it was time to build some shelving, so back to Home Depot I went. A couple hours later, shelf space to spare. Then I sat back and played a game of Hearts. I won on the last hand by shooting the Moon!

After picking me up at the Salt Lake City airport, Will, the quintessential tour guide, introduced me to some of the many natural wonders Utah offers. To begin with was Antelope Island, a peninsula surrounded by the Great Salt Lake. Also, we visited Bear Lake on the Idaho border, and Tony Grove up in the Wasatch Mountains with snow still about and birds bountiful. The tour also included some manmade marvels; that is, the Temple Square in Salt Lake City where the Mormon Tabernacle is located and its famous pipe organ; an Elgar piece shook the seats. I took a couple memorable photos of the production; unknown to me, there was a photography prohibition. Forgiveness was in order since I didn't know to ask for permission. Back at Nick's place, we enjoyed some savory dishes, fine wine, and entertaining TV. Also, I got to hang out a bit with his brother and family. Fine folks for sure.

When I got back from Utah, my idea was to begin the final edit of this chronicle. I thought being out of work would lend itself to editing what I'd written. Nada, nothing. I despaired about the lack of inspiration; I thought more about home improvement. One afternoon Layla stopped by after work. We drank wine while she kicked my ass in Zilch. The next morning, I woke up hungover...again. Moderation continued to be a vexing varietal to cultivate. For most folks two or three alcoholic beverages was a nice buzz; for me, it meant I was just warming up. My habitual wine overindulgence wasn't dissimilar from my tobacco addiction I overcame years before. A few subconscious rationalizations would kick in, and I was off to races, so to speak, with a couple of bottles of cabernet sauvignon. I had to find a resolution; willpower only worked for a while.

Life is a play of polarities with ego intermittently refereeing. However, ego is prone to boastfulness; it is easily seduced by self-importance. News anchor Brian Williams apologized on national TV for lying; that is, spicing up his role in some stories he reported. He said, "I'm sorry for what happened. I am different as a result and I expect to be held to a different standard. This was clearly ego driven, a desire to better my role in a story I was already in." It seemed to me a lot of what we do is ego driven; the little one clamoring for more and/or demanding less. In my case, I added vino to my vanity, alcohol to my arrogance, which made the shadow of deceit harder to see through.

151

A shadow of a different sort was spreading across our society: mass shootings. On June 17th, 2015, another mass shooting was committed by a psychotic 21-year-old white man hoping to ignite a race war. He was invited to join a prayer meeting in the spirit of fellowship before killing nine congregants of a historic African American church in Charleston, SC. It's safe to say that we are exhausted by the gun violence, stunned by the suffering. Once again, a shooter with a muzzleloader couldn't have accomplished the horrific act. President Obama had this to say: "We as a country will have to reckon with the fact that this type of mass violence does not happen in other advanced countries." Think about it.

A month later my good friend Terry committed suicide by wrapping her mouth around a pistol barrel and pulling the trigger. Her husband, Leo, called me in the middle of the night in a state of shock with cops and investigators all about (his niece was on her way to keep him company). When I got there the next morning, Leo looked ragged but was able to provide me with more details. He had gone to bed earlier than Terry which was usually the case. Sometime after he fell asleep, she walked down to the cul-de-sac and shot herself which awakened him. Terry had a drinking problem and feared early-onset Alzheimer's (which hadn't been diagnosed). She was seeing a psychologist and taking an anti-depressant.

Layla stopped by after I got back from visiting Leo. Like me, she was dumbfounded and heartbroken; she was very fond of Terry. Earlier that week, Layla and I had a charming conversation with Terry on the phone. We wondered how she could be so delightful and engaging just a few days before killing herself. We reminisced about our favorite times, especially in Birmingham hanging out in the kitchen or on the back of her beat-up pickup truck. Synchronistically, a few days later, I was in my office straightening up when a picture of us on the back of her pickup truck fell onto the carpet. Unknown to me, it was stuck behind another photo I had moved.

Five days later Layla and I attended the celebration ceremony of Terry at a funeral home meeting room to officially say goodbye. Upon signing in both of us burst into tears. We chuckled as we dabbed our tears with tissue; both of us surprised by our sudden emotion. From that point on, I had no idea when I'd get choked up as I exchanged anecdotes with the other guests, mostly Terry's family and gardening club friends. After the celebration, family and friends gathered at their home. It afforded me the opportunity to meet Leo's sons and, most significantly, converse with Terry's daughter; I hadn't seen her in twenty years since I lived with her mother. In addition to grief, she was angry; her mother wouldn't be around to enjoy her two grandchildren. There was no religious ceremony; that would be conducted at the funeral in Birmingham the following week for the benefit of her mother.

> Suicide rates have increased in nearly every state over the past two decades, and half of the states have seen suicide rates go up more than 30 percent. Suicide is a major public health issue, accounting for nearly 45,000 deaths in 2016 alone. (Centers for Disease Control and Prevention)

Layla had become discontent with her job due to a combination of factors from workload to office personalities and politics. She was recruited by a headhunter which resulted in her accepting a job offer with a substantial raise that was home-based. I figured she'd appreciate working from home; I had done so for twenty years and found it superior to an office environment. Our creative juices flowed as we figured out how to convert her guest bedroom into a home office. Layla found a desk that moved up and down allowing for sitting as well as standing. Sharing these moments with her was priceless.

There's no arguing about aspects between planets such as conjunctions, oppositions, squares, trines, and sextiles; they're astronomical fact measured by degree and minute. Ascertaining the meaning is where astrology shines. Back in May, I mentioned I was looking forward to seeing the correspondence with my experience concerning the transit of Jupiter conjunct natal Pluto and the transit of Pluto trine Jupiter/Midheaven. It was a double dose of Jupiter and Pluto that boded well for personal freedom and career change. Well, I looked around and, lo and behold, such had manifested. In the meantime, another Pluto transit was dawning that promised stimulating transformation; that is, Pluto conjunct my Venus (relationships, aesthetics, creativity, etc.) and sextile my Moon (mood, needs, etc.). I was curious to see what the Storehouse came up with.

Thoughts of officially retiring started to multiply. I had applied for a handful of jobs which I was qualified for and rejected or not responded to. I figured it was my age which could be ascertained from my resume. I started gathering more information on health insurance and Social Security. Health insurance costs were steep; close to $900/month and I'd have to wait until next calendar year for Social Security due to my income. This prompted me to dust off the option of retiring in Central America; I decided an investigatory trip to Panama was in order. It offered a cheaper cost of living, good healthcare, and dependable transportation. In preparation for my trip, I read David McCullough's *The Path Between the Seas: The Creation of the Panama Canal*. I didn't realize the amount of effort it took to build the canal, initially by France *and* then the US. It was an impressive feat; the equivalent of landing on the Moon for that generation.

My trip to Panama at the end of August '15 was the last of my frequent flier points on Delta. I was scheduled to arrive late Monday night and return the following Sunday. Upon my return from Panama, I would decide what course to pursue; the pros and cons would align and feel right about remaining in Durham or relocating. I opted to disregard a dull headache thinking it might be HBP (I was dealing with another unreliable monitoring device). The plane flight was uneventful. However, the next morning I woke up in Panama City feeling undeniably worse. After some deliberation, I decided to cancel the rest of my Panama plans. It was best that I wasn't thousands of miles away from home feeling under the weather. Not feeling well while traveling is a drag; while overseas it's drag squared. I returned home the following day. It was another lesson about listening to my body. For unknown reasons flying aggravated my symptoms. I set an appointment to see my GP.

The GP wasn't concerned with my EKG and blood pressure numbers which were slightly above average. Whatever was causing the headaches, dizziness, and ringing was non-cardiac in nature. That was good news. The bad news was my GP didn't know what was causing the symptoms. After my appointment, I took a walk and noticed inner ear stuffiness. I wiggled my jaw like I would after a plane trip to pop my ears which produced some minor relief. I informed my GP about such thinking that information might provide him with valuable insight. He prescribed a nasal decongestant which didn't help but led him to recommend an ENT (ears, nose, and throat) specialist. Long story short; TMJ (temporomandibular joint disorder) was the diagnosis. The symptoms were aggravated by my air travel, ear popping, and gum chewing habit. Minus those activities the symptoms subsided.

Via an Amazon recommendation, I downloaded *The Art of Memoir* by Mary Karr. She highlighted the role of memory and how it filters experience based on personal proclivities; even more so when writing a memoir. Truth can suffer along the way. To illustrate this, unknown to her students, she purposely engaged in a disagreement with a co-conspirator. Then she had her students describe the argument. The differences in their accounts were substantial. Each of us filters or interprets things or situations differently. I felt a stirring regarding my memoir.

I figured my journals were an advantage; they described incidents and provided details I had entirely forgotten. I didn't have to rely as much on my memory. That's not to say there wasn't room for my dusty ego, a trickster at times, to loiter. What I found most difficult was deciding what stories to include and not. I wanted to write an honest account of my journey, the enlightenments and embarrassments, the failures and successes. However, I had some unfinished business… my drinking problem. Trying to spiritually bypass it with various rationalizations hadn't worked.

> No matter how much you're gunning for truth, the human ego is also a stealthy, low-crawling bastard, and for pretty much everybody, getting used to who you are is a lifelong spiritual struggle. (Mary Karr; *The Art of Memoir*)

Speaking of low-crawling bastards, the Republican presidential candidates certainly qualified with their encouragement of sectarianism, provincialism, and nationalism. Trump's "make America great again" was another one of his con jobs (i.e., Taj Mahal casino, Trump University, etc.). Exactly when was this great age? It couldn't have been during slavery days; a disgrace beyond explanation. It couldn't have been during the American apartheid period after slavery when Jim Crow segregation was enforced through violence and intimidation. It couldn't have been during the Trail of Tears and other violent relocations of Native Americans. It couldn't have been during the 1930s when tens of thousands of Mexican-American *citizens* were forcefully deported to Mexico because of their ethnicity.

Every era is a mix of good and evil. In WWII the US was instrumental in freeing occupied Europe and Asia from fascism but also incarcerated Japanese *citizens* in concentration camps. During the '60s the Peace Corps, a volunteer program was initiated by the US government, provided social, economic, and technical assistance to developing countries while promoting mutual understanding around the world. Simultaneously, the US conducted the Vietnam War; a military failure with huge environmental, psychological, and societal effects still felt today.

Regardless of political affiliation, Congressional members were taking advantage of an empty democracy all the way to the bank. Even though elections took place, representative democracy in the US had been gerrymandered to a ridiculous extent. Also, even though Congressional approval was at record lows, close 90% of incumbents were reelected. 50% of members of Congress were millionaires with the net worth of most members increasing dramatically during office. Special interests and oligarchs had purchased our democracy leaving a façade festooned with rising economic immobility and inequality. Fareed Zakaria's *The Future of Freedom: Illiberal at Home and Abroad* presented a cogent analysis of this worldwide trend. By the way, his explanation of why specific services such as healthcare, education, and law/legal systems are best administered by the government and not commercialized should be required reading.

I ran across a phrase in *A Walk in the Woods* by Bill Bryson that describes many locales I have visited or lived in: "a ceaseless unfolding pageant of commercial hideousness." Think Route 19 along the west coast of Florida running north from St. Pete to Crystal River. It is strip mall commercialism run amuck for 80 miles or so. Any attempt to regulate such was deemed unfair or socialism by greedy developers who have controlled the Florida legislature for decades. Don't get me wrong, development isn't bad; it simply needs to be done in an eco-friendly and aesthetically pleasing manner.

Most mornings I walked the same trail, like a cherished song that never gets old. There was always something attractive from sparkling leaves to chirping chickadees to the occasional faint fragrance of a flower. And, along for the walk was the ego/mind, a good servant but a lousy master, occasionally getting wrapped up in idiotic chatter. However, also appearing out the Storehouse were insights, solutions, and edits. Awareness was at hand; not hard to reach but impossible to avoid.

> At every single moment, there is a spontaneous awareness of whatever happens to be present and that simple, spontaneous, effortless awareness is ever-present Spirit itself. Even if you think you don't see it, that very awareness is it. And thus, the ultimate state of consciousness -- intrinsic Spirit itself -- is not hard to reach but impossible to avoid. (Ken Wilber; *The Eye of Spirit*)

At the end of September '15, during the Pope Francis' tour of the US, he met secretly with the government official that denied marriage licenses to gay couples. It was a wrinkle in my opinion of him. The religious Right had a heyday. However, he also met with a gay couple, friends from Argentina. The Left smugly chuckled. Back to the official--she had the right to her religious beliefs; however, she refused to do her job which was civil in nature, not religious. She should have been fired. Our laws are secular; free from religious restrictions for good reasons; laws inspired by religious convictions are often counterproductive such as Prohibition. If a religious restriction happens to coincide with a secular rule set by the Constitution and administered through civil institutions, fine and dandy; otherwise, stay the fuck out my bedroom, wine cabinet, stash box, laptop, and how I opt to die.

Being a Leo ascendant or rising means that I am prone to expressing myself dramatically. For instance, when I entertained the Panera staff with some silly antics which resulted in getting a free cookie. Or, when I stopped by the dry cleaner and performed my rendition of Dick Van Dyke tripping over the ottoman in the iconic opening to *The Dick Van Dyke Show*. The clerk laughed; he was blessed with a sense of humor. I told him how much I loved that routine and "slapdick" in general. My unintentional malapropism led me to pantomime slapping my dick. We laughed until we cried. Maybe you had to be there.

Every couple of months Nora and I reached out via email; she helped edit initial parts of my memoir. She contacted me on her way to visit her fiancé in the mid-West. She recommended catching comic Tom Papa who was scheduled to perform the following night at the classic Carolina Theater in downtown Durham. I figured I could use a good laugh. He was hilarious. His jokes about marriage and family were spot on, and his humorous bit about going to Disneyland with his wife and two daughters reminded me of similar excursions with my daughter and why I'm not a big fan of such entertainment venues. It's a small world.

It came as no surprise that John Cleese's memoir, *So, Anyway,* was a good read. Cleese's tangents about growing up were entertaining and thought-provoking. His reflections on the effect of peer group influence resonated with mine. In a family setting, we are frequently confined or defined by the opinions of family members, namely our parents, but equally significant, our siblings. As the youngest of four children, I was often told how to behave by the whole corps. Once I developed independent friendships with my peer group, I discovered a freer expression of my personality. Cleese's take on humor was spot on as well. Over the years I have encountered some truly humorless people. I feel sorry for them. Laughter and love go hand in hand.

> A good sense of humour is the sign of a healthy perspective, which is why people who are uncomfortable around humour are either pompous (inflated) or neurotic (oversensitive). Pompous people mistrust humour because at some level they know their self-importance cannot survive very long in such an atmosphere, so they criticise it as "negative" or "subversive." Neurotics, sensing that humour is always ultimately critical, view it as therefore unkind and destructive, a reductio ad absurdum which leads to political correctness. (John Cleese; *So, Anyway…*)

I decided to go ahead and declare for Social Security and register for ACA or Obamacare (which would reduce my health insurance costs by two thirds). Additional financial breathing room was provided when I discovered I could tap into my pension and not have to wait until 65. It put moving to Central America on a back burner. Finances would be tight but manageable. The decision was a relief. And, as a reminder of my small self's mortality, one of Layla's friend's father died of a heart attack at 67. Now is a present; I was celebrating.

Part of that celebration was Liz Gilbert's *Big Magic: Creative Living Beyond Fear.* It was another example of grace, a free and unearned gift from the Storehouse falling into my lap, so to speak. I saw mention of it when I was looking for another book on Amazon. It was a good read and the inspiration I needed. One of my biggest takeaways was the need for courage—courage to create and not let stupid ego/fear chatter fuck things up. Feeling energized and capable, I started editing my memoir.

> Pure creativity is magnificent expressly because it is the opposite of everything else in life that's essential or inescapable (food, shelter, medicine, rule of law, social order, community and familial responsibility, sickness, loss, death, taxes, etc.). Pure creativity is something better than a necessity; it's a gift. It's the frosting. Our creativity is a wild and unexpected bonus from the universe. (Elizabeth Gilbert; *Big Magic: Creative Living Beyond Fear*)

One evening, my local TV meteorologist, recommended stepping outside to see the International Space Station "fly" overhead from the NW to SE after sunset. Wow, that was some magic as well.

Orbit height: 249 miles
Speed on orbit: 4.76 miles/s
Max speed: 17,150 mph
Launch date: November 20, 1998
Cost: $150 billion

Once a month or so, I have a dream that wakes me up. Usually, after some tossing and turning, I fall back to sleep. My dream about Terry woke me up; falling back to sleep wasn't an option. I got up and wrote the following account. I am staying in a dormitory at a meditation retreat. While unpacking my stuff Terry stops by. We are chatting when another dorm mate knocks on the door. I am about to introduce Terry when I notice Terry has decided to hide in the closet which I play along with. Then the lady steps into my room. I figure Terry's ruse will be an embarrassment but over momentarily. The lady notices Terry's foot sticking out of the closet. She gets upset that we engaged in a pretense of sorts at her expense. I walk over to her and say, "Please forgive us. We meant no harm." Poof, I'm awake. Initially, I thought it was Terry's zany way of saying "hi." However, after fifteen minutes or so of letting the dream percolate, it came to me. Terry was asking me to forgive her. She meant no harm. Through tears, I assured her of such. Happy trails, Terry.

My oldest sister's husband died after a long bout with lung cancer. Her grief was compounded by details in the will she knew nothing about. I emailed her the URL to the song, *White Bird*, by one of my favorite groups from the late sixties, *It's a Beautiful Day*. Their harmonies were exquisite, and I hoped soothing. In July of 1970, they played at the Second Atlanta International Pop Festival attended by over 500,000 folks. Overnight a bunch of farmland and pecan orchards was transformed into a city. I was peaking on LSD when they played; everything shimmered, and I was silly happy. Much later that night, better yet, early the next morning, I heard Jimi Hendrix play his rendition of *The Star-Spangled Banner*. He died two months later.

Early Sunday mornings generally isn't bad for air travel. On my way to my brother-in-law's funeral, the morning of November 1st, proved to be otherwise. I arrived at the airport around 5:30 AM to find it busy beyond expectation. After going through security, I grabbed a bite to eat at my favorite restaurant in the terminal garnished by a delightful conversation in Spanglish with the waitress, originally from Honduras. She gave me a pat on the back when I told her there was no way she could have teenage children. Seriously, she looked to be in her early 20's.

Then I headed over to my Delta gate where I was told in no uncertain terms that my chances of catching a flight were slim to none because of the inclement weather, numerous cancellations, and the resulting overflow. I figured I should check out other options via other airlines. I tried United; they were slammed due to storms in the Houston area. Then I tried American. The ticket agent was a pleasant fellow. He said the chances of getting a flight were as likely as getting more hair on his visibly bald head. I suggested maybe he could borrow some of mine which had gotten longish. We had a good laugh.

From there I moseyed over to the Delta customer service counter. At this point, I was looking at securing a refund, but I was going to give it one last shot. I got in the queue for "Special Passengers." Then I noticed an Asian woman struggling with a large cardboard box. It was held together by a cinch strap which was far from sufficient. In her broken English, she asked the counter agent for packing tape; no luck. I realized her predicament. There wasn't any place in the terminal to purchase tape. On the other side of the terminal, I saw a Starbucks.

Using international sign language, I told her to look after my luggage. I scurried over to Starbucks and asked the associate if she had packing tape. She looked at me incredulously; sitting on her sales counter was packing tape coupled with the dispenser. She handed me the device which I assured her I'd return. I scooted back and taped the Asian lady's box every which way much to her appreciation. She insisted on taking a selfie with me before her flight to Beijing. I secured my refund and return home.

I was getting used to retirement and liking it. I received confirmation from Social Security about my monthly payment scheduled to start the beginning of the new year along with my pension check. My fixed income was substantially less than what I used to make, but I wasn't complaining. Feeling energized, I spent the morning vacuuming and mopping floors. At one point I walked into the master bedroom and spontaneously said "thank you" to the Universe for my comfortable abode which was aesthetically pleasing and functionally efficient. I had to sit on the bed as waves of bliss caressed me. That evening, feeling celebratory, I drank wine. I woke up hungover and listless. I was tired of my drinking problem; I asked Spirit, Who I really am, to remove my wine habit and let me abide in abstinence.

Complete abstinence is easier than perfect moderation. (St. Augustine)

For my 63rd birthday celebration, Layla and I had dinner at Antonia's, one of our favorite downtown restaurants. The evening came together spontaneously; we had no firm idea where we were going until the last minute. The corvina or drum with the mango salsa normally used on salmon was a perfect combo. In her typical thoughtful manner, Layla gave me a couple of adult coloring books along with the necessary colored pencils. A couple days later we celebrated Thanksgiving at Layla's home with her mother and boyfriend which had become a tradition. The dinner spread was impressive with the creamed cauliflower, pecan pie, and pumpkin pie taking top honors.

I received the following email from Ben.

Yo, Bro...
Ya, finally pulled the plug ay!?! Good for you, I'm sure it actually takes a load off your situation and the "whatta I'm gonna do?" issue. You'll find when you hit 65 and are eligible for Medicare that other considerations become easier to deal with too. I get to start chemo Monday for lymphoma. Seems that bad boy sat indolently in my system for many years (just watching the cars going by), and has now decided to become active. It's stage 4, BUT, all lymphoma is stage 4. Since it is present throughout your bone marrow that's just the way it works. I'll be in chemo for 6 months, then we'll reassess. The regimen isn't bad. Two days of chemo totaling about 8 hours, then repeating that on a 28-day basis. The potential side effects are huge in number and all over the place. But some people have little or none and some get whacked. I've got plenty of backup and support on that front. So, in the meantime, we just keep taking our vitamins and putting one foot in front of the other. Be well, Ben

Stunned and saddened, I replied with a short get well soon note and let's talk when convenient request.

In reaction to President Obama's speech on terrorism and Islam, Trump outdid the vitriol of his previous statements about Muslims. His comments about Mexican immigrants was no better. Instigating hate and fear didn't strike me as an effective means of creating a better world. The fact that most Republicans didn't condemn him was despicable. Bill Maher pinned the tail on the elephant with this observation: "I've been watching the Republican debates. I watched these eight clowns on the stage and at the end I wanted to raise my hand and say, 'I don't believe in evolution.'" The GOP was an embarrassment.

The Golden Rule has nothing to do with gold and everything to do with how gold is acquired; that is, don't treat others as you would have them not treat you. The negative and positive versions of the Golden Rule are found in religions and cultures throughout the world except on Wall Street. You might say my attitude towards Wall Street was evolving, or better yet, devolving. This development had picked up speed since the 2008 debacle, "the worst financial crisis of modern times." According to an extensive survey, there was still a shitload of shenanigans on Wall Street; the basic mindset had not changed. Big banks were still conjuring up derivatives pieced together from questionable loans and pawning them off as higher rated securities. I lost confidence; I no longer trusted the system. I converted my index funds into cash just in time to not profit from one of the best upticks in the market history.

> So, if the financial industry is to put people before profits, and society before shareholders, we need to see a change in the values and behavior of individuals themselves. We need a culture that holds individuals accountable for the consequences of their behavior—good and bad. (Christine Lagarde, managing director of the International Monetary Fund)

Towards the end of December, Johnny drove up to Chicago to stay with a friend in poor health that needed some help getting about. Johnny was recovering from PDS (Post Divorce Syndrome) but sounded happier than I had heard in a long time. He had lived with his brother the last few months where they had carpentry jobs on a big mansion being built in the Blue Ridge Mountains. He made some good money and was able to upgrade his transportation. However, Johnny's brother asked him to leave which I gathered was because of his drinking. My concern was whether in sweet home Chicago his problems and peccadilloes would worsen.

Layla and I spent Christmas Eve together. We saw *Star Wars* at the local theater complex at the mall. The plot was thin and the heartstrings missing. Unimpressed, we gave it a C. Then we had dinner at California Pizza. Layla enjoyed her salad on top of pizza; my southwestern salad was so-so. Christmas morning Layla drove to Savannah to go on a tour (think: *Midnight in the Garden of Good and Evil*) with her mother and boyfriend; eventually ending up in Jacksonville for a few days. Then she drove back to NC and spent New Year's with some girlfriends at Carolina Beach. I was left in charge of tending her animals in her stead.

The New Year began with news of my brother's prostate cancer diagnosis. Due to my early onset of such and his ongoing BHP, he wasn't surprised, handling the development with equanimity. A couple weeks later Ben's son sent me a text about Ben's hospitalization due to pneumonia since the beginning of January (I suspected something was amiss because of his not responding to my emails and voicemails). So, in addition to debilitation from prostate cancer and leukemia treatment, he was struggling to breathe. A few days later Ben's wife called and informed me that he had been moved to a hospice facility in preparation for his transition. Three days later Ben died from pulmonary hypertension and congestive heart failure. Working with Ben for six years was the highlight of my professional career. He was an astute manager, an intuitive salesman, and a good friend. I will miss him dearly.

Later that week I woke up hungover...again. The previous afternoon after a café con leche at my favorite coffee shop, I stopped by my preferred wine market and purchased three bottles of cab instead of my typical two. Being that it was early afternoon, I didn't want to run out later in the evening. As usual, I drank alone while I read, wrote, browsed the net, and watched TV. The end of the night was a blur with a faint recollection of dancing to *Santana*. I had no memory of a snack I ate evidenced by dishes in the kitchen sink I found in the morning fog. I felt forlorn.

Synchronistically, one of my emails that morning was a notification from Amazon Kindle about the delivery of an order I placed months before for *The 30 Day Sobriety Solution: How to Cut Back or Quit Drinking in the Privacy of Your Own Home* by Jack Canfield and Dave Andrews. I was familiar with Jack's *Chicken Soup for the Soul* series which lent credence. However, the mention of "in the privacy of your own home" was the hook. The recommendation for keeping a journal was a big plus as well. I decided on a bold thirty-day time frame with complete abstinence in mind. Three solutions or steps sealed the deal.

1) I acknowledged my problem drinking and the accompanying pain and shame.
2) I acknowledged how my problem drinking was incompatible with my core values (dependability, gratitude, honesty, clarity, etc.).
3) I acknowledged and reprogrammed pesky subconscious beliefs or lies (I have an addictive personality; drinking reduces stress; abstinence is too hard; etc.).

I reminded myself regularly that problem drinking didn't mix with my core values. And, whenever I encountered those pesky subconscious lies, I would reprogram them (i.e., problem drinking is an addiction, not a personality; problem drinking increases stress, not the opposite; abstinence can't be that hard since millions of folks don't drink alcohol). If you are a problem drinker and want to quit, I recommend *The 30 Day Sobriety Solution*. The solutions that appealed to me may be different for you. Without a doubt, moderation didn't work for me; abstinence was easier because it wasn't complicated by equivocation or rationalization. And, I was able to effortlessly enjoy my favorite meal, Awareness with a side of gratitude.

Naturally, there was an astrological correlation to my commitment to abstinence. Saturn and Uranus were a significant part of the play. Saturn, the shadow master, the maturity manufacturer, was transiting 4th house which has to do with home, private self, "something dark and like a web, where a hundred roots are silently drinking." (Rainer Maria Rilke) Saturn, which had been conjunct my Sun (ego, identity, etc.), had moved into conjunction with my Mercury (insight, communication, learning, etc.) and square my Moon (reactions, moods, etc.) in 8th house (wounds, healing, etc.). *And,* transiting Uranus was square natal Uranus which corresponded with the unexpected breakthrough. By the way, a big shout-out to Dana Gerhardt and Elizabeth Spring for their astrological eloquence, honesty, and the Rilke and Goethe quotes, respectively.

> Whatever you can do, or think you can do, begin it; boldness has genius, power and magic in it. (Johann Wolfgang von Goethe)

Even though I felt confident, I waited a couple of months before disclosing my abstinence and making amends to various friends and family; the feedback was varied (what follows is a sample). Layla was supportive and saw no need for my amends. My sister was complimentary and appreciated my apologies; she had borne the brunt of a number of my drunken rants. Johnny was a different story. I regarded him as potentially hazardous due to his drinking problem. I was right. He was dubious verging on disdainful. However, a few days later he called and said straight up "I need help" and asked about *The 30 Day Sobriety Solution*. I gave a rundown of the solutions that worked for me and encouraged him to buy the book. We spoke a few days later; he hadn't bought the book. We talked more in-depth about his drinking problem; it was major league. He was considering a treatment program again; I encouraged him to do so.

Chapter 23: Relaxation

> Life is an adventure, it's not a package tour. (Eckhart Tolle)

A couple of news articles I read about LSD's creative aspects prompted an unexpected adventure. It had been over twenty-five years since I last tripped. I decided to experiment again. My curiosity paid off; the handful of trips were very enjoyable. There was a pattern to the journey, if you will. Initially, there was a burst of physical energy; I walked, gardened, and/or cleaned house. Then the ego, the little one, quieted down and stillness became pronounced. During meditation, the normally faint vortexes of multi-colored light afforded a fractal ride. In conclusion, tripping provided some nice peak experiences, some moments of heightened clarity. This isn't a blanket endorsement. There are risks with any drug; individual physiology and/or psychology can react differently resulting in adverse effects. This is especially so with psychoactive drugs not benefiting from standardized production methods that assure dosage. By the way, in 1968 the federal government defined LSD as a Schedule I drug and outlawed personal use or possession. Be careful.

My road trip to visit Reyna and her husband was a pleasant change of pace with some lovely sights along the highway. From Asheville to Knoxville, I-40 goes through the beautiful Blue Ridge Mountains. Reyna and I picked up where we left off; we chatted nonstop about family, friends, and home improvement. After dinner, we watched *American Idol* which I enjoyed to my surprise (earlier versions' tone of criticism had turned me off). I was on the road early the next morning to visit my sister-in-law and brother. He had just undergone prostate cancer surgery.

"Shit doesn't happen" was my brother's understated and humorous assessment of his post-operative condition. Due to pain medication, he was constipated and uncomfortable; the doctor assured him his system would return to normal. Before calling it a night, we watched the Democratic primary question and answer session with Clinton and Sanders. Hillary came across canned whereas Bernie was more likable and genuine. Regardless of the outcome, I would be voting for the Democrat again. The Republican candidates and platform were beyond consideration to the point of, as I said, embarrassment.

> I am very much the internationalist. And I am also an idealist insofar as I believe that we should be promoting values, like democracy and human rights and norms and values, because not only do they serve our interests the more people adopt values that we

share—in the same way that, economically, if people adopt rule of law and property rights and so forth, that is to our advantage—but because it makes the world a better place. (Barack Obama)

Much to the surprise of political prognosticators, narcissism, aggression, dishonesty, and pompousness carried the day. Trump won the GOP primaries; a pathetic pissing contest worthy of tabloid headlines. However, I didn't give Trump a chance of winning the presidency given his numerous negatives including being a political apprentice. I was confident that Clinton, regardless of her imperfect past, would win because of her experience and well-informed approach to international relations, cultural issues, immigration concerns, economic inequities, and environmental deterioration.

Life is an opera of opposites like war and peace or health and disease. When it comes to health and disease, genetics, epigenetics, and lifestyle are significant factors. *The Gene* by Siddhartha Mukherjee was a riveting and sobering read. Gene-editing techniques, namely CRISPR, has given us the ability to transform our genetic code and eliminate various diseases. However, there are ethical and sociological considerations with genetic engineering that must be considered. Mukherjee's observation concerning the number of males and females in India and China was alarming. For years the technological ability to determine the sex of the fetus has been available. This has resulted in a substantial imbalance between the number of male and females because boys are favored. Projections are between 30 to 40 million more men than women in each country by 2020! It is essential that we consider what unintended consequences could occur with advanced gene-editing.

> Whether nature—i.e., the gene—or nurture—i.e., the environment—dominates in the development of a feature or function depends, acutely, on the individual feature and the context. The SRY gene determines sexual anatomy and physiology in a strikingly autonomous manner; it is all nature. Gender identity, sexual preference, and the choice of sexual roles are determined by intersections of genes and environments—i.e., nature plus nurture. The manner in which "masculinity" versus "femininity" is enacted or perceived in a society, in contrast, is largely determined by an environment, social memory, history, and culture; this is all nurture. (Siddhartha Mukherjee: *The Gene: An Intimate History*)

After not sleeping well for months, Will was diagnosed with sleep apnea or OSA. It's a sleep disorder caused by numerous pauses in breathing during sleep resulting in fatigue. A mask that delivers continuous air pressure during sleep provided him comfort. Research indicates there is a genetic factor; two of his brothers have been diagnosed with OSA as well. However, a few months later he was diagnosed with COPD as well. In this case, lifestyle is the cause; he is a smoker. A steroid inhaler has provided relief.

By September '16 the presidential campaigns of Trump and Clinton were in full swing; normal and abnormal bullshit was hitting the fan. Trump's mendacity, mocking, maligning, and fear mongering was unlike anything witnessed before in American politics. Given those negatives, he still managed to secure the support of the religious Right in large part by selecting Mike Pence, a self-righteous religious reactionary, as his vice-presidential candidate. Given Trump's toxic temperament along with his numerous sexual, social, and business improprieties, many of us doubted his electability including some notable GOP members who publicly supported Clinton. She was a bitter pill for some to swallow given her mistakes comically characterized by Samantha Bee in *Full Frontal* as the "only woman I know who can trip over her own dick."

Layla and David got married on the spur of the moment by a justice of the peace; the honeymoon would follow when convenient. I got a call the day before requesting my presence as a witness. David's parents were also in attendance. The ceremony was short and sweet. Because neither of their homes was adequate for their needs as a couple, they bought a new house which gave them plenty of room and over five acres to accommodate their goats, chickens, cats, and dog. They sold her old house readily while keeping his home as rental property. With David's mother's help (his dad's bum knee prohibited him from helping) we moved the small stuff from her old home including the master bedroom mattress which almost killed us. The movers handled the rest of the large items and furniture.

The family reunion in October in Atlanta was prompted by my younger sister's colon cancer operation. Regardless of the reason, it was nice visiting family. I stayed with my brother and sister-in-law; spending time with them was always a treat. My oldest sister stayed at my younger sister's place; she was lending a hand cooking—her shrimp black bean gumbo was a knockout. Par for the course, there was alcohol being imbibed. I was pleased to observe not the slightest desire on my part to partake. While there I finished reading Bryan Cranston's memoir, *A Life in Parts;* a funny, coming-of-age story that I tried not to read too quickly. His description of how some ideas came to him was a gem; "you never know who's going to give you the gift of a good idea."

Later that month I attended a Headless Way workshop conducted by Richard Lang at the Unity Church in Raleigh. The non-verbal experiments utilize gadgetry, if you will, like pointing your index finger at where you imagine or remember your face is and, *based on present evidence*, accepting what you really see (do it; see for yourself). The experiments may seem silly, but they are understatedly meaningful; think of them as doors you can open to your Self. I have attended half a dozen workshops over the years and found them insightful and fun, a guided tour of the One. Again, possibly my favorite experiment was the placement of colored dots on everybody's forehead without knowing the color. The heart of the experiment is trying to figure out what color group one belongs to while moving about the room. This requires relying on nonverbal cues from other participants which interactively highlights the "crazily heavy and absurd subscription" of the adult stage; thinking we are a conditioned, mortal thing coupled with the propensity to ignore our ever-present Awareness, the One.

> Seeing you are the One doesn't mean you stop experiencing the drama of being a person, the unpredictability of life, your lack of control of others and even yourself, the feeling of being separate and mortal, but now you have access at the same time to who you really are. This makes all the difference. (Richard Lang; *Celebrating Who We Are*)

Much to the surprise of political prognosticators, narcissism, aggression, dishonesty, and pompousness carried the day...again. Trump won the presidency with his platform of right-wing populism, economic nationalism, anti-immigration, and resentment. Unlike Obama, Clinton had to contend with FBI Director Comey's untimely imposition concerning the email imbroglio. Also, she lost Michigan, Pennsylvania, and Wisconsin as well by less than 1% in each (totaling 79,646 votes). Like Gore in 2000, Clinton won the popular vote (by more than 2.86 million) but not the Electoral College and thus lost the election. This undemocratic dinosaur was created by the Founding Fathers as a concession to southern slave states; they feared that a direct popular vote would favor the northern abolitionists (we could at least apportion delegates according to the percentage of the vote). I was saddened and sobered; I found it helpful to remind myself there is no division or distance with my fellow citizen based on present evidence. We are built for loving.

Thankfully, I had plenty of TV entertainment options. *Jeopardy* was a regular evening feature. I got thrilled when there was a category where I had a chance of asking the right question. My standard comedy fixes, sitcoms such as *Mom* and *Big Bang Theory*, had been supplemented by reruns of *The Office*; an offbeat, hilarious comedy whose characters found a place in my heart including Pam, Andy, Jim, Dwight, Erin, Oscar, Michael, Angela, Darryl, Kelly, Kevin, and Robert. Next in the queue was *30 Rock*. The latest drama series to ensnare me was *Sons of Anarchy*. I had my doubts based on the title thinking it would be a dark, violent, shoot 'em up; it was. However, I was familiar with Katey Sagal and Ron Perlman, so I figured it had to be good. I became a big fan of the entire cast including Charlie Hunnam and Maggie Siff. It was *The Sopranos* for bikers full of captivating storylines and good acting.

Thanksgiving was held at David and Layla's home which easily accommodated the attendees: David's parents, Layla's mother and boyfriend, and Tara, Layla's good friend. Topics of conversation ranged from rock & roll to politics which could have been contentious, but all of us liked rock & roll and had voted Democratic. The food was delicious topped off by ice cream and pecan pie. In the flash of an eye, Christmas Eve dawned. Layla and I went to the movies. *Jackie* was our choice with Natalie Portman, Billy Crudup, and Peters Sarsgaard. It was an engaging period piece about Jackie Kennedy shortly before and after the assassination of her husband, the president, JFK, in Dallas on November 22, 1963 (for people around my age an iconic event). It portrays how she dealt with the shock, horror, grief, and her two young children along with planning for the funeral that she hoped would establish an enduring legacy based on preservation and revision.

My problem drinking habit had disappeared; the mirage of moderation discarded as an illusion. For me, the advantage of abstinence was simplicity and calm certainty. There were rare occasions when I would hear the faint whisper of wine, usually stimulated by a TV or movie scene. Quickly, I dismissed it. Johnny fell off the ship, so to speak, when he hit a reef; that is, a romantic repeat with his ex-wife but was back on dry land with the help of SMART Recovery and Campral, a drug that reduces alcohol craving. Bert's sobriety was aided by AA meetings.

Our stories are unique, but the dilemma was the same, problem drinking. A conservative estimate is that 10% of the US adult population suffers from alcohol and/or drug addiction.

Trump was not fit to be president. He was transforming the highest office in the land into a travesty of tragic proportions. The professional psychological diagnosis of his condition was malignant narcissism. Trump's blatant lies, personnel appointments, and executive orders rolling back regulations across numerous industries were especially troubling. The Russian electoral interference was spy novel material. I hoped the investigation by Special Counsel, Robert Mueller, would either prompt Trump to resign or lead to impeachment. One thing for sure, it was going to be a political roller coaster ride for the next few years enhanced by the world transit of Pluto (purging) conjunct Saturn (responsibilities); as with the previous opposition and square mentioned earlier in this account, think airing dirty laundry and general house cleaning.

Elect a clown, expect a circus. (Bumper sticker)

Layla's digestive issues continued giving her fits, at times becoming bedridden. A few years back she thought it was a gallbladder issue, but the doctor misdiagnosed her condition and dismissed her suffering opting for the ever-popular CYA diagnosis, stress. Layla avoided certain foods and tried various diets, all to no avail. Finally, her symptoms were diagnosed correctly and her gallbladder was successfully removed at a nearby hospital. The post-op pain was more substantial than anticipated based on what she was led to believe. A couple weeks later she was feeling much better.

With time on my hands, I embarked on another home improvement kick; the driveway was in dire need. The results of the patching and painting were so spectacular that I decided to paint the exterior of the house. As I poked around checking for wood rot and the like, I discovered much to my chagrin a termite infestation around the dining room window. A few thousand dollars later the infestation was exterminated and extensive repair work was completed. The exterior paint job proved to be a more sizable undertaking than I anticipated. Then the interior beckoned to be painted. Again, it proved to be a more sizable undertaking than I anticipated. Despite the aches and pain, the home improvement projects continued to provide creative focus and sense of accomplishment.

Sometimes one thing leads to another and a catchy song. Inspired by how good the newly painted interior looked I decided to paint the office shelves and desk. They looked so good I resolved to add bookshelves on each side of the fireplace and mount the existing TV. Well, that evolved in ways I never foresaw. The vertical books shelves presented too many conflicting lines, so I had an electrician/carpenter I've relied on over the years cut them down and create one horizontal piece along with installing the necessary electrical supply and HDMI cables for the TV. I opted for an asymmetrical arrangement placing the bookshelf on the right side of the fireplace. However, the TV proved to be too small for the new space. I quickly talked myself into buying a larger TV. I had to say, the evidence was overwhelming, the whole ensemble looked great!

Retirement has been graced with relaxation; a spiritual retreat, if you will, with minimal distractions and distress; a gift of solitude and simplicity from the Storehouse to further enhance my identity as Aware Capacity. It also provided me time to create this memoir; a more difficult undertaking than I expected, especially the syntax and grammar. At one point early on in the editing process I lost my confidence and didn't edit for a couple of months. It may amuse you given the narrow appeal of this memoir, but what brought me out my funk was an interview in the AARP magazine with Laurence Fishburne. Under the 'Words to live by' section, he shared some advice a friend gave him years ago, "You can't be all right with everybody."

> In a sense, admittedly, it's the easiest thing in the world to see what nobody else can see, namely what it's like to be Oneself. But in another sense it's the most difficult thing in the world to see and go on seeing. Of all ambitions this is the most far-reaching, and no other adventure is anything like so daring or so 'difficult' - till we see how the difficulty was of our own making. (Douglas Harding)

Over forty-five years ago, I embarked on an adventure, waking up to my True Nature. During my initial spiritual awakening, I was informed I had lessons to learn; that was an understatement, to say the least. These lessons were part of growing up, cleaning up, and the inevitable problems that arise on occasion with self, family, friends, career, society, etc. Some problems have waxed and others have waned, others have remained the same. That's okay; I am problem-free Aware Capacity. Busted wide open I bow in gratitude to life, the play of Sun and shadow.

Namaste,
Brian Esmond

Facebook: The Play of Sun and Shadow
playsunandshadow@gmail.com
11/24/52; Baton Rouge, LA; 10:28 PM

Made in the USA
Middletown, DE
20 September 2019